BIBLICAL LAW AND ITS RELEVANCE

---

*A Christian Understanding
and Ethical Application for Today
of the Mosaic Regulations*

Joe M. Sprinkle

University Press of America,® Inc.
Lanham · Boulder · New York · Toronto · Oxford

Copyright © 2006 by
University Press of America,® Inc.
4501 Forbes Boulevard
Suite 200
Lanham, Maryland 20706
UPA Acquisitions Department (301) 459-3366

PO Box 317
Oxford
OX2 9RU, UK

Library of Congress Control Number: 2005935783
ISBN 0-7618-3371-4 (clothbound : alk. ppr.)
ISBN 0-7618-3372-2 (paperback : alk. ppr.)

To my colleagues at Crossroads College
for the opportunity to serve God together,
and to Christilee, my wife and best friend.

Deuteronomy 11:1

וְאָ֣הַבְתָּ֔ אֵ֖ת יְהֹוָ֣ה אֱלֹהֶ֑יךָ וְשָׁמַרְתָּ֣ מִשְׁמַרְתּ֗וֹ ¹
וְחֻקֹּתָ֥יו וּמִשְׁפָּטָ֖יו וּמִצְוֺתָ֑יו כָּל־הַיָּמִֽים׃

Table of Contents

Preface

I first became interested in the relationship between the Christian and the Mosaic law while a student at Trinity Evangelical Divinity School (T.E.D.S.) in Deerfield, Illinois. Up until that time I had simply ignored that portion of the Bible, writing it off as merely for the "Jews" and of no particular relevance to me as a Christian. I pretty much felt that way about the whole Old Testament, except for its messianic prophecies. I was a "New Testament Christian."

At Trinity I became much more interested in the Old Testament due to the influence of my teachers Thomas McComiskey and Walter Kaiser. They showed me what a wonderful book the Old Testament really is, and how it was much more relevant to me as a Christian than I had ever imagined. Kaiser's book, *Toward Old Testament Ethics*, which I read after graduating from seminary, proved to my satisfaction that pentateuchal laws were of relevance in formulating Christian ethics. The influence of these two scholars, along with my growing interest in Hebrew language studies, eventually led me to change my career goals. I had hoped to pursue Ph.D. work in New Testament after seminary. After going to T.E.D.S., I made plans to pursue a Ph.D. in Old Testament instead.

What I had not worked out at T.E.D.S. to my satisfaction was the place of Old Testament law in the life of the Christian. While in seminary I had learned of some controversy concerning the place of the law, particularly the ideas of the Theonomists (or Christian Reconstructionists) who argued that the Mosaic civil regulations should be incorporated into modern law codes. I was not convinced that they were right, but I was sure that the usual Christian practice of ignoring completely the civil regulations had to be wrong. As a budding Christian Old Testament scholar, I wanted to know how, if at all, these laws contribute to the Christian faith and practice.

I had the opportunity to pursue the question of the meaning and relevance of biblical law by virtue of attending a Jewish seminary, Hebrew Union College–Jewish Institute of Religion in Cincinnati. In Jewish circles, unlike Christian ones, the laws are not merely peripheral to religion, but at its center. Moreover, at Hebrew Union I had the opportunity to investigate the ancient Near Eastern backdrop of the biblical regulations, studying in Akkadian the Laws of Eshnunna, as well as a selection of the other ancient law codes under the Assyriologist Samuel Greengus. As these laws were taught and studied, comparisons were regularly made with biblical regulations. A fascinating course in biblical law under my teacher Rabbi H. C. Brichto peaked my interest. Brichto's always creative and sometimes brilliant analyzes of biblical regulations inspired me to pursue under him and Samuel Greengus a dissertation on the laws of the so-called Book of the Covenant (Exodus 20:22-23:19), a dissertation that was later published as a book, *'The Book of the Covenant': A Literary Approach.*

By the end of this process, I had developed a profound appreciation for biblical laws. I could even say I came to like them!

In the years since my dissertation, I have continued to think, write, and (when possible) teach in the area of biblical law with a view towards its relevance religiously and ethically to Christian believers. The book that follows is the fruit of my pursuit of this topic, incorporating works that I have either taught, read as scholarly papers, and/or previously published.

The thesis of this book is that all biblical laws, not just the Ten Commandments, are relevant for Christian believers today; and we ignore the law to our own impoverishment morally and spiritually. This thesis will then be demonstrated by specific examples of how biblical laws provide insight into moral and spiritual matters.

The first three chapters give backdrop for the rest of the book.

Chapter 1 ("The Mosaic Law and the Christian") seeks to determine an appropriate methodology for Christians to find relevance in the Mosaic law for today. Various approaches are laid out and evaluated, and the principalizing approach is defended as the best approach.

Chapter 2 ("Is There Truth in the Law [John 1:17]?") seeks to correct the erroneous notion sometimes drawn from John 1:17 that the OT is a book of law without true grace. In fact, John's Gospel, like the Psalms, affirms that God's law is true—predicting and foreshadowing the ministry of Jesus Christ—and draws its language about the grace of God in John 1:14-17 from a passage in the law (Exod 33-34; particularly Exod 34:6) where Yahweh shows himself especially gracious. The best reading of John, it will be argued, indicates that he affirms both the truth and the gracious character of the law, and he sees that law as embodied in the person of Jesus Christ.

Chapter 3 ("Near Eastern and Biblical Laws Compared") returns to theoretical issues as to how to relate the civil laws in the Bible to cuneiform laws found in ancient Mesopotamia and dating from biblical times. It is argued in that chapter that the formulations of biblical civil laws were influenced by the cultural milieu where these other laws were known, and yet biblical laws are not slavishly dependent on these other law collections. Biblical law, indeed, often expresses an ideology quite different from that found in cuneiform law. Thus comparisons between these law collections are helpful in two ways: First, these other laws can clarify the cultural milieu of similar biblical laws and so aid in interpretation. Second, the comparison between Israel's laws and Mesopotamian laws indicates a contrast in ideology between Israel's legal tradition and that of her neighbors.

The rest of the book deals with more specific issues.

Chapter 4 ("Law and Narrative in Exodus 19-24") shows the context of grace and the purpose of a personal, I-Thou relationship with God in the giving of the law at Sinai. It shows in some detail how the law paints a portrait of the character of God and conveys certain theological truths. Hermeneutically, this chapter shows how the narratives affect the way we read the laws (its structure, its emphasis on slaves, its use of the number seven, and so forth) and the way the laws in turn affect how we read biblical narratives (the creation accounts, the Golden Calf story, the Patriarchal narratives, and the like), thus showing law and narrative to be closely intertwined.

Chapter 5 ("Exodus 21:22-25 [*Lex Talionis*] and Abortion") deals with a hot-button ethical issue and the exegesis of the passage about a pregnant woman struck during a brawl that Christians on both sides of that issue point to for defense of their position.

Chapter 6 ("'Do not Steal': Biblical Laws about Theft") discusses the regulations and the logic behind the regulations regarding theft and deprivation of property.

Chapter 7 ("Understanding the Laws of Clean and Unclean") tries to make sense of these very confusing ceremonial laws. That chapter seeks to find the principles behind the laws of purity that led God to give these rules to Israel. Although literal application of these laws is no longer obligatory under the new covenant, I argue that the principles that led to them are still relevant.

Chapter 8 ("The Red Heifer") discusses in some detail one of the laws concerning purity, namely the purification ritual in Numbers 19 involving the ashes of a red cow.

Chapter 9 ("Old Testament Perspectives on Divorce") takes on another hot-button, ethical issue. There it is argued that the OT regulations about divorce are compatible with NT teachings about divorce, and that greater attention to the OT teachings on this matter is necessary for a fully biblical divorce ethic.

Chapter 10 ("The Law's Theology of Sex") discusses other aspects of biblical sexual ethics, including polygamy, adultery, bestiality, seduction, rape, incest, prostitution, and homosexuality, showing how these regulations are based on the Bible's theology of creation.

Chapter 11 ("'Just War' in Deuteronomy 20 and 2 Kings 3") takes on yet another hot-button, ethical issue: war. This chapter argues that the rules for war in OT law were far more humane and sophisticated than is generally recognized, and these laws in fact anticipate the rules for just war developed in the early Church. Far from being barbaric, this chapter argues that Israel's ethics of war are in no way inferior to modern conceptions of "just war." It also argues that understanding the rules for war in Deuteronomy 20 helps us to make sense of a perplexing passage in 2 Kings 3.

Chapter 12 ("Law and Justice in the Historical Books") traces how pentateuchal laws came to be applied or not applied in Israel's history. In particular it shows how the laws were kept or distorted, lost and found, administered by various sorts of persons (fathers, elders, priests, judges, kings, and governors), and reinstituted at various points in Israel's history after Moses. It also shows the contrast between OT law and its administration in OT history and the more developed legal system of the rabbis that developed by NT times.

Although I approach my subject from the standpoint of an evangelical Christian, I have learned much not only from Jewish scholars (under whom I studied) but also from scholars of other Christian traditions. It is my hope that those of various interpretative communities will find value in what I present.

Joe M. Sprinkle
Professor of Old Testament
Crossroad College
Rochester, Minnesota
August 2005

Acknowledgments

I would like to thank my current employer, Crossroads College (Rochester, Minnesota), and my former employer, Toccoa Falls College (Toccoa Falls, Georgia), for the opportunity to serve and grow as a Bible scholar-teacher. Both institutions have supported my attending professional meetings where many of these chapters were first presented. The librarians at both institutions (Gene Mahan and Sarah Dodge, respectively) have helped me obtain many interlibrary loans that made the research for this book possible. Chapters 1 and 3 are derived from course lectures on Biblical Law presented first at Toccoa Falls College and later at Crossroads.

Scholars at Toccoa Falls College who have read and made suggestions about earlier versions of one or another of these chapters include Daniel Evearitt, Michael Hildenbrand, and Donald Williams. I appreciate their help and friend-ships. Those who have contributed to proofreading the book version include my wife Christilee (who has also had to put up with the foibles of her scholar-husband) and my mother-in-law Elaine Keller. Of course, the errors that remain are my own.

I am grateful also for Daniel G. Reid, editor for InterVarsity Press, for granting me IVP's permission to reuse my contributions to *The Dictionary of the Old Testament: Pentateuch* and the material to be published in *The Dictionary of the Old Testament: Historical Books*. In the former, my article on "Theft and Deprivation of Property" forms the basis for Chapter 6 of this book; my article on "Red Heifer" is the basis of Chapter 8; and my article on "Sexuality, Sexual Ethics" is the basis for Chapter 10. In the latter, my article on "Law in the Historical Books" is the basis for Chapter 12.

Moreover, I am in debt to the journals that have previously published my essays for their generous policies that allow authors to reuse the material after publication. Chapter 4 is based on my article, "Law and Narrative in Exodus 19-24," published in *The Journal of the Evangelical Theological Society* 47 (2004): 235-252. Chapter 5 is based on my article, "The Interpretation of Exodus 21:22-25 (*Lex Talionis*) and Abortion," in the *Westminster Theological Journal* 55 (1993): 233-253. Chapter 7 is based on "The Rationale for the Laws of Clean and Unclean in the Old Testament" published in the *Journal of the Evangelical Theological Society* 43 (2000): 637-657. Chapter 9 is based on "Old Testament Perspectives on Divorce and Remarriage" published in the *Journal of the Evangelical Theological Society* 40 (1997): 529-550. And Chapter 11 first appeared as "Deuteronomic 'Just War' (Deut 20:10-20) and 2 Kings 3:27" in the *Zeitschrift für altorientalische und biblische Rechtsgeschichte* 6 (2000): 285-301. I have not merely reprinted earlier materials, but I have felt free to revise and supplement my earlier writings as I have edited them into this book. The editors of these publications (R. Youngblood and A. Köstenberbger for *JETS*, M. Silva for *WTJ,* and E. Otto for *ZABR*, along with Daniel Reid of InterVarsity) have improved my prose here and there along the way.

I am grateful to Bob Buller, Editorial Director of the Society of Biblical Literature, for permission to quote translations of ancient Near Eastern laws from Martha Ross, *Law Collections from Mesopotamia and Asia Minor.*

Bible translations used in this book are taken from various standard translations as noted, though I have often freely translated the Hebrew and Greek text on my own. For most of the period when these essays were first being written, my primary English translation of the Bible was the New American Standard Bible (1977 edition). This was the standard translation used at Toccoa Falls College when I taught there. Some of my free translations are no doubt influenced by the version I was regularly using.

Scripture taken from the NEW AMERICAN STANDARD BIBLE®, © Copyright 1960, 1962, 1963, 1968, 1971, 1972, 1973, 1975, 1977 by The Lockman Foundation is used by permission.

Scripture taken from the Holy Bible, NEW INTERNATIONAL VERSION®, copyright © 1973, 1978, 1984 International Bible Society, is used by permission of International Bible Society.

The style used in this book is derived from *The SBL Handbook of Style* (Hendrickson, 1999).

I would like to thank Richard Averbeck of Trinity Evangelical Divinity School for his leadership in organizing and chairing the Biblical Law Group at the Evangelical Theological Society, and his encouragement of work in the area of biblical law. Chapter 2 ("Is there Truth in the Law [John 1:17]?") was originally written at his suggestion and presented at the Biblical Law sessions of the annual meeting of the Evangelical Theological Society in San Antonio, Texas, in November of 1994. Chapter 4 ("Law and Narrative in Exodus 19-24") was also first read before the Biblical Law Group at E.T.S. (Toronto, November 2002) as was Chapter 7 (originally entitled, "The Laws of Clean and Unclean and their Relationship with the Concept of Sacred Space," E.T.S. annual meeting, Boston, November 1999).

Abbreviations

AB	Anchor Bible
ABD	*Anchor Bible Dictionary.* Edited by D. N. Freedman. 6 vols. New York, 1992
AHw	*Akkadisches Handwörterbuch.* W. von Soden. 3 vols. Wiesbaden, 1965-1981.
AJT	*Asia Journal of Theology*
Akk.	Akkadian (Assyrian)
ANET	*Ancient Near Eastern Texts Relating to the Old Testament.* Edited by James Pritchard. 3rd ed. Princeton, 1969
Ant.	*Jewish Antiquites.* By Flavius Josephus
AOAT	*Alter Orient und Altes Testament*
b. B. Qam.	Babylonian Talmud, tractate *Baba Qamma*
b. Ketub.	Babylonian Talmud, tractate *Ketubbot*
b. Sanh.	Babylonian Talmud, tractate *Sanhedrin*
BA	*Biblical Archaeologist*
BAR	*Biblical Archaeology Review*
BBR	*Bulletin for Biblical Research*
BDB	F. Brown, S. R. Driver, and C. A. Briggs. *A Hebrew and English Lexicon of the Old Testament.* Oxford, 1907
Bib	*Biblica*
BJS	Brown Judaic Studies
BRev	*Bible Review*
BSac	*Biliotheca sacra*
BT	*The Bible Translator*
BZAW	Beihefte zur Zeitschrift für die alttestamentliche Wissenschaft
CAD	*Chicago Assyrian Dictionary.* Chicago, 1956-
CahRB	Cahiers de la Revue biblique
CBQ	*Catholic Biblical Quaterly*
CC	Continental Commentaries
CEV	Contemporary English Version
De spec. leg.	*On the Special Laws (De specialibus legibus).* By Philo of Alexandria
DJG	*Dictionary of Jesus and the Gospels.* Edited by J. B. Green and S. McKnight. Downers Grove, Illinois, 1992.
Dtr	Deuteronomistic (history, writer); Deuteronomist
EncJud	*Encyclopaedia Judaica.* 16 vol. Jerusalem, 1982
ESV	English Standard Version
EvQ	*Evangelical Quarterly*

EVV	English versions
ExpTim	*Expository Times*
FCG	Feminist Companion to the Bible
Gk.	Greek
GOODSPEED	*The Complete Bible: An American Translation.* By E. J. Goodspeed
HALOT	*Hebrew and Aramaic Lexicon of the Old Testament.* By L. Koehler, W. Baumgartner, and J. J. Stamm. Translated and edited by M. E. J. Richardson. 5 vols. Leiden, 1994-2000
HCSB	Holman Christian Standard Bible
Heb.	Hebrew
Hist.	*The Histories.* By Herodotus
HL	Hittite Laws
HSM	Harvard Semitic Monograph
HtD	Hithpael (an intensive-reflexive verbal stem in Hebrew)
HUCA	*Hebrew Union College Annual*
IBHS	*An Introduction to Biblical Hebrew Syntax.* Bruce Waltke and M. O'Connor. Winona Lake, Indiana. 1990
ICC	*International Critical Commentary*
IDBSup	*Interpreter's Dictionary of the Bible: Supplementary Volume.* Edited by K. Crim. Nashville, 1976
JB	Jerusalem Bible
JBL	*Journal of Biblical Literature*
JESHO	*Journal of the Economic and Social History of the Orient*
JETS	*Journal of the Evangelical Theological Society*
JJS	*Journal of Jewish Studies*
Joüon	P. Joüon. *A Grammar of Biblical Hebrew.* Trans. and revised by T. Muraoka. 2 vols. Subsidia biblica 14/1-2. Rome, 1991
JPS	Jewish Publication Society
JSNTSup	Journal for the Study of the New Testament Supplement Series
JSOT	*Journal for the Study of the Old Testament*
JSOTSup	Journal for the Study of the Old Testament Supplement Series
JTS	*Journal of Theological Studies*
KJV	King James Version
LCL	Loeb Classical Library
LE	Laws of Eshnunna
LH	Laws of Hammurabi
LL	Laws of Lipit-Ishtar
LU	Laws of Ur-Nammu
LXX	Septuagint (early Greek translation of the Old Testament and the Apocrypha)
m. B. Qam	Mishnah, tractate *Baba Qamma*
m. Ketub.	Mishnah, tractate *Ketubbot*
m. 'Ohalot	Mishnah, tractate *'Ohalot*

m. Parah	Mishnah, tractate *Parah*
m. Tem.	Mishnah, tractate *Temurah*
MAL	Middle Assyrian Laws
Mek.	*Mekilta* (a rabbinic work)
MT	Masoretic Text (traditional Hebrew Bible)
NAB	New American Bible
NASB	New American Standard Bible
NBC	New Century Bible
NEB	New English Bible
NIBCOT	New International Bible Commentary on the Old Testament
NICNT	New International Commentary New Testament
NICOT	New International Commentary Old Testament
NIDNTT	*New International Dictionary of New Testament Theology.* Edited by C. Brown. 4 vols. Grand Rapids, 1975-1985
NIDOTTE	*New International Dictionary of Old Testament Theology and Exegesis.* Edited by W. A. VanGemeren. 5 vols. Grand Rapids, 1997
NIV	New International Version
NJPS	*Tanakh: The Holy Scriptures: The New Jewish Publication Society Translation according to the Traditional Hebrew Text*
NKJV	New King James Version
NLT	New Living Translation
NRSV	New Revised Standard Version
OTS	*Old Testament Studies*
PEQ	*Palestine Exploration Quarterly*
Presb	*Presbyterion*
Rashi	Rabbi Solomon ben Isaac (medieval Jewish commentator)
RB	*Revue biblique*
REB	Revised English Bible
RevExp	*Review and Expositor*
RSV	Revised Standard Version
SBLDS	Society of Biblical Literature Dissertation Series
SBLSP	*Society of Biblical Literature Seminar Papers*
SBLWAW	Society of Biblical Literature Writings from the Ancient World
SBT	Studies in Biblical Theology
ScrHier	Scripta hierosolymitana
SJLA	Studies in Judaism in Late Antiquity
SLEx	Sumerian Laws Exercise Tablet
SP	Sacra pagina
SSN	Studia semitica neerlandica
t. B. Qam.	Tosefta, tractate *Baba Qamma*
TDOT	*Theological Dictionary of the Old Testament.* Edited by G. J. Botterweck and H. Ringgren. Grand Rapids, 1974-

TDNT	*Theological Dictionary of the New Testament.* Edited by G. Kittel and G. Friedrich. 10 vols. Grand Rapids, 1964-1976
TEV	Today's English Version (Good New Bible)
Tg. Onq.	*Targum Onqelos* (an early Aramaic Translation of the Old Testament)
TJ	*Trinity Journal*
TLNT	*Theological Lexicon of the New Testament.* C. Spicq. Translated and edited by J. D. Ernest. Peabody, Mass., 1994
TOTC	Tyndale Old Testament Commentary
TWOT	*Theological Wordbook of the Old Testament.* Edited by R. L. Harris, G. L. Archer Jr. 2 vols. Chicago, 1980
VT	*Vetus Testamentum*
VTSup	Supplements to Vetus Testamenum
WBC	Word Biblical Commentary
WTJ	*Westminster Theological Journal*
ZABR	*Zeitschrift für altorientalische und biblische Rechtsgeschichte*
ZAW	*Zeitschrift für die alttestamentliche Wissenschaft*

Chapter 1

THE MOSAIC LAW AND THE CHRISTIAN

An important theological question for the Christian is this: What is the role of the Mosaic law under the new covenant? This task has challenged interpreters from the beginning of the church age and continues to challenge exegetes to this day, for New Testament (NT) statements about the law are hard to harmonize with each other.

On the one hand some NT statements indicate that we are "not under law but under grace" (Rom 6:14), that "Christ is the end of the law" (Rom 10:4), and that "If you are led by the Spirit you are not under the law" (Gal 5:18). Laws of ritual and worship are de-emphasized to the point of elimination: clean and unclean foods, circumcision, Sabbath, sacrifices, temple, and priesthood all appear to be superceded in Christ (Mark 7:19; Acts 11:8-9; Rom 14:5, 14; 1 Cor 7:19; Heb 7:11-19, 28; 8:13; 10:1-9). Christ has abolished in his flesh the commandments and regulations that separated Jew from Gentile (Eph 2:15).

On the other hand "All Scripture is inspired by God and is profitable for teaching" (2 Tim 3:16-17). "All Scripture" presumably applies to the laws as well as the rest of the Old Testament (OT). Jesus came not to "abolish the law" and till heaven and earth pass away "not the smallest letter or the least stroke" will disappear from the law (Matt 5:17-20). Jesus rebukes fellow Jews for not keeping the law (John 7:19). According to the Apostle Paul, Christians "establish the law" (Rom 3:31), and he states that women are to be in submission "as the law also says" (1 Cor 14:34). James tells his audience to keep the law, not sit in judgment over it (James 4:11). There are also authoritative quotations and allusions to the Mosaic laws, especially but not exclusively from the Decalogue. For instance, Rom 13:9 refers to the Decalogue's prohibitions of adultery, murder, theft and coveting; and it quotes Lev 19:18: "Love your neighbor as yourself." James 2:8 also cites authoritatively Lev 19:18. James 2:9 and 2:11 condemn partiality along with adultery and murder as contrary to the law. 1 Peter 1:16 quotes as authoritative Lev 19:2: "Be holy, for I am holy." A number of examples of this will be noted in the discussion below.

There have been a number of Christian approaches to the Mosaic law: the Reformed approach, the approach of classical dispensationalism, the Lutheran approach, the approach of Meredeth Kline (intrusion ethics), the approach of theonomy (Christian Reconstructionism), and finally the principalizing approach, which will be the one adopted here. I leave out of consideration views that say, for example, that Jesus contradicted and corrected errors of the Mosaic law or that Paul's statements about the law are simply self-contradictory or that various

NT authors contradict each other on this matter. The fundamental answer to negative conclusions such as these is to construct a plausible alternative. This chapter will also serve to lay out the approach to the Christian and the law that is assumed in the other chapters of this book.

I. THE APPROACH OF REFORMED THEOLOGY TO THE LAW

The first approach to the law, and one that remains influential, is that of Reformed theology.

1. *The approach of Reformed theology to the law defined.* Reformed theology's approach to the law is spelled out in the Westminster Confession of Faith (A.D. 1646) in Chapter XIX "Of the Law of God," a confession still affirmed by many conservative Presbyterian denominations. This approach begins by dividing the laws into three categories: moral, ceremonial, and civil.

The *moral law* refers to the broad moral principles of the law, especially as expressed in the Decalogue (Ten Commandments). These are often formulated as absolute moral statements ("Do not commit adultery") without qualifications or specified penalty. Modern scholars label such absolute statements *apodictic law.* In Reformed theology, only the moral law is directly applicable to both the Christian and the non-Christian, as the Westminster Confession states:

> The moral law does forever bind all, as well justified persons as others, to the obedience thereof; and that, not only in regard of the matter contained in it, but also in respect of the authority of God the Creator, who gave it. Neither does Christ, in the Gospel, any way dissolve, but much strengthen this obligation.

The explanation sometimes given is this: The moral law, being based on the character of God that does not change, remains forever applicable.

The second category is *ceremonial law.* Ceremonial law (modern Bible scholars often label these *cultic laws*) refers to laws having to do with religious ritual or ceremonies: the sacrifices, the festivals, the tabernacle, laws of clean and unclean and the like. According to the Reformed approach, unlike moral law, ceremonial laws are no longer directly applicable to Christians but have been supplanted by Christ. The Westminster Confession states:

> Besides this law, commonly called moral, God was pleased to give to the people of Israel, as a church under age, ceremonial laws, containing several typical ordinances, partly of worship, prefiguring Christ, His graces, actions, sufferings, and benefits; and partly, holding forth divers instructions of moral duties. All which ceremonial laws are now abrogated, under the New Testament.

Under the Reformed approach ceremonial law has typological value since the tabernacle and the sacrifices and the festivals foreshadow Christ. But now that the reality has come, there is no need for the shadow.

The third category is *civil law*. Civil law gives regulations to be enforced by the theocratic, national state of Israel in order to maintain a civil society. These include laws prescribing penalties for theft or murder or kidnapping or adultery. Mere prohibitions of such things represent moral law. Civil laws ordinarily go on to include the penalties associated with violation of the law. Hence "Do not commit murder" (Exod 20:13) is moral law, but making premeditated murder punishable by death while making unintentional manslaughter punishable by confinement to a city of refuge till the death of the high priest (Exod 21:12-14; Numbers 35; Deut 19:1-10) represents civil law. Often civil laws are formulated "If X occurs, Y is the legal consequence." That formulation is labeled *casuistic law* or *case law* by modern scholars. According to the Westminster Confession, since the Church is not a nation, civil laws are not directly applicable to the Church, though they sometimes illustrate the moral law that is applicable. The Westminster confession states:

> To them also, as a body politic, He gave sundry judicial law, which expired together with the state of that people; not obliging any other now, further than the general equity thereof may require.

The Reformed approach concludes that though Christians are not under the law as Israel was, the law is still of value to Christian believers. The Westminster Confession states:

> Although true believers be not under the law, as a covenant of works, to be thereby justified, or condemned; yet is it of great use to them, as well as to others; in that, as a rule of life informing them of the will of God, and their duty, it directs and binds them to walk accordingly; discovering also the sinful pollutions of their nature, hearts and lives; so as, examining themselves thereby, they may come to further conviction of, humiliation for, and hatred against sin, together with a clearer sight of the need they have of Christ, and the perfection of His obedience. It is likewise of use to the regenerate, to restrain their corruptions, in that it forbids sin: and the threatenings of it serve to show what even their sins deserve; and what afflictions, in this life, they may expect for them, although freed from the curse thereof threatened in the law.

Thus the Reformed approach sees value in the law, especially the moral law. The law is a guide for living. It is a means of discovering one's own sinful nature and guilt, and therefore one's need of salvation in Christ. It helps restrain moral corruption in the life of a Christian. It also leads the Christian to be grateful to God for his having delivered the believer from the law's punishments.

2. *Strengths of the approach of Reformed theology to the law.* There are strengths to this Reformed approach to the law.

First, the Reformed approach rightly recognizes that some laws are more important than other laws. Not all the laws are on the same order. Jesus indicates there are "weightier" and by implication lighter matters in the law (Matt 23:23) in which justice and mercy and faithfulness are weightier than tithing mint and dill.

Similarly the OT prophets regarded laws of justice as more important than laws of ceremony and regarded cultic observance as less important than treating people decently. For example when the prophet Samuel rebukes Saul for ignoring God's instructions on how to conduct war against the Amalek, he states: "to obey is better than sacrifice" (1 Sam 15:22-23). Isaiah indicates that following ritual laws of sacrifice, festivals, Sabbaths, and prayer are unacceptable to God if major moral violations are occurring, specifically, if one's "hands are covered with blood" (Isa 1:11-15). Isaiah also teaches that treating people justly is better than "fasting" (Isaiah 58). Amos points out that festivals and sacrifices without justice are offensive to God (Amos 5:21-24). Hosea asserts that "knowledge of God" is better than sacrifice (Hos 6:6). Finally, Micah says that what God really wants is not more expensive sacrifices, but justice, faithfulness, and walking humbly with God (Mic 6:6-8).

The fact that cultic rituals were, even in the OT, considered of secondary value as compared with moral regulations prepares the way for the elimination of cultic regulations in Christ.

A second strength of the Reformed approach is that it is compatible with NT statements about the abrogation of the ritual laws. Christ indicated that food laws are no longer obligatory (Mark 7:19, "Thus he declared all foods clean"). The writer of Hebrews also indicates that the Levitical priesthood, the Mosaic covenant, the temple/tabernacle, animal sacrifices, and the like were intended to be temporary. These things have now been set aside because what they foreshadowed is fulfilled in Christ's sacrifice on the cross (Heb 7:11-13, 18-19, 28; 8:13; 9:23-25; 10:1, 8-9, etc.).

3. *Weaknesses of the approach of Reformed theology to the law.* Although the Reformed approach to the law is helpful in many ways, it does not resolve every issue satisfactorily.

The most important problem with the Reformed approach is that the categories are not completely distinct. For example, sometimes there are ceremonial elements among moral laws: The ceremonial Sabbath law—the only one of the Ten Commandments that is nowhere repeated in the NT—is among the moral precepts of the Decalogue (Exod 20:8-11).[1] Also the civil goring ox law (Exod 21:28) has a ceremonial aspect in that the flesh of the stoned animal could not be eaten, presumably because of impurity. The civil law on murder allows freedom for a manslayer to leave the city of refuge conditioned upon a ceremonial element: the death of the high priest (Num 35:25, 28, 32). The ceremonial law's prohibition against going up by steps to an altar (Exod 20:26) is related to moral decency in worship (not exposing one's nakedness). The ceremonial admonition

---

1. Seventh Day Adventists argue that the Saturday Sabbath is not a ceremonial law but, like the other nine in the Decalogue, is a moral law to be obeyed by Christians.

not to eat flesh torn by animals (Exod 22:31) is probably based on the moral notion that such behavior is dehumanizing—reducing man to the level of vulture. The ceremonial prohibition against cooking a kid goat in its mother's milk (Exod 23:19) is probably related to avoiding human cruelty nurtured by such a practice. Thus the categories moral, civil, and ceremonial are not strictly distinct. David Dorsey adds the question: "Which of the 613 laws is not moral?"[2] The obvious answer is that they were all moral, and for an Israelite to have disobeyed any of them would have been immoral.

John Frame, himself a Reformed theologian, astutely observes:

> The traditional distinction between moral, civil, and ceremonial law is still useful as a catechetical device, but not helpful in resolving concrete problems of application. In asking how a particular law applies to us, we do not assign it first to one of those three categories and then deduce from that its applicability. Rather we ask first concerning its applicability, and on the basis of that conclusion we assign it to one (or more) of these three categories. The Law does not, of course, come to us with the labels "moral," "ceremonial," and "civil" attached to its provisions. . . . Those we apply most literally we call "moral," those we apply least literally we call "ceremonial."[3]

Division of the law into the categories moral, civil and ceremonial is of heuristic value in allowing us to discuss different kinds of laws with differing degrees of direct application, but the categories are not wholly distinct.

Theonomists (to be discussed below) raise another question against the Reformed approach: On what basis does the Reformed approach exclude the civil law? The NT provides ample evidence for excluding ritual laws and clearly affirms moral law, but the case for excluding the civil laws seems less compelling. Theonomists think that the civil laws should be models for modern jurisprudence in so far as Christians are able to incorporate such laws into modern law codes. Why should the civil laws not apply today just as the moral law does? In any case, how does 2 Tim 3:16-17, "All Scripture is . . . profitable," apply in the case of civil regulations under the Reformed approach?

From the opposite direction, theologically speaking, dispensationalists (see below) raise another issue: How is the Reformed approach compatible with the law being nullified in Christ (Rom 6:14; 10:4; Gal 5:18)? Romans 6:14 says "you are not under law, but under grace," and Rom 10:4 says, "Christ is the end of the law . . . to everyone who believes." Dispensationalists argue that these verses prove that the Mosaic law's applicability has been terminated, a view incompatible with the Reformed use of the law.

---

2. D. Dorsey, "The Law of Moses and the Christian: A Compromise," *JETS* 34.3 (1991): 330. Jews since Maimonides traditionally reckon there to be 613 laws in the Pentateuch: 248 positive commands and 365 negative commands—one for each day of the year.

3. John Frame, "Towards a Theology of the State," *WTJ* 51 (1989): 203.

The arguments of the theonomists and dispensationalists will be addressed below.

II. CLASSICAL DISPENSATIONALISM'S APPROACH TO THE LAW

A major theological system that has taken an approach to the law quite different from that of Reformed theology is that of classical dispensationalism.

1. *The dispensational approach to the law defined.* Classical dispensational-ism[4] is a theological system developed in the nineteenth century by John Nelson Darby and associated in the twentieth century with such names as C. I. Scofield, Lewis Sherry Chafer, and Charles C. Ryrie. Classical dispensationalism as a system emphasizes a sharp distinction between Israel and the Church and dis-continuity between OT and NT.

A classical dispensational approach to the law was spelled out by Ryrie.[5] This can be used as the basis of our discussion. According to Ryrie, Christians are not under the law of Moses in any way at all. We are not under law but under grace (Rom 6:14). The Christian's relationship with the Mosaic law has been terminated because "Christ is the end of the law for righteousness to everyone who believes" (Rom 10:4) and "If you are led by the Spirit you are not under the law" (Gal 5:18). Hence the Mosaic law in its totality is abrogated in Christ and is no longer applicable. That includes the Decalogue. Thus the Mosaic law is nei-ther a means of salvation nor a guide for Christian living. This view is not anti-nominian,[6] however, for Christians are under another law: the "law of Christ" (1 Cor 9:21; Gal 6:2). Although we are under a completely different system—the law of Christ rather than the law of Moses—that new system incorporates some individual Mosaic commands and thus overlaps with the Mosaic law. But it is not the Mosaic law that is authoritative for us as Christians. It is the law of Christ.

2. *Strengths of the classical dispensational approach to the law.* The classi-cal dispensational approach to the law is not without its merits.

First, classical dispensationalists rightly warn against *legalism* and *letterism.* Legalism (as defined here) refers to a theological system where one seeks to earn one's salvation by means of works of the law. Certain of Paul's Jewish oppo-

---

4. A new branch of dispensationalism, known as progressive dispensationalism, has developed in recent years. It is less rigid in dogma and draws fewer and less sharp distinctions between Israel and the Church as compared with classical dispensationalism (though more such distinctions than do non-dispensationalists). I am not sure how progressive dispensationalists would treat the Mosaic law, but I suspect this system is not incompatible with the principalizing approach defended here.

5. C. C. Ryrie, "The End of the Law," *BSac* 124 (1967): 239-47.

6. Antinomianism (from *anti* "against" and *nomos* "law") holds that under the gospel dispensation of grace the moral law is of no use or obligation because faith alone is necessary for salvation. (*Webster's New Collegiate Dictionary*, 1981).

nents evidently held to a form of salvation by works of the law (see Rom 2:6-8; Gal 3:10-13; 5:3-4), though the NT teaches salvation is by faith apart from works (Eph 2:8-9). Letterism refers to an unhealthy and obsessively scrupulous interest in details (the "letter") of the law. Those who fall into letterism often "miss the forest for the trees" so to speak – missing the big questions of morality in the pursuit of legal minutia. Jesus rebuked the Pharisees for letterism: "You tithe mint and dill and cumin, but have neglected the weightier matters of the law: justice, mercy and faithfulness" (Matt 23:23). Letterism is oppressive and is a hindrance to spiritual growth.

Second, classical dispensationists rightly emphasize that we are under a new covenant. One cannot simply assume that regulations under one covenant (namely the Mosaic) necessarily apply to another one (the new). Laws can change with a change of covenant, a point the writer of Hebrews makes to his Jewish audience (Heb 7:12).

Third, certain verses do seem supportive of this view, particularly Rom 6:14; 10:4, and Gal 5:18, though alternative interpretations are possible (see below).

3. *Weaknesses of the classical dispensational approach to the law.* Although classical dispensationalism makes some good observations, there are some problems with this view as well.

First, "law versus grace" is a false dichotomy. The law was in fact a gracious gift of God to his people to guide them and show them whether or not they were in compliance with the covenant. It was never a means of salvation or meriting a relationship with God, not even theoretically, even though some of Paul's opponents were legalists. The prologue to the Decalogue (Exod 20:2) begins, "I am the LORD your God who brought you forth from the land of Egypt." The concept of salvation actually comes before the laws are even given. Salvation from Egypt comes to Israel before Israel is given the law to keep. The law was thus given to a people who were already "saved." Laws were not the means of salvation, but were guidelines for those already saved. Similarly, Israel was not given the covenant because they were so good, for they were a stubborn people (Deut 9:6). The covenant was not granted because they were so great but because God loved them (Deut 7:7-9). Similarly, a covenant relationship with God came to Abraham not by any merit of law-keeping, but through God's gracious offer accepted by faith (Gen 15:6; Rom 4:3-4). Paul points out that Abraham was saved before the legal "work" of circumcision (Rom 4:9-16; compare Genesis 15 with Genesis 17). Thus before the Mosaic law (Abraham), after the Mosaic law, and during the Mosaic law, salvation was and is a matter of God's grace rather than human merit.

Second, classical dispensationalists underestimate the degree of continuity between the OT and NT covenants. For example, Jer 31:31-34 (quoted in Hebrews 8) announces the coming of the new covenant for "the house of Israel and the house of Judah" in which God will put his law on his peoples' hearts. That the new covenant is explicitly for Israel and Judah, but is applied in the NT to the Church, and that in this new covenant God's law is written on the hearts of Christians seem to imply more continuity between OT law and the NT than classical dispensationalism allows.

Third, certain verses in the NT are problematic for classical dispensationalism's neglect of the law. 2 Timothy 3:16-17 states that "all Scripture is inspired by God and is profitable for teaching," but in practice classical dispensationalists regularly ignore Mosaic law. Jesus' statement that he "did not come to abolish the law . . . but to fulfill" (Matt 5:17-20) seems hard to reconcile with the dispensational approach to the law that sees the Mosaic law as abrogated. Bahnsen[7] notes that interpreters often take "fulfill" in Matt 5:17 as if it meant "bring to an end," but he argues that to read the verse that way is to make the verse self-contradictory: "I did not come to abolish the law, but to bring it to an end." Jesus certainly fulfilled the law by carrying it out. But the contrast between "fulfill" and "abolish" in this verse suggests some sort of abiding value to the law. Paul considers the law the embodiment of truth by which the Jews are instructed (Rom 2:18-19), but in Romans 3:31 Paul also affirms that in some sense the law is for Christians: "Do we nullify the law by this faith? On the contrary, we uphold the law." The law is holy (7:12) and spiritual (7:14). Love is the fulfilling of the law (13:10). How could Paul say these things if the classical dispensational view of the law were true?

1 Corinthians 7:19 pertains to this discussion: "Circumcision is nothing, and uncircumcision is nothing; what matters is keeping the commandments of God." This verse is ironic since what is circumcision but an OT command of God? But the sense is perhaps this: Though ceremonial matters like circumcision cease to be essential for Christian believers, the "commandments of God" still play a vital role for Christians. According to Paul, the law is not opposed to the promises of God (Gal 3:21). Paul delighted in the law of God (Rom 7:22), and considered it good if used lawfully (1 Tim 1:8). All this seems contrary to dispensationalism's law-versus-grace dichotomy.

Fourth, the NT use of OT laws seems contrary to the classical dispensational limitation of law to the law of Christ. Paul quotes various commandments from the Decalogue and applies them to believers (Rom 7:7; 13:9; Eph 6:1-3). James quotes and applies the law of love command (James 2:8; see Lev 19:18), and condemns partiality, adultery, murder, and slander as contrary to "the law" (James 2:9, 11; 4:11). Peter quotes and applies Leviticus' command to "Be holy for I am holy" (1 Pet 1:16; Lev 19:2). Finally, as Luke T. Johnson[8] has argued, James seems to derive many of his moral statements directly from Leviticus 19 of the Holiness Code, as the following table (from Kaiser)[9] shows.

---

7. Greg Bahnsen, *Theonomy in Christian Ethics* (Nutley, NJ: Craig Press, 1979), 54.

8. Luke T. Johnson, "The Use of Leviticus 19 in the Letter of James," *JBL* 101 (1982): 391-401, cited by Walter Kaiser, *The Uses of the Old Testament in the New Testament* (Chicago: Moody, 1985), 221-224.

9. Kaiser, *Uses of the Old Testament in the New Testament*, 223.

Leviticus 19:12-18	James' Use of Leviticus 19
19:12 Do not swear falsely by my name and profane the name of your God.	**5:12** Do not swear . . . so that you will not be condemned.
19:13 Do not hold back the wages of a hired man overnight.	**5:4** Behold, the wages you failed to pay the workman who mowed your fields are crying out against you.
19:15 Do not show partiality.	**2:1** Do not show favoritism. **2:9** If you show favoritism . . .
19:16 Do not go about spreading slander among your people.	**4:11** Do not slander one another, brothers.
19:17b Rebuke your neighbor frankly so that you will not share his guilt.	**5:20** Know that whoever turns a sinner back from his error will save him from death and cover a multitude of sins.
19:18a And your hand will not avenge you and you shall not be angry with the children of your people.	**5:9** Don't take out your resentments on each other, brothers.
19:18b You shall love your neighbor as yourself.	**2:8** You shall love your neighbor as yourself.

Fifth, as Waltke[10] observes, the classical dispensational approach to the law ignores the important concept of the lordship of Christ in every area of life. A weakness of dispensationalism is that it concentrates almost exclusively on personal, individual piety, but does not seek to implement into society the political and social implications of the gospel. Should not the truth that "Jesus is Lord" find practical expression in civil law as well as every other area of existence?

Finally, the proof texts used by dispensationalists—namely Romans 6:14; 10:4; and Gal 5:18—are subject to alternative interpretations that do not demand the conclusion that the law is completely abrogated.

Romans 10:4 states, "Christ is the end of the law for righteousness for everyone who believes." One key word is "end" (Gk. *telos*). Dispensationalists (among others) take this verse to mean that Christ is the termination of the law for Christian believers, but there are other possibilities: Christ could be the "end" of the

---

10. B. Waltke, "Theonomy in Relation to Dispensational and Covenant Theologies," in *Theonomy: A Reformed Critique* (eds. W. Barker and W. R. Godfrey; Grand Rapids: Zondervan, 1990), 66.

law in the sense of its goal (Cranfield).[11] The law looks forward to Christ, being the one of whom Moses wrote (John 1:45); and Christ fulfills the law's predictions and promises. Although it is possible that the application of the law is modified upon reaching its goal in Christ, it does not necessarily follow that Christ terminates the law altogether.

Even if "end" in Rom 10:4 means "termination," it does not necessarily follow that there is no abiding application of the Mosaic law. Another view is that Christ is the end of the Pharisaic heresy of "law-for-righetousness justification" (Longnecker).[12] According to this view, Paul does not mean that Christ is the end in the sense of termination of the OT law itself, but that Christ is the end or termination of "the law-for-righteousness." That is, Christ is the end of the Pharisaic heresy of trying to merit salvation on the basis of legal righteousness. The lack of the article with *nomos* could mean Paul has legalism rather than the Mosaic law in view. In any case, the general context (Rom 9:30-32) suggests Paul is discussing the use of law as a means of salvation, something for which OT law was never intended.

Although dispensationalists argue Romans 6:14 ("we are not under law, but grace") implies that Christians are not subject to the law, this too is not a necessary conclusion. Classical dispensationalists themselves do not argue that Christians are not under any law at all, for they affirm we are under "the law of Christ." It is the Mosaic law that dispensationalists believe Christians not to be under. But another view of "not under law" is that Christians are not under Pharisaic merit theology. In Rom 6:14 law (Greek *nomos*) may have the limited sense of Pharisaic merit theology or works righteousness rather than Mosaic law (Bahnsen).[13] Or alternatively, "law" may be a metonym for the condemnation of the law (Cranfield).[14] If so, it refers to the Mosaic law as it condemns us as sinners. Because of God's grace we are not under the law's condemnation. But that does not mean we are not under law as a guide for holy living.

Similar arguments can be made for Gal 5:18 "If you are led by the Spirit you are not under the law." Law in Galatians relates specifically to the nomistic viewpoint of certain Jewish Christians who were teaching the Gentile Christians at Galatia the false dogma that Christians were obligated to keep ceremonial laws such as circumcision in order to be saved (Gal 5:1-6). Christians led internally by the Spirit are not to be under law in that sense for several reasons: First, contrary to the teaching of these Judaizers, Christians are not fully under the law's dominion since under the new covenant they are no longer obligated to keep ceremonial aspects of the law such as circumcision. Paul teaches that becoming a new creature in Christ is what matters, not circumcision (Gal 6:15). Second, they

---

11. C. E. B. Cranfield, *Romans* (2 vol.; ICC; Edinburgh: T & T Clark, 1975, 1979), 520.

12. R. Longnecker, *Paul, Apostle of Liberty* (Grand Rapids: Baker, 1976), 144-153.

13. C. K. Barrett, *A Commentary on the Epistle to the Romans* (New York: Harper, 1957), 129; Bahnsen, *Theonomy,* 221.

14. Cranfield, *Romans,* 320.

are not under the Judaizers' (mis-)understanding of the law because salvation has always been based on faith, not based on keeping the law (Gal 2:16). If it were based on law-keeping, then Christ died for no reason (Gal 2:21). But the problem with this merit theology is that they would have to keep all the law to merit salvation, which is impossible, and so they would be lost (Gal 3:10-11; 5:2-3). Third, the Galatians should not put themselves under the Judaizers' laws because being led internally by the Spirit empowers a believer to overcome the sins of the flesh (Gal 5:16-17) and to keep the law of love (Gal 5:14), whereas the Judaizers' external, letteristic rule-books provided no such empowerment, but only slavery (Gal 5:1). So Christians are not under ceremonial law, legalistic merit theology or letteristic and fleshly rule-keeping. And yet none of this implies that the law's moral and religious principles cannot continue to serve as a guide for Christian thought and life.

The above shows that there are plausible alternatives to the dispensational interpretation of Rom 10:4; 6:14; and Gal 5:18 that allows for the possibility that Christians could be under the Mosaic law in some sense.

III. THE APPROACH OF LUTHERAN THEOLOGY TO THE LAW

Another approach to law comes from Martin Luther and the Lutheran movement.

1. *The Lutheran approach to the law defined.* Traditional Lutheran theology developed its own distinctive approach to the law. This is laid out in the *Book of Concord* (A.D. 1580).[15] In Lutheran theology, the law is given for several purposes: (1) The law maintains external discipline. (2) The law leads men and women to a knowledge of sin and prepare them for the grace of the gospel. In this system law and gospel must be strictly distinguished. (3) For those reborn in Christ, the law regulates the lives of Christians. This "third function of the law" is disputed by antinomians who reject the preaching of law, and others who say the sole purpose of the law is to convict unbelievers. But denial of the third function is dangerous to and subversive of Christian discipline. Because the lingering effects of the old nature remains, Christians also need the guidance of law.

It must be understood, however, that Lutheran theology does not mean by "law" what other theological systems do. The "law" in Lutheran theology is not the law of Moses; but rather it is "the unchangeable will of God," the moral law as epitomized in the Decalogue, and natural law. The judicial laws of Moses were binding only on the Jews except in so far as they reflect natural law. Luther puts it in his typically pungent way:

Moses was an intermediary solely for the Jewish people, to whom God gave the law. . . . Moses does not concern us. If I accept Moses in *one* commandment, I

---

15. *Book of Concord: Confessions of the Evangelical Lutheran Church* (A.D. 1580) (tr. Theodore Tappert; Philadelphia: Fortress, 1959), 478-479, 223, 87, 561-568.

must accept all of Moses. Thus it would follow if I accept Moses as master, then I must let myself be circumcised according to Jewish custom, eat, drink and dress thus and so, and observe all that stuff . . . Now if anyone confronts you with Moses and his commandments and wants to press you to keep them, say 'Go to the Jews with your Moses; I am no Jew, don't entangle me with Moses.'"[16]

Christians according to Luther are bound to obey the civil laws of their own nations and not reinstitute the Mosaic laws. Luther allows that some laws of the Jews might be incorporated into the civil laws of Gentile nations, but this is the same "as when one nation follows examples from laws of other nations, as the Romans took the Twelve Tables from the Greeks,"[17] and not a matter of authority. Luther's view thus contrasts with that of the Calvinists in theocratic Geneva who made religious offenses capital ones on the basis of Mosaic laws. Spiritual and temporal authorities are not to be mingled or confused. According to Lusther, Catholicism, by attaching sin to foods and days, was misled by the Levitical law of Moses and inappropriately burdened the Church with bondage to the law.

2. *Strengths of the Lutheran approach to the law.* Lutheran theology, building on the insights of Martin Luther who rediscovered the concept of justification by faith alone apart from works of the law, has formulated an approach to the law that successfully avoids legalism (meriting salvation via works of the law), letterism, and antinomianism. There are NT verses that seem to contrast law and grace that fit well with Lutheran theology: "The law was given through Moses; grace and truth came through Jesus Christ" (John 1:17), "We are not under law, but under grace" (Rom 6:14). It also fits in well with Paul's teachings in Romans 13 that demand that Christians acknowledge the laws of the state. Its emphasis on discontinuity between OT law and the NT grace is reminiscent of the sharp distinctions found in classical dispensationalism with which Lutheran theology shares both strengths and weaknesses.

3. *Weaknesses of the Lutheran approach to the law.* The Lutheran approach to the law has several weaknesses. First, the sharp law-gospel dichotomy in Lutheranism appears more the imposition of a dogmatic construct than a necessary deduction from Scripture. Law and grace are not necessarily opposites. The alternative views of Rom 6:14 have been already been discussed, and an alternative view of John 1:17 will appear in Chapter 2. Second, Luther's affirmation of Mosaic laws insofar as they overlap with "natural law" leaves open how one determines what is or is not "natural law." In the modern debate, some say homosexual behavior is contrary to natural law, while others say it is in accord with

---

16. Quoted by Heinrich Bornkamm, *Luther and the Old Testament* (tr. E. W. and R. Gritsch; ed. V. Gruhn; Philadelphia: Fortress, 1969), 122.

17. Bornkamm, *Luther and the Old Testament,* 123.

the homosexual's nature and is therefore consistent with natural law. The selection of which of the Mosaic laws overlap with natural law seems similarly subjective. Third, the ignoring of the civil laws in practice is inconsistent with 2 Tim 3:16 that "All Scripture . . . is profitable for teaching." Finally Lutheranism's sharp contrast between temporal powers and spiritual authority seems to deny the lordship of Christ in every area of life.

IV. MEREDITH KLINE'S INTRUSION ETHICS

A variation on the Reformed approach to the law, though not one that has been widely adopted, was proposed by OT scholar Meredith Kline.[18]

1. *Meredith Kline's approach to the law defined.* Meredith Kline argues that the OT political and social laws are not immediately applicable today because they were tailored to a special situation of Israel. Though the civil laws have no direct application today, says Kline, he does see typological value in the civil law just as Reformed theologians (and others) have always seen typological value in the ceremonial law. In particular, Israel as a holy nation prefigured the holiness of God's heavenly kingdom and the holiness belonging to the consummation of all things. For example, the wars against the Canaanites prefigures the second coming of Christ who will wage war against all the enemies of God (Rev 19:11-21).

Vern Poythress[19] has attempted to identify typological elements in the laws in a way not inconsistent with Kline's approach. The following chart is based on Poythress' analysis as well as Kline's thoughts.

---

18. See M. G. Kline, *The Structure of Biblical Authority* (Grand Rapids: Eerdmans, 1972); idem, "Comments on an Old-New Error [Review of Bahnsen, *Theonomy*]," *WTJ* 41 (1978-79): 172-189; John Frame, "The One, the Many, and Theonomy," in *Theonomy: A Reformed Critique,* 89-99; V. S. Poythress, "Effects of Interpretative Frameworks of the Application of Old Testament Law," in *Theonomy: a Reformed Critique,* 103-123; Bahnsen, *Theonomy,* 571-84.

19. V. Poythress, *The Shadow of Christ in the Law of Moses* (Brentwood, Tenn.: Wolgemuth & Hyatt, 1991).

MATTER IN LAW	WHAT IT PREFIGURES
Tabernacle	Presence of Christ now & in Heaven
Sacrifices	The Sacrifice of Christ on the Cross
Priesthood	Priestly role of Christ in relating to his people
The Whole Cultic System	*Union with Christ*
Moral and Civil Laws	The Righteousness of Christ
The Promised Land	The Future Kingdom of Christ
Penalties in the Law	Christ's Last Judgment
Destruction of the Canaanites	Condemnation of the Wicked in Hell

Another point made by Kline is that the civil law has intruded the ethics of the eschatological kingdom into Israel. What he means by that is that the civil law prefigures aspects of the kingdom of God in its final manifestation. Its ethics have been intruded in certain ways into the practice of ancient Israel.

2. *Strength of Meredith Kline's approach to the law.* Kline's bringing out of typological elements of the civil law supplements the approach of Reformed theology and is a valuable and valid contribution to the discussion of the law.

3. *Weaknesses of Meredith Kline's approach to the law.* In practice, Kline's view is much like the dispensational and Lutheran views in that the civil law is essentially not applicable for today. He finds some value in it typologically, but little practically. In fact, Kline argues that the proper government for today is a religiously neutral state rather than a Christian one in which no one religion has an advantage over another. But wherein is the lordship of Christ in every area of life under such an arrangement? Frame rightly argues against Kline that there is insufficient reason to exclude governments from the influence of Christ.[20] If Kingdom Ethics could be intruded into the life of Israel, why could they not be intruded into modern states as well? Kline has prematurely precluded allowing modern civil law to be influenced by the Scriptures, including its civil laws.

---

20. Frame, "The One, the Many, and Theonomy," 95.

V. APPROACH OF THEONOMY (CHRISTIAN RECONSTRUCTIONISM)

Another variation on the approach of Reformed theology is that of theonomy or Christian Reconstructionism.

1. *Theonomy's approach to the law defined.* Theonomy means "law of God." Theonomy is part of a broader movement known as Christian Reconstructionism (associated with such figures as Greg Bahnsen, Gary North, and Rousas John Rushdooney) that gained some notoriety in Christian circles in the 1970s and 1980s,[21] though its strength as a movement appears to have waned. Christian Reconstructionism seeks ultimately to recapture all social and political institutions for Christ and create a Christian culture. One element of that is to seek to establish "the law of God" as the law of the modern state.

As an ideology theonomy represents a modification of the Reformed approach to the law. Theonomists agree with the advocates of the Reformed approach that the ceremonial law is superceded under the new covenant but disagree with them over the continued applicability of the civil law. Whereas the traditional Reformed approach to the law says only the moral law is directly applicable today, Christian Reconstructionists (theonomists) argue that both the moral and the civil regulations of the Mosaic law are directly applicable today.

Theonomists believe that Christians should work towards establishing a theocratic state in the world. Society, they believe, needs to be reconstructed through changing its laws so that modern legal codes are made to conform with the Mosaic civil laws as found in the Pentateuch. Even the sanctions of those laws must be enforced as the Bible describes them. Hence offenses such as striking parents, idolatry, witchcraft, Sabbath breaking and worship of gods other than Yahweh should become capital offenses as they were in the OT.

The choice then, say theonomists, is God's law or man's law: theonomy or autonomy. God's law, they argue, is much better.

2. *Strengths of theonomy's approach to the law.* Although we will ultimately find theonomy/Christian Reconstructionism wanting, as an approach it has some merits.

---

21. Among works defending or critiquing Theonomy: Bahnsen, *Theonomy in Christian Ethics*; William S. Barker and W. Robert Godfrey, eds., *Theonomy: A Reformed Critique* (Grand Rapids: Zondervan, 1990); Kenneth L. Gentry, *God's Law in the Modern World: The Continuing Relevance of Old Testament Law* (Phillipsburg, N.J.: Presbyterian & Reformed, 1993); H. Wayne House and Thomas Ice, *Dominion Theology: Blessing or Curse?* (Portland, Oregon: Multnomah Press, 1988); Kline, "Comments on an Old-New Error [Review of Bahnsen, *Theonomy*]," 172-189; Gary North, *Tools of Dominion: The Case Laws of Exodus* (Tyler, Texas: Institute for Christian Economics, 1990); Douglas A. Oss, "The Influence of Hermeneutical Frameworks in the Theonomy Debate," *WTJ* 51 (1989): 227-258; Rousas John Rushdooney, *The Institutes of Biblical Law* (Nutley, N.J.: Craig Press, 1973).

First, Christian Reconstructionists are rightly concerned about the lordship of Christ in every area of society. Christians are not simply to sit around and wait for Jesus to come and establish the age to come, but rather believers are to be the salt of the earth allowing Christian teaching to leaven society even now. This should include every sphere of life, including the legal.

Second, Christian Reconstructionists rightly question approaches which totally ignore the civil law. The teaching of 2 Tim 3:16-17 that "All Scripture is inspired . . . and profitable" must apply to civil law too.

Third, theonomists have stimulated thoughtful critiques of modern legal practices based on comparisons with biblical law. How might biblical civil law provide a critique of modern law? The following, collected from both theonomists and non-theonomist sources, are some critiques of modern jurisprudence based on biblical law: Modern Law emphasizes *rights*; whereas biblical law emphasizes *duties*. Modern law is conceived of as "a delicate balance of competing interests"; whereas the Bible conceives of law as an expression of morality and justice. Modern judges merely "apply the law" whether or not the law is just, whereas, biblical judges were to do justice. In modern law the secular state imposes its will from above down upon the people, whereas the Bible emphasizes the need for personal morality based on religion to undergird the law from below. The Bible makes theft a matter of tort between the offender and the victim and obligates the criminal to make restitution directly to the individual wronged. This is arguably more just than the modern system that makes theft a crime against the state in which the offender pays his debt to "society" through prison but not to the victim. Restitution to victims is both more just and more cost effective than incarceration.

2. *Weaknesses of theonomy's approach to the law.* Although the approach of theonomy/Christian Reconstructionism is in some ways attractive, it also has serious weaknesses.

First, theonomy takes insufficient account of the new theological setting of the church age. In particular, its error is the opposite of that of classical dispensationalists: It underestimates the discontinuity between OT and NT covenants. The Church is not a nation, and America is not the promised land. Since we are not a theocracy, theocratic laws do not seem directly relevant. Hebrews 7:12, 18 argues that with a change in covenant, there is necessarily a "change of law" and a "setting aside of the former commandment." Theonomy, in denying that there has been substantive change of law, has denied the newness of the new covenant (Jer 31:31-34).[22]

Change in covenant circumstance can affect how sanctions are meted out. John Frame and Vern Poythress[23] both argue that the death penalties for cultic

---

22. T. David Gordon, "Critique of Theonomy," *WTJ* 56 (1994): 39.
23. Frame, "Theology of the State," 222-223; Poythress, "Effects of Interpretive Frameworks," 117-19.

offenses were based on the special holiness of Israel with the tabernacle of God among them. Cultic violation under those circumstances could bring God's wrath on the entire community. Now that God's tabernacle is no longer in our midst, however, the rationale for punishments such as those in Deuteronomy 13 and 17 arguably no longer apply.

If the civil law were directly applicable to Christians as theonomists claim, one would expect them to show up in NT discussions of the Christian and the state. Paul discusses matters of civil obedience in Romans 13 but makes no reference to the Sinai regulation.[24] Arguments from silence such as this are by nature weak, yet theonomy's case could easily have been confirmed had NT authors explicitly used the Mosaic law along Christian Reconstructionist lines.

Christopher Wright[25] argues that in the OT there is a vital link between family, ownership of land, and God: "An Israelite's land and property were the tangible symbols of his personal share in the inheritance of Israel." Hence an attack on a family's property was also an attack on their relationship with Yahweh who had given them the land. But Wright also observes that in the NT the expression "in Christ" has replaced the expression "in the land," and fellowship with the church has replaced the clan.[26] These changes reflect both a change of culture (tribal to nuclear family) and the change of redemptive setting. This results in a change in application of the property laws.

Second, theonomy fails to take into sufficient account the change in cultural and historical settings between pentateuchal times and today that make certain laws inapplicable. Some laws have become impractical and unenforceable in the modern age. Are we to dispossess the Canaanites? How can we, for Canaanites no longer exist. This "law" was time and place specific. Others are culturally antiquated. For example, cities of refuge regulations (Deuteronomy 19; Numbers 35) that call upon manslayers to flee to a city of refuge for a trial to determine whether the offense is unintentional or deliberate murder, and having a relative (the kinsman-redeemer of blood) serve as pursuer and executioner, might have been a practical means for dispensing justice in a tribal, immobile, agrarian, low-population society where everybody knew everybody, but such an arrangement would hardly work in the mobile, urban, high population cities of today.

Moreover, some laws seem never to have been enforced as law even in the OT. One such law is that of the Year of Jubilee (Leviticus 25, 27) in which once a lifetime land was to be returned to the descendants of its original owners. There is no evidence that a Year of Jubilee was ever proclaimed in OT times. There are historical reasons why this was so. The Year of Jubilee law would only go into effect forty-nine years after conquering the land, and the law is formulated on the assumption that Israel would conquer and settle the land quickly. In fact, however, during the time of the book of Judges Israel got bogged down and did not

---

24. Gordon, "Critique of Theonomy," 28.

25. Christopher Wright, *God's People in God's Land* (Grand Rapids: Eerdmans, 1990), 135-136.

26. Wright, *God's People in God's Land,* 111-114.

completely conquer the land. During Judges Israelites were often under the political control of foreigners rather than Israelites, and so Israel had little opportunity to apply the Jubilee regulations. Only at the time of David, centuries after
Joshua, did Israel finally conquer the whole land of promise. But by that time
records of the original owners of the land would have been lost or so confused as
to make fair implementation of the Year of Jubilee difficult. After further complications of the division of the monarchy at Solomon's death, the matter appears
never to have come up.

Some laws assume (without commanding) cultural conditions that do not occur in Western societies: debt slavery (Exod 21:1-11); fat-tailed sheep (Exod
29:22); flat-roofed houses where people regularly walk (Deut 22:7); the custom
of brideprice and dowry (Exod 22:16-17); climate of Palestine for festival dates
(Lev 23:33-39) and the like. [27]

Third, theonomy/Christian Reconstructionism is tied to a questionable eschatology: postmillennialism. Most theonomists hold to a postmillennial interpretation of the end times. Postmillennialism holds that eventually the whole
world will be evangelized and christianized by the Church. This will lead to a
golden age, the millennium of Revelation 20, that will occur before Christ returns
to earth in the second coming. Christian Reconstructionists hope to introduce the
law of God into modern societies as part of that christianizing process during the
millennial golden age.

Of the three common eschatological views—premillennialism (that Christ
returns before the thousand years of Revelation 20), amillennialism (that the
thousand years of Revelation 20 is concurrent with the church age, at the end of
which Christ returns), and postmillennialism (Christ returns at the end of the
thousand years of Revelation 20)—postmillennialism is clearly the least popular
position among contemporary theologians. To the extent that theonomy is tied to
postmillennialism, those who on other grounds reject postmillennialism will tend
to reject theonomy. This is not a conclusive argument, however, because one in
principle could hold to a form of Christian Reconstructionism without its postmillennial eschatology. Televangelist and 1988 presidential candidate Pat
Robertson, who is premillennial, is said to have toyed with a modified form of
Christian Reconstructionism. [28] Nonetheless, postmillennial eschatology has in
practice been a key foundation for Reconstructionist thought and theonomy.

Fourth, theonomy could degenerate into oppression. James Dobson argued
this way,

> Do you agree that if a man beats his slave to death, he is to be considered guilty
> only if the individual dies instantly? If the slave lives a few days, the owner is

---

27. Dorsey, "The Law of Moses and the Christian," 325-329, who also gives many
more examples.

28. R. J. Neuhaus, "Ralph Reed's Real Agenda," review of R. Reed, *Active Faith:
How Christians are Changing the Soul of American Politics, First Things* 66 (Oct. 1996):
n.p. Cited 29 June 2004. On-line: www.firstthings.com/ftissues/ft9610/neuhaus.html.

considered not guilty (Exod 21:20-21)? Do you believe that we should stone to death rebellious children (Deut 21:18-21)? Do you really believe that we can draw subtle meaning about complex issues from the Mosaic law, when even the obvious interpretation makes no sense to us today? We can hardly select what we will and will not apply now. If we accept the verses you cited, we are obligated to deal with every last jot and tittle."[29]

House and Ice likewise imagine hypothetical scenarios that paint "A Christian Reconstructed America" in terms reminiscent of the oppressive Muslim theocracy created by the Taliban of Afghanistan.[30]

In my view both Dobson and House & Ice wrongly portray the law of God as inherently unjust. If it is unjust, how could a just God have given it to Israel? Some of their interpretations of how the law was applied are in my opinion not accurate interpretations of the Mosaic law. For example Dobson's interpretations of beating and or maiming slaves misses the real point of these laws which was to provide slaves with rights and protection, as will be argued below in the chapter on the *Lex Talionis*.

Nonetheless these authors have a point. In the past the attempts to tie church and state too closely have not worked out well and have degenerated into oppression, as when Protestant "heretics" were tortured and killed by Catholics during the Spanish Inquisition or when Reformers in Calvin's day burned and drowned Anabaptists for their alleged heresies. Even just laws in the hands of fallible human administrators could be twisted into something unjust and oppressive. Ralph Reed, who believes in religiously informed political action by Christians, repudiates Christian Reconstructionism because of its potential for oppression: "Reconstructionism is an authoritarian ideology that threatens the most basic civil liberties of a free and democratic society."[31]

Fifth, contrary to theonomy's approach to the law, the NT does not indicate that the sanctions (penalties) of Mosaic laws are eternally abiding. Instead the NT applies the principle of the law apart from the original sanctions to the church age. Kaiser[32] points to the case of incest in 1 Cor 5:1-5 in which a man slept with his father's wife. There Paul does not even hint that the law's death penalty should be applied (cf. Lev 18:29) but directs that the individual should receive church discipline until he repented, at which time he could be restored to fellowship. In this case the principle of the law (that incest of this sort is condemned by God) is affirmed, but the sanction (death) is not. Rather a different sanction, appropriate to the new redemptive setting, is substituted: excommunication. Even though the original sanction is not applied, the biblical law remains valuable in pointing out sin. As a matter of fact, apart from OT law or direct revelation from God Paul could not have been able to define this activity as sinful.

---

29. Quoted by North, *Tools of Dominion,* 360.
30. House and Ice, *Dominion Theology: A Blessing or a Curse,* 63-82.
31. Quoted by Neuhaus, "Ralph Reed's Real Agenda," n.p.
32. W. Kaiser, "God's Promise Plan and his Gracious Law," *JETS* 33.3 (1990): 292.

Tremper Longman[33] observes that Jesus allowed divorce in the case of adultery but made no suggestion that one should apply the death penalty for this offense, even though adultery was punishable by death in the OT. This difference is further evidence of adjustment of the sanction due to the changed redemptive situation.

VI. THE PRINCIPALIZING APPROACH TO BIBLICAL LAW

The final approach to the law is the one accepted and labeled by this author[34] as the principalizing approach. This approach is also adopted by the Evangelical OT scholars Walter Kaiser,[35] David Dorsey[36] and J. Daniel Hays.[37] It has affinities with the approach to the law by Jewish biblical scholar Moshe Greenberg.[38]

1. *The principalizing approach to the law defined.* According to the principalizing approach, it is necessary to look at each law and ask what principle—moral or religious—underlies this regulation. Kaiser calls this the "most common method of finding contemporary relevance from particular laws of another time and culture."[39]

Fundamental to this approach is to recognize that the law has changed since the advent of Christ. Whereas Christ did not come to abolish the law . . . but to fulfill" (Matt 5:17), the fulfillment of the law by Christ nevertheless has transformed the way in which we apply OT laws. Now they must be read in the light of the dawning of the new, eschatological age.[40] In this eschatological, Messianic Age, Mosaic laws no longer apply directly to the Christian. This is in part because those laws were written for a particular historical-cultural setting that no longer exists. But more significantly, they do not apply directly because in fulfilling the law, Christ brought us under a different theological setting of the new covenant.

---

33. Tremper Longman, "God's Law and Mosaic Punishments Today," *Theonomy: A Reformed Critique,* 53.

34. J. Sprinkle, "Law," *Evangelical Dictionary of Biblical Theology* (ed. W. Elwell; Grand Rapids: Baker, 1996), 467-471.

35. Walter Kaiser, *Toward Old Testament Ethics* (Grand Rapids: Zondervan, 1983); idem, *The Uses of the Old Testament in the New;* idem, *Towards Rediscovering the Old Testament* (Grand Rapids: Zondervan, 1987); idem, "God's Promise Plan and his Gracious Law," 289-302.

36. Dorsey, "The Law of Moses and the Christian," 321-334.

37. J. Daniel Hays, "Applying the Old Testament Law Today," *BSac* 158 (2001): 21-35.

38. Moshe Greenberg, "Some Postulates of Biblical Criminal Law," in *Yehezkel Kaufmann Jubilee Volume* (ed. M. Haran; Jerusalem: Detus Goldberg, 1960), 3-28; idem, "More Reflections on Biblical Criminal Law," *Studies in Bible: 1986* (ScrHier 31; ed. S. Japhet; Jerusalem: Magnes, 1986), 1-17.

39. Kaiser, *Towards Rediscovering the Old Testament,* 157.

40. After Frank Thielman, *Paul & the Law* (Downers Grove: InterVarsity, 1994).

Despite the changed cultural, historical and theological setting, Christians can and should continue to derive moral and religious principles from Mosaic laws. The underlying principles of the law transcend their original cultural and covenantal setting. This is achieved by a process of principalization: starting with a particular law, then going up the "ladder of abstraction" (Kaiser's term)[41] to find a more general moral or religious principle that undergirds that law. The principle so derived is then reapplied today taking into consideration the changed cultural and theological setting under the new covenant. Hermeneutically this is the same process by which we apply Paul's commands to the Corinthians or to Timothy to ourselves. We ask the question, "What principle led God through the writer to say this under those circumstances?" Once the principle is derived, then we can apply that same principle to analogous situations today. This is true not only for Paul's directives but also for the Mosaic laws. The moral and religious principles derived by this procedure can then be equated with the "law of Christ."

This approach can be compared with the categories of the Reformed approach. What the Reformed approach calls moral law is already in the form of principles that transcend the covenants and cultural conditions, so such laws are directly applicable today. The Reformed approach is correct to say civil laws do not apply directly since the Church is neither a theocracy nor a political state. It is also true that the ceremonial laws do not apply directly because we are under a new covenant for which the sacrifices and festivals and other ceremonies are not mandated. Nevertheless the principles behind both civil and ceremonial laws still apply.

For example, a civil law with some ceremonial elements is the cities of refuge regulations. God commanded Israel to set up cities of refuge to which someone could flee after committing manslaughter (Numbers 35; Deut 19:4-7). Those guilty of intentional murder (Num 35:12, 18-19) and those who fail to flee immediately to the city of refuge (Deut 19:6) were subject to being killed by a member of the deceased person's clan labeled "the kinsman-redeemer of blood" (Heb. *go'ēl haddām*). But if someone was only guilty of accidental or unintentional manslaughter, the perpetrator of this act was not to be executed. Instead he was to be confined to the city of refuge until the death of the high priest (Num 35:25, 28).

In today's modern urban, mobile societies, it would be absurd and impractical to try to reinstitute the cities of refuge regulations, designed as they were for a primitive, rural, non-mobile population. Nonetheless, certain moral principles can be deduced: (i) Murder is terribly wrong, as seen by its being subject to the extreme penalty of the law. (ii) Intentional murder is a more serious crime than unintentional or accidental manslaughter. This is indicated by the lesser penalty for the latter offense. Every legal system needs to make that distinction if it is to be just. (iii) Even negligent manslaughter is a very serious offense that requires some punishment, though much less severe than the punishment for intentional

---

41. Kaiser, *Toward Rediscovering the Old Testament*, 166.

murder. (iv) From the religious point of view, the connection between the release from the city of refuge and the death of the high priest implies the religious doctrine of substitutionary atonement, reminding Christians of the atoning power of the death of Jesus Christ, our high priest.

Another example is the Day of Atonement regulations. Leviticus 16 describes the Day of Atonement (Yom Kippur), the most solemn and sacred of all of Israel's holy days. The Day of Atonement dealt with the purging of Israel's sins and its ceremonial impurities. Impurities are described in Leviticus 11-15. In one sense one could say that this holy day has no relevance for Christians at all because we are not required to perform animal sacrifice for sin and the distinction between clean and unclean was abolished by Christ (Mark 7:19). Nonetheless some religious principles can be rightly discerned in the Day of Atonement regulation that continue to be valid under the new covenant: (i) the holiness of God, (ii) the moral contamination of human beings, (iii) the incompatibility of a holy God abiding with impure people, and (iv) the need for atonement to remove people's impurity so as to experience God's presence.

To continue to dwell in their midst, God required, in addition to the regular sacrifices, an annual purging of the people's sins and impurities lest he break out in wrath against them. The NT, especially Hebrews 7-10, picks up on these principles, seeing the Day of Atonement as a type of the atoning work of Christ on the cross, though Christ's work is in every way superior. Unlike Aaron, Christ as high priest is sinless and needed no sacrifice for himself (Heb 7:26-27). Unlike the Day of Atonement sacrifice, Christ's sacrifice of himself needed to be offered only once, not annually (Heb 9:25-26). And whereas Aaron entered the earthly sanctuary, Christ enters heaven itself to do his priestly work (Heb 9:24). Nonetheless the fundamental religious principles behind the Day of Atonement provide the framework for Christians to understand the meaning of the death of Christ that reconciles a holy God and sinful man through the atoning sacrifice of his own blood. Thus the Day of Atonement remains useful for Christians as they reflect on the meaning and significance of the death of Christ for their sins.

2. *Strengths of the principalizing approach to the law.* There are many positive aspects to the principalizing approach to the law.

First, the principalizing approach to the law affirms 2 Tim 3:16-17 ("All Scripture . . . is profitable for teaching") in the case of all the laws: moral, civil and ritual. It allows Paul's positive statements about Christians keeping the law (Rom 3:31, etc.) to be true.

Second, the principalizing approach to the law avoids arbitrary and sometimes misleading labels such as moral, civil, ceremonial laws. These terms may be used for their heuristic value, but are not essential to the approach.

Third, the principalizing approach to the law fully recognizes modifications required by the new cultural and theological setting of the new covenant. For example, sacrifices and the food laws (Mark 7:19) are obsolete in terms of literal application. Nevertheless even here moral and religious principles are contained in them (e.g., the sacrifices teach the concept of blood atonement).

Fourth, the principalizing approach to the law can affirm the lordship of Christ in every area of life, even the judicial. The moral principles that can be derived from civil laws are still applicable and should, whenever feasible, be promoted by Christians in modern jurisprudence.

Fifth, the principalizing approach to the law can explain certain ironic and difficult verses. For example, it helps explain how Abraham could be said to keep the "commands, statues and laws" (Gen 26:5), terms used elsewhere for the Mosaic regulations, before the Mosaic law was given. This could be said of Abraham because he kept the principles later codified into specific laws. Specifically, through living by faith Abraham in essence kept the law. Similarly, Paul makes the ironic statement, "neither circumcision nor uncircumcision counts for anything, but keeping the commandments of God" (1 Cor 7:19). What could Paul mean given that circumcision was one of the commandments of God? What I think he means is that the literal command of circumcision could be practiced or not with indifference because it was the sign of the now obsolete Abrahamic-Mosaic covenant, and yet the moral and religious principles of the law represent God's commandments for believers under the new covenant. This is true even of the circumcision command, for it was a symbolic reminder for believers to "walk before [God] and be blameless" (Gen 17:2). Even though circumcision need not be practiced by Christians, what it symbolized should be.

Sixth, there are a number of places where the Bible appears to principalize the laws.[42] For example, in Ezra 9:1-2 Ezra refers to a law proscribing marriage to "Canaanites" (Deut 7:1-5) and uses it to condemn Jewish intermarriage with non-Canaanite foreigners. This was justified because the same principle applied: Marriages with Canaanites would lead Israel astray spiritually. So marriages to the peoples of the land in Ezra's day would do the same.

There are several cases where Paul seems to principalize the law. In 1 Cor 9:9-14 Paul takes a law from Deut 25:4 ("do not muzzle an ox while he is threshing") and uses it to argue that Christian ministers should be supported economically. How did he get that out of this law? Deuteronomy 25:4 essentially allows oxen to dip down and eat some of the grain that would from time to time fall across their path while threshing. This among other things teaches people to be kind to animals that would otherwise be driven to distraction by smelling grain they could not eat. But Paul evidently sees a deeper, more abstract principle in this law: Those that work for you should benefit from the work that they do. The law about oxen reflects a larger principle that workers should receive material benefit from their labors. That principle can in turn be applied back to ministers who ought to be paid for their ministries.[43] Note that Paul repeats this use

---

42. Some of these examples are after Dan G. McCartney, "The New Testament Use of the Pentateuch: Implications for the Theonomic Movement," in *Theonomy: A Reformed Critique,* 129-149.

43. Kaiser, *Toward Rediscovering the Old Testament,* 164-166.

of Deut 25:4 to justify paying ministers in 1 Tim 5:18. There he quotes Deut 25:4 in parallel with a saying of Jesus, as if both were equally authoritative.

Another example where Paul uses the law is in 2 Cor 13:1. There he alludes to Deut 17:6-7 and 19:15 that require "two or three witnesses" in court cases, but Paul applies this by analogy to a church conference. The common principle is that judgments need to be based on solid evidence.

2 Corinthians 6:14 ("do not be unequally yoked together with unbelievers") is derived by analogy from Deut 22:10, a law about not yoking an ox and a donkey together. This law is among laws of inappropriate mixtures that teach Israel the concept of holiness or separation. That principle applies to Christians who are to maintain a separation from unbelievers in certain kinds of relationships.

In 1 Cor 5:1-3 Paul affirms the principle found in Lev 18:8, 29 that incest between a man and his father's wife is wrong. Yet he does not apply the law with its death penalty directly. Instead, in view of the new redemptive setting under the new covenant, he substitutes excommunication for execution. Here we see that the morality of the law applies directly, but the sanction does not.

Paul also appears to derive sexual morality from the law in 1 Cor 6:9. There Paul condemns, among other things, homosexual acts. The second of Paul's terms for homosexual is Gk. *arsenokoitai*. This Greek word seems to have been derived from the Septuagint (LXX), an early Greek translation of the Hebrew Bible. The LXX renders Leviticus 20:13 as "Whoever sleeps with a male in the manner of bedding (intercourse with) a woman (*meta arsenos koitēn gunaikos*), they have both committed an abomination." Paul's term for homosexual *arsenokoitai* combines the elements "male" (*arsēn*) and the word "bed/intercourse" (*koitē*). The compound word, not found in any extant Greek text earlier than 1 Corinthians, is probably derived directly from the LXX translation of Lev 20:13.[44] Thus Paul is reaffirming the morality of Leviticus that condemns homosexual intercourse, though he does not reaffirm its earthly sanction: the death penalty. Instead Paul announces a heavenly sanction: Such persons will not inherit the kingdom of God (1 Cor 6:10).

In 1 Cor 5:13 Paul quotes from Deut 17:7, "You must purge the evil from among you." In the original usage, purging involved capital punishment. Again, the morality of this law is applied by Paul via principalization to the Church, but the sanction has changed: Excommunication substitutes for the law's implication of execution. Yet the underlying principle remains the same: God's people must be visibly holy.

Hebrews 9:22 affirms the principle found in Lev 17:11 and elsewhere of the importance of blood for atonement. But it sees the ultimate application of that principle in Christ's bloody sacrifice of himself on the cross (Heb 9:25-28). This illustrates how religious principles of the law still find application in the NT.

---

44. Richard B. Hays, *The Moral Vision of the New Testament* (San Francisco: HarperSanFransisco, 1996), 382-383.

These examples appear sufficient to show that the NT use of the law seems supportive of the principalizing approach proposed here.

3. *Weaknesses of the principalizing approach to the law.* The most serious question raised against the principalizing approach to OT laws is this: Is it possible to derive principles from particular laws? B. S. Jackson,[45] discussing the "underlying principles" approach of M. Greenberg to the laws, questions the degree to which one can derive general principles from specific laws. In the case of one man's ox goring another man's ox to death in which no one is at fault, the law (Exod 21:35) says the two owners are to split the losses. But how far can we generalize this conclusion? No abstraction—only applies to oxen, not other animals? Some abstraction—applies to when one man's animal kills another man's animal? Broad abstraction—applies when one man's property damages another man's property? Such decisions appear arbitrary and hermeneutically open the door for the interpreter to read his or her own ideology into the laws.

While Jackson is right to say that deducing principles is tricky; nonetheless, principles can be derived from particular laws. Jackson's own approach falls into the error of reading the law as if it were modern *positive law,* the modern legal theory that tries to regulate by enacting law in exhaustive detail. Instead of being positive law, both biblical and ancient Near Eastern laws represent paradigmatic law, giving illustrations of justice and providing examples to inform judges when they dealt with analogous cases. Raymond Westbrook comments on Jackson: "Jackson . . . argues that Babylonian law dealt in cases, not principles. We would argue that it dealt in principles but could only express them as cases. The principles can be extracted, but by applying the *native* cultural and social concepts." He also states, "[The court] looked to the code, not for an exact, mechanical precedent, but for the *principle* [italics mine] that the code indirectly laid down through its examples."[46]

To Westbrook one can add that for the Bible, the *"native* cultural and social concepts" are found hermeneutically through the application of the principle of analogy of Scripture (or analogy of faith). The assumption that the laws form a harmonious whole allows some erroneous abstractions to be weeded out. Any principle derived from a law must be compared with other laws and biblical cultural and social concepts to see if the derived principle is consistent. If it is not, then the interpreter has probably derived the wrong conclusion. Similarly it is necessary to compare biblical laws with other laws in the ancient Near East as a means of checking whether a supposed principle is consistent with the contemporary cultural milieu.

---

45. B. S. Jackson, *Essays in Jewish and Comparative Legal History* (Leiden: Brill, 1975), 25-63.

46. Raymond Westbrook, *Studies in Biblical and Cuneiform Law* (Paris: Gabalda, 1988), 77 n. 156.

VII. VALUE OF MOSAIC LAW FOR CHRISTIANS TODAY

I conclude my discussion of the Mosaic law and the Christian by summarizing some ways in which the Mosaic law is still of value for Christians today.

1. *The law serves to restrain sinners.* The just principles of the Mosaic civil laws when instituted into the actual laws of nations (whether directly through Scripture or indirectly through natural revelation, cf. Rom 2:14 and Romans 13) serve to restrain evildoers (1 Tim 1:9-10) and maintain order in society. This aspect of law is indispensable to a just society.

2. *The law is a prelude to the gospel.* For all humanity knowing the moral standards of the law is a necessary prerequisite for the gospel. The law gives the "bad news"—we are sinners who fall short of the glory of God—that is indispensable for appreciating how good the good news really is. No one can be declared righteous on the basis of the law (Rom 3:20), but the law does make the sinner conscious of sin (Rom 3:20; 4:15; 5:13; 7:9-10). The moral law is necessary to help sinners see their need of a mediator or priest between themselves and God and see that they are in need of a savior.

3. *The law is a guide for Christian living.* The believer, through the Spirit, keeps the righteous requirements of the law (Rom 8:3-4), following the principle of love which is the fulfillment of the law (Rom 13:8-10; Gal 5:14; Mark 12:31; see Lev 19:18). As the NT references to the laws indicate, the moral principles of the law still define proper and improper behavior for the Christian, supplementing NT morality by addressing some issues not directly treated in the NT. The promises of life associated with obedience to the law can be applied to the NT believer (Eph 6:2-3; Exod 20:12). And the religious principles found in the ceremonial laws provide the conceptual framework for understanding Christ and his salvation.

4. *Biblical civil laws are suggestive for modern jurisprudence.* Even Luther, who as we have seen rejected the Mosaic civil law's authority over the Christian, nonetheless recognized that Mosaic laws could be suggestive for the law codes of modern states. The examples concerning biblical law's underlying legal philosophy and its emphasis on monetary penalties to the family (tort) instead of imprisonment are discussed above under the strengths of the theonomy approach.

5. *The law has value in that it shows the holy yet merciful character of God.* As the law reveals God's character, the law can therefore be a source of doxology, as it is in Jewish tradition: "Blessed are you, O LORD our God, King of the Universe, who has sanctified us by your commandments." "Blessed are you, O LORD our God, King of the Universe, who has chosen us from all peoples, and

has given us your Law." "Blessed be he who in his holiness has given the Law to his people Israel."[47]

6. *The law points to Christ who is the fulfillment of the law.* He fulfills its types and foreshadowing. He fulfilled its righteousness by his sinless character. He will fulfill its judgments when he comes as judge of the world. He is the sacrifice to which OT animal sacrifices pointed. He is the ultimate great high priest who mediates God to the world. He is God who tabernacled among us.

The chapters that follow will seek to elucidate the law's value for Christians today through discussing some particular topics where the law and its teaching are prominent. The present chapter, however, has defined and defended the theological outlook that is presupposed in all my treatments of the Mosaic law— namely, the principalizing approach as a means of finding value in the law for today.

---

47. After H. Adler, *Service of the Synagogue: Day of Atonement* (New York: KTAV, n.d.), 14, 109, 111.

Chapter 2

IS THERE TRUTH IN THE LAW (JOHN 1:17)?
On the Gospel of John's View of the Mosaic Revelation

The New King James of John 1:17 reads, "For the law was given through Moses, *but* grace and truth came through Jesus Christ." Taken at face value, this verse suggests a stark contrast between the law and the combination of grace and truth. C. K. Barrett states, "In this verse the main emphasis lies on the contrast between Moses and Christ, Law and Gospel."[1] C. I. Scofield, who a century ago popularized dispensationalism, quotes this verse as a proof text of the key contrast between the Jewish and Christian dispensations: "The most obvious and striking division of the Word of truth is that between law and grace."[2] But the verse speaks of truth as well as grace. John 1:17 might be taken so far as to suggest that the Mosaic law was neither gracious nor truthful, or at least substantially less so than the new covenant under Jesus. There have indeed been readers who have understood this verse as a "polemic against the Synagogue,"[3] and that "the Evangelist is only concerned with the contrast" between the law and the revelation in Jesus Christ.[4] This was the view of Martin Luther whose theology drew a sharp distinction between law and gospel. He comments on John 1:17: "This grace and truth were not taught by the Law or given by Moses. Grace and truth draw a line of demarcation between Christ and Moses."[5]

I. TRUTH OF THE LAW AFFIRMED IN THE OT

If John were denying the truth of the law, he would be denying explicit statements in the Old Testament about the veracity of the law. These statements espe-

---

1. C. K. Barrett, *The Gospel According to St. John* (2nd ed.; Philadelphia: Westminster, 1978), 169.

2. C. I Scofield, *Rightly Dividing the Word of Truth* (1886) Chapter 6. Cited 20 May 2004. On-line: http://www.biblebelievers.com/scofield/scofield_rightly06.html.

3. Raymond E. Brown, *The Gospel According to John* (AB 29-29a; Garden City: Doubleday, 1966-1970), 36.

4. R. Bultmann, *The Gospel of John* (tr. G. R. Beasley-Murray; Philadelphia: Westminster, 1971), 79.

5. Martin Luther, *Luther's Works on CD-Rom* (Augsburg, 1999; print edition, *Luther's Works*, vol. 22: Sermons on the Gospel of St. John: Chapters 1-4; ed. J. J. Pelikan, et al.; Saint Louis: Concordia Publishing House, c. 1957), n.p., s.v. Sermons on the Gospel of John, John 1:17.

cially use the term *'emet* "truth, stability, reliability, trustworthiness" and other forms (*'emûnâ; ne'emānâ*) that like *'emet* are derived from the root *'amēn* "to be steady, firm, trustworthy." A number of such statements occur in the Psalm 119, the great wisdom psalm that indirectly praises God by praising his law or *tôrâ*.[6] There the psalmist refers to the law (under various terms) as "the word of truth (*'emet*)" (v. 43) and states more directly "all of your commandments are trustworthy (*'emûnâ*)" (v. 86); "all your commandments are true (lit. "truth"; *'emet*)" (v. 151); "your law (*tôrâ*) is truth (*'emet*)" (v. 142); and "the sum of your word is truth (*'emet*)" (v. 160, NASB & NRSV).

Psalm 19 also speaks in praise of God's law. It states that "the law of the LORD (*tôrat* YHWH) is perfect (*tamîmâ*)" and "the statues/testimony (*'ēdût*)[7] of the LORD are trustworthy (*ne'emānâ*)" (v. 7). Moreover, Psalm 19 goes on to call the precepts of the LORD "upright" and his commandments "pure" (v. 8). And in one more synonym for the law, the psalmist states "the judgments (*mišpāṭim*) of the LORD are true (lit. "truth"; *'emet*), they are altogether right/righteous" (v. 10b).

Elsewhere Psalm 111:7 places in parallel "The works of your hand are truth (*'emet*) and justice" with "all your precepts are trustworthy (*ne'emānîm*)." Nehemiah 9:13 speaks of God's "laws of truth/true laws" (*tôrôt 'emet*). Malachi 2:6 refers to what Mosaic instructions or *tôrâ* dispensed by priests should be: "teaching of truth (*tôrat 'emet*)."

It is thus clear that the OT claims that the *tôrâ* is God's word and true. Is it possible that John is contradicting that claim?

---

6. *Tôrâ* is used in the Hebrew Bible about 220 times. It means more specifically "teaching instruction," though it has usually been translated "*law*" because it was translated in the LXX with the Greek work *nomos* "law." The Greek word *nomos* was an unfortunate translation, however. The word *nomos* comes from the realm of commercial transactions, being derived from a Greek word meaning "to distribute, deal out, apportion (especially of property)" from which it develops to mean "the coercive law of the state" (*NIDNTT* 2:438-439). *Tôrâ*, on the other hand, is at heart a pedagogic term, referring to God's instructions to Israel, only some of which involve state enforcement. Laws by definition are regulations of society enforced by the state; however, not all of the regulations labeled *tôrâ* are able to be so interpreted.

7. Heb. *'ēdût* was traditionally understood to mean "testimony," but in this context it is parallel with various terms for God's word, and is specifically parallel with *tôrâ* in the present verse. The expression "ark of the *'ēdût*" is used as a synonym with "ark of the covenant" in a way that suggests that *'ēdût* has a meaning similar to covenant. Heb. *'ēdût* is probably cognate with Akk. *adu* "a type of formal agreement" (*CAD* 1.1:131-4; *AHw*, s.v. "*eid*" [oath]). The term *'ēdût* in the context of Psalm 19 has come to mean "instruction conveyed by the covenant."

II. JOHN AND THE TRUTH OF THE MOSAIC LAW

Any interpretation of John 1:17 that sees in John a sharp contrast between law and truth is rendered dubious on the basis of John's statements elsewhere that assume the truth of the Mosaic law.

John quotes Jesus' affirmation of scriptural reliability, "The Scripture cannot be broken" (John 10:35). "Scripture" here obviously refers to the Old Testament and the text is affirming its infallibility. John also quotes Jesus' prayer to the Father, "Your word is truth" (John 17:17). Again, as was shown above, God's "word" can be a synonym of God's *tôrâ* or teaching as found in his commandments and laws of the OT. Thus by these quotations John is making a strong affirmation of scriptural trustworthiness in general; and given that the law is a part of that Scripture, he affirms thereby the law's reliability as well.

But there may be more here. *Codex Sinaiticus* of the LXX of Psalm 119:142 reads "your word is truth" (*ho logos sos alētheia*), nearly identical with the Greek of John 17:17b (*ho logos ho sos alētheia estin*).[8] So words of John 17:17, "your word is truth," may be echoing the LXX rendering of Psalm 119:142 that speaks particularly of the truth of the law. If so this would make a sharp distinction between law and truth in John 1:17 even more implausible.

John's use of the law shows that he indeed affirms its validity. According to John's Gospel, the Scriptures bear genuine witness of Christ (John 5:39). Jesus is the one of whom Moses in the law wrote (John 1:45), so Jesus can rebuke his audience with the words, "If you believed Moses, you would believe me, for he wrote about me" (John 5:46). The Mosaic law was clearly Scripture to any first century Jew, and (as the Pentateuch portrays itself) the law was recognized as the word of God to Moses. Though Jesus' opponents were not keeping it, Jesus affirms that the law ought to be obeyed (John 7:19), and John probably agrees with the Pharisees' words (though not its particular application) that ignorance of the law brings a curse on the people (John 7:49).

In particular, the "law" in the broad sense of the Pentateuch[9] finds fulfillment in Christ according to John: Jesus' claims are confirmed by two or three witnesses as the law concerning evidence demands (Deut 19:15; John 8:17). Jesus is the fulfillment of the serpent lifted in the wilderness (Num 21:4-9; John 3:14). Jesus is the I AM who spoke to Moses (Exod 3:14; John 8:58). Jesus is the fulfillment of the bread (manna) that comes down from heaven (Exod 16:4-35; John 6).[10] To John the law's statement about the Passover lamb "not one of his bones will be broken" (Exod 12:26 and Num 9:12 with Ps 34:20) was fulfilled

---

8. Barclay M. Newman and E. A. Nida, *A Translator's Handbook on the Gospel of John* (Helps for Translators; London: United Bible Societies, 1980), 540.

9. John can use law (Gk. *nomos*) in the sense of the Pentateuch (John 1:45, in parallel with the "Prophets") and even in the sense of Scripture (John 10:34 where "law" refers to a quotation from Psalm 82:6; John 15:25 where "law" refers to Psalm 35:19 or 69:4).

10. Stephen J. Casselli, "Jesus as Eschatological Torah," *TJ* 18.1 (Spring 1997): 18 n. 11.

when the soldiers did not break Jesus' legs on the cross (John 19:36). John in this way identifies Jesus as the fulfillment of the Passover regulations.

John as a follower of Jesus clearly concludes that the Mosaic law is in fact unfailing, reliable truth that bears genuine witness to Christ who is its fulfillment. This in turn must influence the interpretation of John 1:17. As Raymond Brown states, "The theory that vs. 17 contrasts the absence of enduring love in the Law with the presence of enduring love in Jesus Christ does not seem to do justice to John's honorific reference to Moses."[11] It hardly seems likely in view of John's high respect for the truth of the Mosaic law that John 1:17 is mounting a polemic against it.

In sum, statements about the law in John complement the statements about the law found in the OT. John affirms with the OT that God's law is "truth," that is, something that is reliable and even goes on to see in it a foreshadowing of the life and ministry of Jesus. Any interpretation that takes John 1:17 as denying the truth of the law must therefore be ruled out of court.

III. "GRACE AND TRUTH" IN JOHN 1:14, 17 DERIVED FROM EXOD 34:6

Yet another factor confirms John's high view of the Mosaic revelation: the observation that he has derived his vocabulary of "grace and truth" from the law, Exod 34:6 in particular.

The "grace and truth" (*charis* and *alētheia*) in John 1:14, 17 seems to echo the expression "lovingkindness and truth" (*hesed* and *'emet*) that occurs often in the Hebrew Bible (Gen 24:27, 49; 32:11; 47:29; Exod 34:6; Josh 2:14; 2 Sam 2:6; 15:20; Hos 4:1; Mic 7:20; Ps 40:11; 85:11; 89:15).[12] The expression *hesed ve'emet* is properly understood as a hendiadys meaning "lasting, constant *hesed*" that conveys the sense of certainty or reliability of the promised *hesed*.[13] Likewise, "full of grace and truth" in John 1:14 could also be understood as a hendiadys, "truly full of grace"[14] or similar.

This connection between John's "grace and truth" and *hesed* and *'emet* in the Hebrew Bible is widely accepted by commentators.[15] Against it is the fact

---

11. Brown, *John,* 16.

12. C. Spicq, *TLNT* 1:77 n. 46.

13. A. Jepsen, "*'emet*" *TDOT* 1:311; H. –J. Zobel, "*hesed,*" *TDOT* 5:48.

14. Henry Mowvley, "John 114-18 in the Light of Exodus 337-3435," *ExpTim* 95 (1984): 137, citing Lightfoot.

15. Barrett, *John,* 167; G. R. Beasley-Murray, *John* (WBC 36; Waco, TX: Word, 1986), 14; Brown, *John,* 14, 35; F. F. Bruce, *The Gospel of John* (Grand Rapids: Eerdmans, 1983), 42; D. A. Carson, *The Gospel According to John* (Grand Rapids: Eerdmans, 1991), 129-130; Edwin Hoskyns, *The Fourth Gospel* (2nd ed.; London: Faber & Faber, 1947), 150; Craig S. Keener, *The Gospel of John* (vol. 1; Peabody, MA: Hendrickson, 2003), 416-417; B. Lindars, *The Gospel of John* (NCB; Greenwood, S.C.: Attic Press, 1972), 95; F. J. Moloney, *The Gospel of John* (SP 4; Collegeville, MN: Michael Glazier, 1998), 39; Leon Morris, *The Gospel According to John* (NICNT; Grand Rapids: Eerdmans, 1971), 107 n. 96.

that Gk. *charis* is only used to render *hesed* rarely in the LXX (Esth 2:9; Sir 7:33 and 40:17;[16] see also Esth 2:17 where *charis* translates *hēn vāhesed* "grace and *hesed*") whereas *eleos* ("mercy") and its cognates predominate. This problem has led some to see the allusion as going back to Exod 33:16 where the LXX uses *charis* and a cognate of *alētheia* together in the same context.[17] However, the Syriac Bible translates both the Greek expression in John 1:14 and the Hebrew expression *hesed ve'emet* with the same rendering in Syriac, *taibuta* ("goodness, kindness, grace") and *qushta* ("truth, right, justice").[18] Moreover, John's "full of grace and truth" (John 1:14) is arguably a literal translation of Exod 34:6's *rab hesed ve'emet* ("abounding in *hesed* and truth").[19] It will be argued below that John 1:14-18 is in fact meditating on Exodus 33-34.

But is *charis* an acceptable translation of the Heb. *hesed*? The LXX's own preference for rendering *hesed* as Greek *eleos* "mercy" (213x) is itself problematic and widely questioned by Hebraists as too specific, though pinning down the exact nuance of *hesed* is a challenge and has led to a number of monographs.[20] Glueck's highly influential monograph on *hesed* (first published in German in 1927) emphasized that *hesed* has to do with someone with whom one has a relationship (relatives, guests, allies, friends, subordinates).[21] Glueck went on to argue that *hesed* primarily has to do with "merited obligations, rights, and duties" rather than "grace."[22] Scholarship since Glueck, however, while accepting Glueck's view that *hesed* is a term related to covenants or relationships, has tended to back away from his legalistic emphasis on merit, rights and mutual obligation.[23]

---

16. For the Hebrew text of Ben Sirah, see P. C. Beentjes, *The Book of Ben Sira in Hebrew* (VTSup 68; Leiden: Brill, 1997), 31, 70, 159.

17. "How will it be truly (*alēthos*) known that both I and this people have found favor (*charin*) with you?" Exod 33:16 LXX.

18. Brown, *John*, 14.

19. Lindars, *John*, 95.

20. Nelson Glueck, *Hesed in the Bible* (tr. A. Gottschalk; Cincinnati: Hebrew Union College Press, 1967); K. Sakenfeld, *The Meaning of Hesed in the Hebrew Bible* (HSM 17; Missoula, MN: Scholars Press, 1978); G. R. Clark, *The Word Hesed in the Hebrew Bible* (JSOTSup 157; Sheffield: Sheffield Academic Press, 1993).

21. Glueck, *Hesed*, 35-36.

22. Glueck, *Hesed*, 7-55. Glueck does not deny any role for "grace" in *hesed*. Glueck puts it this way: "The *hesed* of God, while it is not to be identified with His grace, is still based on the latter, insofar as the relationship between God and people, structured by him as a covenantal relationship, was effected by electing Israel through an act of grace" (p. 102).

23. K. Sakenfeld, "Love (OT)," *ABD* 4:377. R. L. Harris, "*Hesed*," *TWOT* 1:305-307, is even stronger in rejecting the Glueck thesis. Likewise, S. Romerowski, "Que signifie le mot *hesed*?" *VT* 40 (1990): 89-103, argues that the word means "kindness, benevolence, affection, friendship, love, favor, grace, mercy or piety" rather than loyalty or mutual obligations. On the other hand Zobel, "*hesed*," *TDOT* 5:44-64, still argues "the one who receives an act of *hesed* is justified in expecting an equivalent act in return" (p. 47).

There are a number of places where acts of *hesed* are acts of grace or mercy rather than duty or obligation. For instance, in 1 Kgs 20:31, when the servants of Ben-Hadad ask to go to Ahab in sackcloth to seek to save Ben-Hadad's life, they do so because the kings of Israel had the reputation of being "merciful kings" (lit. "kings of *hesed*"). Even though Ahab grants mercy using the language of covenant ("he is my brother"—v. 32), there was no covenant duty that would demand that Ahab spare the Aramean king's life, for Ben-Hadad had abrogated any treaty that may have existed by engaging Israel in war at Aphek (v. 26). In this case *hesed* implies acting in mercy and grace.

Likewise when Psalm 51:1 in its confession of sin pleas to God, "Have mercy upon me, O God, according to your *hesed*; according to the greatness of your compassion, blot out my transgressions," there is no question of merit on the part of the psalmist whose sins have violated the covenant conceivably to the point of breaking, nor any duty or obligation on the part of God to grant him that forgiveness. Forgiveness depended on God's "compassion" (*rahamîm*), not on David's merit. Other passages also emphasize God's gracious "compassion" (root *rāham*) as motivating God's *hesed* and forgiveness or help (Ps 25:6-7; 103:3-4; Isa 54:8, 10; Lam 3:32; Ps 40:11; 69:16; Isa 63:7).

While no single word in either Greek or English catches the semantic range of *hesed,* Gk. *charis* ("grace") catches some genuine elements of the semantic range of *hesed*, so that if John has rendered it as *charis* as commentators suspect, that is defendable. One reason for John's rendering of *hesed* as *charis* rather than *eleos* may be diachronic: *eleos* in the LXX is used in the sense of "undeserved favor"; whereas early Christian writings tended to use *charis* instead.[24] John, then, may be an early instance of this when he rendered Heb. *hesed* with Gk. *charis* rather than *eleos* in John 1:14 and 17.

Spieckermann rightly sees the semantic range of *hesed* as including grace, mercy, compassion, kindness and love.[25] That observation allows him to make "God's self-determination towards love" the foundation not only of NT theology (as one might expect), but also of his concept of OT theology.[26] His prime example of this is the theophany of Exod 34:6-7 and especially that phrase arguably quoted by John where God speaks of himself as "abounding in *hesed ve'emet*":

---

24. Keener, *John,* 417. It is difficult to confirm Keener's thesis in John's writings. After John 1:14-17, the Johannine literature never uses *charis* again, nor *eleos* at all, except in the greeting "grace [*charis*], mercy [*eleos*] and peace. . . in truth and love" in 2 John 3. But little can be deduced from a usage in a greeting formula about distinctions John might make between *charis* and *eleos*. The Revelation uses a cognate of *eleos*, namely *eleeinos* "miserable, to be pitied" in Rev 3:17, but again not much can be deduced from that.

25. H. Spieckermann, "God's Steadfast Love: Towards a New Conception of Old Testament Theology," *Bib* 81 (2000): 311.

26. Spieckermann, "God's Steadfast Love," 308.

6 The LORD passed before him, and proclaimed,
"The LORD, the LORD,
a God merciful and gracious,
slow to anger, and abounding in steadfast love and faithfulness (*hesed ve'emet*),

7 keeping steadfast love for the thousandth generation,
forgiving iniquity and transgression and sin,
yet by no means clearing the guilty,
but visiting the iniquity of the parents
upon the children
and the children's children,
to the third and the fourth generation." (NRSV)

The context of Exodus 34 is one of betrayed love, for Israel has just violated the law by worshipping the Golden Calf (Exod 32:1-6). That led Moses to break the original tablets of the law (Exod 32:19), symbolizing Israel's violation of the covenant. Because of that violation, God had every right to destroy Israel and even floated the idea of doing so to Moses (Exod 32:9-10). But in his grace God chose not to do so. Rather, as a symbol of renewal of the covenant, he had Moses carve new replicas of the original tablets of the Decalogue (Exod 34:1). God then goes on to proclaim his gracious character. As Spieckermann puts it, despite the covenant violation, "God's love takes the shape of mercy and grace, of abstaining from anger and of being ready to forgive the thousands (i.e. numerous) of generations without any limit, although the punishment restricted to four generations would not fail to come."[27] Again *hesed* does not seem to connote duty or obligation here, but grace.

It is hard to exaggerate the degree of God's grace and favor as described in Exod 34:6-7. As Brichto puts it, "that favor is characterized not just by carrying *iniquity* on the books, but *iniquity, transgression and sin*, that is, offenses of every kind and degree."[28] God here shows himself a God of love, mercy, forgiveness and grace, though without denying his holiness and justice. This is picked up in Jonah where the prophet explains why he did not want to go to Nineveh to preach by alluding directly to Exod 34:6, "For I knew that you are a compassionate and kind God, slow to anger and abounding in grace (*rab hesed*)" (Jonah 4:2). For Jonah, God was just too gracious. Jonah suspected from the beginning on the basis of Exod 34:6 that God being so merciful would find some lame excuse to forgive those despicable Assyrians, so Jonah did not want to go.

Thus love and grace are not alien to the theology of the OT. As Romerowski observes, the theological usage of the word *hesed* in various passages teaches the OT saint what the Apostle John teaches in the NT: that God is love (1 John

27. Spieckermann, "God's Steadfast Love," 310.
28. H. C. Brichto, *Towards a Grammar of Biblical Poetics* (New York: Oxford University Press, 1992) 108.

4:16).[29] John's theology of God's grace and love are thus informed from Exod 34:6-7 to which John alludes.

IV. THE USE OF EXODUS 33-34 IN JOHN 1:14-18

Not only does John 1:14 draw the wording of "full of grace and truth" from *rab ḥesed ve'emet* in Exodus 34:6, but John 1:14-18 can be seen as a meditation on Exodus 33-34.[30]

John says, "The word became flesh and dwelt among us" (John 1:14a). This can be taken as an allusion to the tabernacle in the book of Exodus. "Dwelt" is from Gk. *skēnoō* that is cognate with *skēnē* "tent" and meant etymologically "to pitch a tent, live in a tent."[31] The Hebrew term for tabernacle (Heb. *miškēn*) means "dwelling place"[32] but this structure is also called the "tent of meeting." The LXX renders the term "tent" in Greek as *skēnē*. John 1:14 thus may have the sense, "The Word . . . tabernacled among us." The construction of the tabernacle is described in Exodus 25-31 and 35-40, but there is a more specific reference contextually in Exodus 33-34: At the "tent of meeting" Moses had the conversation with God that led God to reveal his character (Exod 33:7-9).

The point John is making is this: In the tabernacle, God "dwelt" among his people (Exod 25:8) in a "tent" and God spoke to Moses "face to face as a man speaks to his friend" (Exod 33:7-9) and spoke through his word, the law written on tablets of stone (Exod 34:1, 28). So likewise God metaphorically pitched his tent among his people in Jesus Christ and speaks to his people now through the Word made flesh in the person of Jesus Christ.[33] In making this allusion, John probably saw Jesus as the antitype or fulfillment of the tabernacle and of the law.

John goes on to say, "and we have seen his glory . . . full of grace and truth" (John 1:14b-d). This is a more specific allusion to the glory of the LORD found in Exodus 33-34. In Exod 33:9 the pillar of cloud had descended to the tent of meeting, the pillar elsewhere said to veil the glory of the LORD (Exod 24:16), as does the curtains of the tabernacle itself. In Exod 33:18 Moses requested of God, "Let me behold your glory!" God responds that no one can see him and live (33:20). However, God would allow his goodness to pass before Moses and pro-

---

29. Romerowski, "Que signifie la mot *ḥesed*?" 92. G. A. Larue, introduction to *Ḥesed in the Bible,* by Nelson Glueck (Cincinnati: Hebrew Union College Press, 1967), 18, cites Dom Rembert Sorg as making the same assertion.

30. Mowvley, "John 114-18 in the Light of Exodus 337-3435," 135-137, for a similar defense of this thesis.

31. W. E. Vine, *Expository Dictionary of New Testament Words* (Old Tappan, N.J.: Revell, 1940), 345; Carson, *John,* 127-128.

32. Bruce, *John,* 40-41, suggests that Jews of the first century would associate (in a kind of folk etymology) the Greek words for "tent" *skēnē* and "dwell" *skēnoō* with the late Hebrew word for "dwelling" *šekînâ* that is cognate with *miškēn* "tabernacle." *Šekînâ* came in Judaism to mean God's glorious Presence. Similarly Keener, *John,* 408.

33. Mowvley, "John 114-18 in the Light of Exodus 337-3435," 136.

claim his name Yahweh all while hiding Moses in the cleft of the rock and shielding him with his "hand"; thus he would allow Moses to see something of his "glory," namely his "back," but not his "face" (33:19, 21-23). The fulfillment of this promise is found in Exod 34:6-7 where God reveals himself as *rab ḥesed ve'emet* "full of grace and truth." In this process God does not show Moses what he looks like, for God's "hand," "back," and "face" are each vivid anthropomorphisms.[34] God's "back" (33:23) is not a literal part of his anatomy, but stands for what God can reveal to Moses, especially his character as revealed in the word of revelation. Even though Moses did not see God's glory in its fullness, his face was radiant, reflecting the glory of God, as he returned from his encounter with God with the tablets of the law (Exod 34:29-32). The glow of that reflected, secondary glory was so strong that, like God himself, Moses required a veil to cover that glory (Exod 34:33-35).

Moses saw something of God's "glory" in conjunction with the spoken word of revelation that described God's character as "full of grace and truth" (Exod 34:6-7). But he also saw God's glory in conjunction with a giving of God's laws that reflect God's character that he commanded Moses to write down (Exod 34:10-27). Therefore, it is unlikely that John 1:17 would be denying that Moses saw something of God's glory as full of grace and truth when he was "given" the law. More likely John is affirming that just as Moses saw the something of the glory of the LORD when he received the law, so God's glory is even more visible though the revelation of the Word-become-flesh. The glory of God shown to Moses in conjunction with the giving of the law may be lesser in degree than the glory of God revealed through Christ, but they are similar in kind.

John comes back to this allusion to Moses wanting to see God's glory in John 1:18. This text shows the greater degree of revelation in Christ: "No one has seen God at any time." This rewords the idea of God's statement to Moses, "You cannot see my face, for no one can see me and live" (Exod 33:20). Not even Moses who asked to do so could see God. Rather it is Christ, who was not merely hidden in the cleft of the rock and allowed to see God's "back," but is one who dwelt intimately "in the bosom of the Father" [that is, in front of him] is the one who "has made him known" (John 1:18).[35] In Exodus 34 those who looked on Moses' shining face saw something of the glory of God. But that is true in a far richer and deeper and more wonderful way in the flesh of Jesus Christ who is (depending of which variant is correct) God's "only son" or "the only begotten God" (John 1:18). In Jesus' own words, "He who has seen me has seen the Father" (John 14:9).

After the parenthetical remark about John the Baptist in v. 15, John returns to the themes of verse 14 in verse 16, "From his *fullness* we have received *grace* upon *grace*" (NASB). This line alludes to 1:14 "*full* of *grace* and truth" that, as we

---

34. U. Cassuto, *Commentary on Exodus* (Jerusalem: Magnes, 1951), 437.

35. Craig A. Evans, *Word and Glory: On the Exegetical and Theological Background of John's Prologue* (JSNTSup 89; Sheffield: Sheffield Academic Press, 1993), 81.

have seen, in turn alludes to Exod 34:6. "Grace *upon* grace" may well be better understood in the sense of "grace *instead of* grace," *instead of* being the most common meaning of Gk. *anti*.[36] If so the sense is, "*Instead of* grace, we received *more* grace."

But if that is the correct understanding, what is the first "grace" for which the revelation of Christ is seen as a substitute? The *hoti* clause of v. 17 seems to be explanatory of v. 16: "For (*hoti*) the law was given through Moses; grace and truth came through Jesus Christ." The first grace can thus be associated with the law of Moses. The gift of the law through Moses was itself a display of grace. Indeed, *charis* "grace" has as one of its secondary meanings "gift" so a "law *given*" does not need to be taken as in contrast with *charis*.[37] Furthermore, the content of the law in Exod 34:6-7 describes God's grace. In that same context Moses requested God's "favor" or grace [LXX *charis*] in seeking to know God's ways (Exod 33:13), a request God granted. Thus the additional grace that now is revealed in Christ substitutes for the earlier grace of the law.[38] In other words, the grace shown to Moses that revealed the reliable *hesed* of Sinai is replaced by the reliable *hesed* of the new covenant.[39]

Further undermining finding any sharp contrast between law and grace-and-truth is the strong possibility that when John says in 1:14 "that the word became flesh," his term for "word" may be intentionally using a synonym for *tôrâ*. Schoneveld argues that *logos* "word" in John 1:14 draws on the use of *logos* "word" as a synonym for *nomos* "law" as seen in Philo and the parallel between "word" and "law" in the OT and Rabbinic midrashim. Schoneveld concludes that "the Word became flesh" in effect means "the Torah/Law became flesh"[40] and is thus not pejorative towards the law.

It now becomes clear that whatever contrast John may be drawing in John 1:17, it is not a law-versus-grace dichotomy. Here some translations have been misleading. The New King James quoted above (similar to the KJV) renders John 1:17 with a sharp contrast: "For the law was given through Moses, *but* grace and truth came through Jesus Christ." However, there is no word *but* represented in the Greek. This is rather an interpretation on the part of the translator. Were that the meaning intended by John, one might have expected a *men . . . de* syntactical construction in the Greek.[41] John uses *men . . . de* less than the other Gospels, but

---

36. Brown, *John*, 15-16; Carson, *John*, 132.

37. E.g., Rom 4:4, "When a man works, his wages is not credited to him as a gift (*charis*) but as an obligation" (NIV). Moloney, *John*, 46, renders John 1:14 not as "full of grace and truth" but as "the fullness of a gift that is truth," and 1:17b as "the gift that is the truth came through Jesus Christ."

38. Carson, *John*, 132-134.

39. Brown, *John*, 16.

40. Jacobus Schoneveld, "Torah in the Flesh: A New Reading of the Prologue of the Gospel of John as a contribution to a Christology without Anti-Judaism," *Immanuel* 24/25 (1990): 77-86. Similarly, Keener, *John*, 360-363.

41. F. Godet, *Commentary on John's Gospel* (Grand Rapids: Kregel, 1978), 279.

it does occur.[42] While the lack of this construction may only reflect John's Hebraic style in composing Greek, it could also be because there is no sharp contrast intended in John 1:17.

It is just as plausible to render John 1:17 as a parallelism of comparison as it is to render it as a contrast: "*Just as* the law was given through Moses, *so* grace and truth [which the law prefigures] came through Jesus Christ."[43] Taken this way, the contrast is not between law and the combination of grace and truth, but with the verbs. The true grace found in the law was "given" through Moses, while true grace "became" (*egeneto*) in the sense of "became flesh" in Christ. This is the meaning of *egeneto* in v. 14 where the same verb is used.[44] A number of early church fathers saw the contrast in John 1:17 as between the law as "type" and Christ as "reality" (*alētheia*), not as between the law as "falsehood" and Christ as "truth" (*alētheia*).[45] Such a view fits well with John's typological use of the law elsewhere. There is certainly something greater about the "grace and truth" that is revealed in Christ. Fernando puts it well: "Though Law was given though Moses, it was something external to him. But grace and truth are the person of Jesus Christ himself."[46] But this in no way denies that there was grace and truth in the law.

V. CONCLUSION

Although John 1:17 might be read as a polemic against the Synagogue in which John denies both grace and truth to the law, this interpretation is unacceptable for many reasons.

John himself many times affirms the truth of the law and in many particular examples sees it as genuinely foreshadowing Jesus Christ who is its fulfillment. Were he to deny truth to the law, John would have to deny both the many statements in the Old Testament that affirm the reliability of God's *tôrâ* (one of which he may have quoted), as well as his own affirmations about the law's authority and veracity and fulfillment in Christ. Nor is it likely that John would deny the gracious character of the law. John's phrase in John 1:17 "grace and truth" echoes 1:14 "full of grace and truth" which in turn is probably John's own translation of the law's *rab ḥesed ve'emet* ("abounding in *ḥesed* and truth") in Exod 34:6. The Heb. term *ḥesed,* despite some controversy, can rightly be translated grace (*charis*) by John. The theological usage of *ḥesed* in the OT generally, and in Exod 34:6 in particular, is that the God of the OT is a God of love and grace

---

42. Nigel Turner, *A Grammar of New Testament Greek* (vol. IV: Style; Edinburgh: T. & T. Clark, 1976), 75, says John uses *men ...de* "one in 264 lines."

43. Carson, *John,* 132; Lindars, *John,* 98; J. Jeremias, *"Mouses,"* *TDNT* 5:873.

44. Caselli, "Jesus as Eschatological Torah," 36.

45. J. H. Barkhulzen, "A Short Note on John 1:17 in Patristic Exegesis," *Acta Patristica et Byzantina* 8 (1997): 18-25.

46. G. C. A. Fernando, "John 1:17 as Window to the Realities of Law and Love in the Fourth Gospel," *AJT* 13.1 (1999): 63.

who forgives and maintains his covenant with Israel despite Israel's betrayal of his love.

John 1:14-18 is itself a meditation on the law; particularly, a meditation on Exodus 33-34. John alludes to the tent of meeting (Exod 33:7-9; John 1:14a) and to God's unwillingness to show Moses the fullness of his glory (Exod 33:20; 1:14b, 18). He finds the foundation of his theology of "grace and truth" as well as the wording for that theology in Exod 34:6. Grammatically John 1:17 need not be rendered as a strong contrast but could be taken as a comparison, "As the law was given through Moses, so grace and truth came through Jesus Christ." Contextually John 1:17 explains 1:16 "we have received grace instead of grace" as meaning that in place of the grace associated with the law we have received the grace incarnated in Jesus Christ. Indeed, in saying "the word became flesh," John may well be saying that "the law became flesh." As Keener puts it, "John does not encourage his readers to forsake their Jewish past, but to recognize that following Christ, the embodiment of Torah, his community fulfills the highest demands of Judaism."[47]

There is a sense in which the grace found in the incarnate Word has displaced the grace found in the law. The law foreshadows Christ, but Christ is its fulfillment. The revelation of God's grace and truth is deeper and more profound in Christ than it was in Moses. Moses *was given* the word; Jesus *is* the Word. Moses sees God's glory from the backside, while Jesus saw it in the bosom of the Father. Those who saw Moses after receiving the law saw a reflection of God's glory emanating from his face, but those who see Jesus see God. In Christ grace and truth and the law and God himself became incarnate so that God's grace and truth became visible.

Nevertheless, far from contrasting "the law" with "grace and truth," John 1:17 is in fact affirming both the gracious character of the law, as well as its veracity. He does so, however, for the purpose of exalting him whose person is grace and truth at its purest and best.

---

47. Keener, *John,* 417.

Chapter 3

NEAR EASTERN AND BIBLICAL LAWS COMPARED

Biblical scholars often compare biblical laws (especially the civil laws) with extra-biblical cuneiform laws written during OT times,[1] so a student of biblical law must be acquainted with these extra-biblical laws. The chapters that follow will refer to these laws from time to time. Biblical law has many of the same categories of legislation as these cuneiform laws. Cuneiform is a type of writing using wedge shapes to form symbols. Sumerian, Akkadian, and Hittite were all written in cuneiform.

I. MAJOR COLLECTIONS OF CUNEIFORM LAW

The major collections of cuneiform law are as follows:[2]

1. *Laws Of Ur-Nammu (c. 2100 B.C.)*. One major collection of laws dates to about 2100 B.C. (middle chronology), the Laws of Ur-Nammu. These were written in Sumerian, the oldest known written language. Ur-Nammu founded the Third Dynasty of Ur. Abraham came from Ur either around this time, or a couple centuries thereafter, depending on which chronology is correct. In any case Ur-Nammu ruled centuries before Moses, who lived in the Late Bronze Age (c. 1550-1200 B.C.). Though these laws originated in Ur around 2100 B.C., our three copies come from later, about the time of Hammurabi (1700s), and were found at three—or perhaps two—different sites: the Nippur Tablet, the Ur tablets, and the "Sippur" Tablet (which may have come from Nippur). The laws are fragmentary: Less than forty laws are still extant, not all of which are translatable. It was preceded by a prologue, much of which can be translated. It is the earliest known collection of laws, dating roughly to the time of the patriarchs.

---

1. For example, Hans J. Boecker, *Law and the Administration of Justice in the Old Testament and the Ancient East* (Minneapolis: Augsburg, 1980), and Shalom Paul, *Studies in the Book of the Covenant in the Light of Cuneiform and Biblical Law* (VTSup 18; Leiden: Brill, 1970), are strongly comparative in approach.

2. Translations of and factual information about ancient Near Eastern laws are found in Boecker, *Law and the Administration of Justice*; *ANET* (3rd ed.; ed. J. B. Pritchard; Princeton: Princeton University Press, 1969), and Martha Roth, *Law Collections from Mesopotamia and Asia Minor* (SBLWAW 6; Atlanta: Scholars Press, 1995).

These laws can be compared with similar biblical laws.[3]

LAWS OF UR-NAMMU	BIBLICAL PARALLELS
LU §1. *If a man commits a homicide, they shall kill that man.*	Exod 21:12 "Whoever strikes a man so that he dies is to be put to death."
LU §§6-7. *If a man violates the wife of another and deflowers the virgin wife of a young man, they shall kill that male. If the wife of a young man, on her own initiative, approaches a man and initiates sexual relations with him, they shall kill that woman; the man shall be released.*	Deut 22:23-24 "If there is a girl who is a virgin engaged to a man, and another man finds her in the city and lies with her, then you shall bring them both out to the gate of that city and you shall stone them to death; the girl, because she did not cry out in the city, and the man, because he has violated his neighbor's wife. Thus you shall purge the evil from among you."
LU §§9-10. *If a man divorces his first-ranking wife, he shall weigh and deliver 60 shekels of silver. If a man divorces a widow, he shall weigh and deliver 30 shekels of silver.*	Return of brideprice/dowry upon divorce unless the woman is a "guilty party" is assumed in the Bible. Compare Deut 24:1 and our discussion of divorce in Chapter 9 below.
LU §18 *If [a man] cuts off the foot of [another man with . . .], he shall weigh and deliver 10 shekels of silver.* LU §22. *If [a man knocks out another man's] tooth with [. . .], he shall weigh and deliver two shekels of silver.*	Compare the *lex talionis* of Exod 21:23-25, and the law that a slave is granted his freedom if the master knocks out his tooth, Exod 21:27; see our discussion in Chapter 5.
LU §28. *If a man presents himself as a witness, but is demonstrated to be a perjurer, he shall weigh and deliver 15 shekels of silver.*	Deut 19:16-21 where a perjurer receives the penalty the accused would have received.
LU §29. *If a man presents himself as a witness but refuses to take the oath, he shall make compensation of whatever was the object of the case*	The false witness of Deut 19:16-21 as with LU §28. Guilt determined by a person's refusal to take an oath in Exod 22:11, and a compensation (guilt) offering required for refusal to answer a call to testify under threat of a curse in Lev 5:1, 5-6.

---

3. Translations of the cuneiform laws in this chapter are from Roth, *Law Collections from Mesopotamia and Asia Minor.*

2. *The laws of Lipit-Ishtar (c. 1925 B.C.).* The laws of Lipit-Ishtar date to about 1925 B.C. (middle chronology). They were also written in Sumerian. Lipit-Ishtar ruled another Sumerian city, Isin, after the collapse of the 3rd Dynasty of Ur. Isin is about 100 miles northwest of Ur. At least a dozen manuscripts of these laws are extant, almost all of which come from the Sumerian city of Nippur (north of Isin) from the Old Babylonian period, although one copy was also found at Kish and one in Sippar, both in the region of Akkad (near Babylon). A prologue, an epilogue, and about thirty-eight laws are extant from Lipit-Ishtar's laws, with an unknown number of laws missing in gaps. A few laws ascribed to Lipit-Ishtar by M. Roth may belong to some other law collection.

LAWS OF LIPIT-ISHTAR	BIBLICAL PARALLELS
LL §17. *If a man, without grounds(?) accuses another man of a matter of which he has no knowledge, and that man does not prove it, he shall bear the penalty of the matter for which he made accusation.*	Deut 19:16-21 where a perjurer receives the penalty the accused would have received.
LL §33. *If a man claims that another man's virgin daughter has had sexual relations but it is proven that she has not had sexual relations, he shall weigh and deliver 10 shekels of silver.*	Deut 22:13-19 where a man who defamed his bride by accusing her of not being a virgin is fined 100 shekels of silver and not allowed ever to divorce her. [If proven true, the woman was subject to stoning.]
LL §§34-35. *If a man rents an ox and cuts the hoof tendon, he shall weigh and deliver one third of its value (in silver). If a man rents an ox and destroys its eye, he shall weigh and deliver one-half of its value (in silver).*	Exod 22:14-15 where one who borrows an animal must make restitution if it is maimed, though not if the owner was present (approving of the use to which his animal was put). Verse 15b is obscure but may state that if the animal is hired out, the owner must take the loss should the animal be damaged: *If it was hired, the risk [which eventuated] was already paid for in the value of the rent paid [by the borrower].* (J. Sprinkle's paraphrase).

3. *The laws of Eshnunna (c. 1800 B.C).* The laws of Eshnunna were written in the Old Babylonian dialect of Akkadian around 1800 B.C. Unlike Sumerian in which the laws of Ur-Nammu and the laws of Lipit-Ishtar were written, Akkadian is a Semitic language like Hebrew. Eshnunna was a city about 100 miles north of Babylon. These laws were discovered in 1947 and 1949 at Tell Harmal (ancient Shaduppum) near Baghdad with a later, student exercise copy found at Tell Haddad. The laws of Eshnunna are considered a few year older than the laws of Hammurabi (c. 1750 B.C.). The laws of Eshnunna show similarities with the

earlier Sumerian codes which suggests literary dependence. The laws of Esh-nunna deal with tariffs and wages, family matters, assault, slave laws, bonds, etc. One law is identical with a biblical law: LE §53, "If an ox gores an(other) ox and causes its death, both ox owners shall divide the price of the live ox and also the meat of the dead ox" is virtually identical in wording with Exod 21:35.

4. *The laws of Hammurabi (c. 1750 B.C.).* The laws of Hammurabi were written in Old Babylonian Akkadian. They date to c. 1750 (middle chronology) when Hammurabi (or Hammurapi) had a small empire whose capital was Baby-lon. The main text of the laws of Hammurabi is a 7 1/2 foot tall black stone stela that was carried by Elamites to Susa around the 12th century B.C. after plunder-ing one of the cities of Hammurabi's former empire, perhaps Sippar. It was dis-covered in 1901-1902 by French archaeologists and is now housed in the Louvre museum in Paris. It was probably one of a number of such stelas erected in cities under Hammurabi's dominion, and fragments of a second and possibly a third were also found in Susa. The stela shows Hammurabi receiving a rod and ring from the god Shamash as symbol of the king's authority to rule. Below this im-age are the laws.

These laws were highly influential in the Akkadian scribal tradition. The text was copied and recopied numerous times over the course of a thousand years, and many later copies have been found. These allow scholars almost completely to fill the portions of the stela that are imperfectly preserved.

The laws of Hammurabi begin with a long prologue and conclude with an epilogue. In both Hammurabi brags about having established justice. The pur-pose of these laws was perhaps propaganda: to allow Hammurabi to prove to readers and to the gods how just he was and why those whom he conquered should be happy he conquered them. There are some 282 laws, almost all of which are extant. Many deal with the same subject matter as biblical laws: per-jury, sorcery, theft, kidnapping, housebreaking, contracts of bailment, marriage, adultery, divorce, bodily injuries, causing a woman's miscarriage, malpractice by physicians or veterinarians or barbers, negligence by builders and boatmen, rules for rental of an ox, goring oxen, hire of persons, and slaves. It is the longest and best organized of the Mesopotamian law collections.

5. *The edict of Ammisaduqa (c. 1560 B.C.).* Another text of relevance to biblical laws is the edict of a Babylonian king named Ammisaduqa. This is an edict, not a collection of laws. An edict is a law by decree of a ruler. This edict declares release (Akk. *andarru*) of debts. It is reminiscent of the Bible's Sabbath Year and Year of Jubilee laws, and shows how those laws might have actually worked.

6. *The Middle Assyrian laws (c. 1300s B.C.).* The Middle Assyrian laws are written in another dialect of Akkadian, namely Assyrian. They were found on a number of tablets dating to the 11th century B.C., but they seem to be based on

roughly 14th century originals. The earliest copies date to the time of Tiglath-Pileser I of Assyria in the 11th Century. A Neo-Assyrian fragment (7th century) from around the time of Assurbanipal has also been found. Tablet A has some 59 laws extant; Tablet B has 20; and Tablet C+G another 11; and further fragments preserve more or less 35 more. In addition, there are some Middle Assyrian palace decrees.

7. *Hittite laws (1650-1200 B.C.).* The Hittite laws were first written down c. 1650-1500 B.C. by the Hittites who were centered in Asia Minor. Hittite was a non-Semitic, Indo-European language unrelated to either Sumerian or Akkadian, and yet the Hittite laws are influenced by other cuneiform laws and are broadly in the Mesopotamian legal tradition. The earliest four copies were written down in the Old Hittite Kingdom period (c. 1650-1500 B.C.). That was before the time of Moses. Later copies are from the New Hittite period (c. 1500-1180 B.C.) and these show evidence of revision rather than mere copying of older laws. In some cases the New Hittite laws revise Old Hittite laws no longer extant in the oldest manuscripts, so both are needed to reconstruct the oldest laws. The Hittites fell as a kingdom c. 1200.

8. *Other laws.* Other ancient Near Eastern laws exist but will only be briefly listed here. There are Sumerian law fragments that date from 2050-1700 B.C. These include laws of X (c. 2050-1800 B.C.), laws about rented oxen (c. 1800 B.C.), Sumerian laws exercise tablet (c. 1800 B.C.), and the Sumerian laws handbook of forms (c. 1700 B.C.). There is also a collection of Neo-Babylonian laws (c. 700 B.C., Sippar).

II. RELATIONSHIP OF BIBLICAL AND CUNEIFORM LAWS

How do biblical and cuneiform laws relate to each other? Is it that there is direct borrowing of biblical laws from cuneiform laws? Or are they completely independent?

Older liberal commentators[4] argued that biblical law simply borrowed from and/or modified Hammurabi or other preexisting, ancient law codes, perhaps drawing on Canaanite laws. But no Canaanite law collections have been found by archaeologists, and biblical laws are not close enough to any known collection of cuneiform laws to prove direct borrowing.

Some parallels between biblical and cuneiform laws do appear too close for chance. It seems unlikely that LE §53 just happens to be virtually identical with Exod 21:35. Moreover biblical and cuneiform categories of law overlap—goring oxen, pregnant women caused to miscarry by blow. Some sort of cultural influence appears to be the best way of explaining these similar categories.

---

4. E.g. J. M. Powis Smith, *The Origin and History of Hebrew Law* (Chicago: U. of Chicago, 1931).

It seems probable that the categories of law in the Bible have at least been influenced by the type cases that are in the cuneiform collections. The Bible assumes the existence of such laws and that readers would have been aware of them in general terms. Where a law is just, the Bible can even adopt it intact, as is the case with LE §53. But that only one biblical law is known to be identical with an earlier extra-biblical law shows the limited nature of such adoptions.

III. BIBLICAL AND CUNEIFORM LAWS CONTRASTED

It is also helpful to contrast biblical and cuneiform laws. The following comparisons are derived from M. Greenberg and Rifat Sonsino.[5]

CUNEIFORM LAWS	BIBLICAL LAWS
1. Essentially secular.	Many ceremonial laws and "religious" motive clauses. Cultic, civil, and moral injunctions freely mixed.
2. Laws are by the king not gods. The god Shamash on the Black Stone Stela of Hammurabi is a symbol of impersonal cosmic truth, not a lawgiver.	Moses mediates laws directly from God.
3. Cuneiform codes meant to glorify the kings who compiled them. Placed in temples outside of public view and in a script only scholars could read.	Laws in Bible represent *Torah* ("instruction") meant both to glorify God and educate the public in order to mold the national character.
4. Reflects unlimited authority of kings.	Limits the authority of kings (Deut 17:14-20).
5. Property crimes are punishable by death (requiring up to 30-fold restitution for theft and the death of the thief if he cannot pay).	Property crimes are not capital offenses: Elevates human life over property *(limited to 5-fold restitution, and servitude—not death—for those who cannot pay).* Exception is stealing God's property under the ban (Achan, Judges 7). Mere property crime is never capital. People are more important than things.

---

5. M. Greenberg, "Some Postulates of Biblical Criminal Law" *Yehezkel Kaufmann Jubilee Volume* (ed. M. Haran; Jerusalem: Detus Goldberg, 1960), 3-28; idem "Biblical Attitudes Towards Power: Ideal and Reality in Law and Prophets" in *Religion and Law* (ed. Edwin Firmage; Winona Lake: Eisenbrauns, 1990), 105, 108; ibid "Reply" 124; Rifat Sonsino, "Characteristics of Biblical Law," *Judaism* 33 (1984): 202-209.

6. Offenses against slaves are placed with offenses against oxen as mere property crime.	Offense against slave is among cases against people, not merely a matter of property; separate from offenses against oxen since even a slave has transcendent life value.
7. Religious sins not generally capital offenses.	Many religious offenses capital: idolatry, false prophecy, sorcery, blasphemy, Sabbath violations (Deut 13:6-9; 18:20; Lev 20:27; 24:10-23; Num 15:32-36).

These contrasts indicate that biblical law and cuneiform laws have rather different ideologies.

IV. CONCLUSIONS

There are both similarities and differences between ancient Near Eastern laws and biblical laws. The similarities listed above show that biblical laws have been influenced by their ancient Near Eastern context, and that in turn suggests (and experience confirms) that comparison with cuneiform laws can be helpful in illuminating the meaning of the laws in the Bible. On the other hand, that influence should not be exaggerated. There is only one law in the entire Bible that finds an exact parallel in cuneiform laws. Furthermore, in many cases biblical laws reflect an ideology that differs fundamentally from the ideology reflected in cuneiform laws. These contrasts in ideology are just as instructive as the similarities in content categories. For this reason any study of biblical law will do well to compare these laws with their cuneiform counterparts, but doing so with the realization that such a comparison will reveal contrasts as well as similarities.

Chapter 4

LAW AND NARRATIVE IN EXODUS 19-24

I. READING BIBLICAL LAWS APART FROM NARRATIVES

James Watts writes, "Lawyers and judges do not usually read law books from beginning to end like novels. Instead, laws are collected, compared, harmonized, codified, and in general arranged systematically so as to preclude the necessity of ever having to read the whole code through from start to finish."[1] As Watts goes on to note, this is exactly how traditional Jewish and Christian readers, as well as modern critical scholars, often have read the regulations of the Pentateuch. The laws of the Pentateuch have regularly been analyzed by themselves without much consideration to the narrative context in which they are embedded.[2] Without denying the usefulness of attempts to systemize biblical regulations, there is also a need to read the laws contextually within their narrative and legal-literary frameworks.

II. WAYS THAT LAWS INTERRELATE WITH NARRATIVES

The laws of Exodus 19-24 interrelate with the narratives of the Pentateuch in a variety of ways.

1. *The Laws are part of the narrative of God's graciously establishing a personal relationship with Israel as distinct from other nations.* From a formal point of view, the laws (Exod 20:1-17; 20:22-23:33) are part of and subordinate to the narrative of God's establishment of the covenant with Israel at Sinai (Exodus 19; 20:18-21; 24). More generally this address is a continuation of the exodus story (Exodus 1-18) in which God graciously initiates a personal relationship with his people so that Israel will come to know Yahweh as their God (Exod 6:6-7; 16:12).

It is important to note how God first establishes the relationship with Israel by saving them and then subsequently regulates that relationship through the covenant and its laws. In other words, a relationship with God was established not by law-keeping, but as a free gift. Israel's relationship with God originates

---

1. James W. Watts, *Reading Law: The Rhetorical Shaping of the Pentateuch* (The Biblical Seminar 59; Sheffield: Sheffield Academic Press, 1999), 11.

2. E.g., Ze'ev W. Falk, *Hebrew Law in Biblical Times* (2nd ed; Provo, Utah: Brigham Young University Press, 2001).

before the giving of the law in the divine-human encounter between God and Israel at the exodus. Bratcher notes that the "exodus precedes the giving of torah at Sinai. . . . God initiated a relationship with his people by entering history and hearing the cries of oppressed slaves."[3] The giving of the Decalogue is prefaced on the assumption that Israel is already "saved" and in personal relationship with God: "I am Yahweh your God who released you from the land of Egypt" (Exod 20:2). The Mosaic law was not, and never was intended to be, the means of establishing a relationship with God. Instead it was a means of regulating Israel's already established relationship with God, being guidelines for those already "saved." Israel's covenant relationship with God did not come because they were so good, for they were a stubborn people (Deut 9:6). The covenant was not granted to them because they were so great, but because God loved them (Deut 7:7-9). The relationship itself was a matter of grace, not law.

The law, rather than being a means of salvation, was a means of helping Israel to become a "holy people" set apart to God (Exod 19:6),[4] for it defines holy behavior. The laws prohibit things that are destructive to Israel's relationship with God (e.g., worshiping other gods, moral breeches that offend God). It promotes things that cultivate a proper relationship with God (e.g. festivals, right kinds of worship activities, righteous behaviors that please God). The fundamental obligation of Israel was to love God (Deut 6:4); the law defines what shape a loving response to God should take. Thus obedience to the law was an expression of faith that cultivated Israel's, and the individual Israelite's, relationship with God. For Israel, a personal relationship with God "places every facet of life under faithful response to God."[5] This is the reason why the laws cover various aspects of life: moral, social and religious.

The law's context in the narrative of God's establishing a personal relationship with Israel explains the frequent use of first and second person personal pronouns, "I-Thou" language, in the laws of Exodus 20-23. This personal language thus shows the laws to be more than a list of "do's and do not's." They are part of God's personal message to his people meant to deepen their personal relationship with him.

The narrator introduces the Decalogue (Exod 20:1-17) in the context of the theophany at Sinai (Exodus 19). There God employs "I-Thou" language as he offers Israel a covenant with himself on the condition "if *you* will obey *my* voice and keep *my* covenant" (Exod 19:5). The words introducing the Decalogue, "God spoke all these words saying" (Exod 20:1), links back to Exod 19:5 by supplying

---

3. Dennis R. Bratcher, "Torah as Holiness: Old Testament 'Law' as Response to Divine Grace" (paper presented at the annual meeting of the Wesleyan Theological Society, Dayton, Ohio, 5 November 1994), n.p. Cited 14 July 2004. Online: http://www.cresourcei.org/torahholiness.html.

4. Gordon Wenham, "Law and the Legal System in the Old Testament," *Law, Morality and the Bible* (ed. B. Kaye and G. Wenham; Downers Grove: InterVarsity, 1978), 27.

5. Bratcher, "Torah as Holiness," n.p.

some of the commands that God expects of a people in covenant relationship with himself to "obey" and "keep." The words of the Decalogue that follow are full of "I-Thou" language that shows this to be Yahweh's personal address to his people: "*I* am Yahweh *your* God who released *you* from the land of Egypt" (v. 2); "*You* are to have no other gods besides *me*" (v. 3); "*you* are not to make for *yourself* an image" (v. 4); "*I* Yahweh *your* God am a jealous God" (v. 5); "*You* are not to take the name of Yahweh *your* God in vain" (v. 6), etc. The "you" in each case is masculine singular, referring to national Israel personified in corporate personality, which as a group had been offered the covenant in chapter 19. No doubt Israelite readers also applied the second person singulars directly to themselves as individuals.

Similarly, the book of the covenant (Exod 20:22-23:33), even if more impersonal in formulation than the Decalogue, is bracketed within an "I-Thou" context. The front bracket is its prologue and introductory cultic laws (Exod 20:22-26) that are full of "I-Thou" language. It is introduced as Yahweh's speech to Israel through Moses. Yahweh said to Moses, "Address the children of Israel as follows: '*You yourselves* have seen how from the sky *I* have spoken with *you* [pl.]'" (v. 22). The second person plural is used here in v. 22 and in the law prohibiting images in v. 23, while the second person singular is used in altar law at verses 24, 25, and 26.[6] Yahweh refers to himself in first person (I, me, my) throughout (vv. 22, 23, 24, and 26).

The back bracket of the book of the covenant consists of social and cultic laws (Exod 22:17-23:19)[7] followed by the epilogue to the book of the covenant (Exod 23:20-33), both of which are also full of "I-Thou" language. "I-Thou" language is less common in Exod 21:1-22:17, perhaps influenced by its civil law genre that in other ancient Near Eastern law collections tend to have impersonal, casuistic formulations.[8] Nonetheless, this section begins with "I-Thou" language (21:1: "These are the norms that *you* [=Moses] are to set before them") and has just enough "I-Thou" language later (Exod 21:2, 13-14, 23) to keep the reader

---

6. Why the text switches from plural you to singular you is not entirely clear. The you plural represents Israel as a group of individuals, whereas the you singular represents national Israel personified as an individual, as in the Decalogue. This is shown by Dale Patrick, "I and Thou in the Covenant Code," in *SBLSP* (1978): 71-86. Perhaps the making of idols was more likely to be an individual activity; whereas, the making of an altar is more likely to be an activity of the collective community, as was the case in Deut 27:5-7 and Josh 8:30-31 where this law is applied.

7. Scripture references here refer to those of the English Bible. Exodus 21:37 in the Hebrew Bible (the MT) is 22:1 in the English Bible. Thus the English Bible references in Exodus 22 are numbered one unit higher than Hebrew Bible references to the same verses in that chapter.

8. The typical source-critical explanation for the impersonal formulation of the civil laws in the book of the covenant is that these laws were derived from an earlier, non-Israelite law-code and incorporated into the book of the covenant with relatively little modification.

aware of the context introduced by the prologue that this is God's personal message to Israel.

"I-Thou" language also occurs elsewhere among the laws. It is common in God's instruction to Moses [=thou] on how to build the tabernacle (Exodus 25-31). Leviticus 1-7 consists primarily of impersonally formulated laws concerning sacrifice; but like the central core of the book of the covenant, the narrator personalizes these laws by the use of personal pronouns here and there. The second person formulation in the introduction at Lev 1:2[9] shows that the whole corpus is God's message to Israel mediated by Moses. There is a highly personal section at Lev 4:4-16 where the second person predominates,[10] and there are a few isolated cases where the first person is used in reference to God (Lev 6:17; 7:34) or the second person singular is used in reference to Israelites (Lev 6:21). All this serves to remind the reader that this is Yahweh's personal message for Israel.[11]

In addition to "I-Thou" language, there is also implied "Us-Them" language in the law and its surrounding narratives. This "Us-Them" language emphasizes how "we," the Israelite readers, should be separate from "them," the nations,[12] as a result of Israel's relationship with God as "Thou." This "Us-Them" dichotomy can be discerned in Exodus 19-24. In Exod 19:5-6 God promised Israel that if they "obey my voice and keep my covenant," that is, if they maintain the covenant by following the laws, Israel would be set apart from other peoples as God's special possession, as a "kingdom of priests and a holy nation." In the Decalogue's prologue Israel is reminded how God separated the Israelites from Egypt physically, and the cultic laws emphasize that they must be separate spiritually as well by avoiding idolatry of any sort and by keeping the Sabbath (Exod 20:2-6, 8). The pagan practices of outsiders, such as sorcery and idolatry, were punishable with death (Exod 22:18, 20). Canaanites in particular must be driven out of the land of promise and their cult objects completely obliterated (Exod 23:23-24, 28-32). The Canaanite "they" were not even to live with the Israelite "us" (Exod 23:33). And yet other foreigners, namely sojourners (Heb. gēr), were to be treated decently by the Israelite "us." They were not to be oppressed or taken advantage of, but the "us"-Israelite readers were supposed to empathize with their plight in view of Israel's own historical experience as sojourners (Exod 22:21; 23:9). Such laws ultimately allow "them" to become integrated into "us,"[13] and thereby come to know God as "Thou."

---

9. [Yahweh to Moses:] "Speak to the children of Israel and say to them, 'When a man from among *you* [pl.] wishes to present an offering to Yahweh from the livestock, *you* [pl] may present *your* offerings from the herd or the flock.'" (Lev 1:3)

10. You [sing.] occurs in Lev 2:4, 5, 6, 7, 8, 12, 13, 14, 15; you [plural] in v. 12.

11. After Watts, *Reading Law*, 63.

12. Bernard S. Jackson, "The Literary Presentation of Multiculturalism in Early Biblical Law," *International Journal for the Semiotics of Law* 8.23 (1995): 183.

13. Jackson, "The Literary Presentation of Multiculturalism," 204.

2. *Laws are a means for the narrator to portray the character of God.* A second purpose of the laws within the narrative is to paint the character of God for the reader. One technique narrators (biblical and non-biblical) can use to paint a mental portrait of a character is through the character's own words.[14] So from the narrative point of view, the law contributes to the characterization of God. Watts states, "Pentateuchal law not only characterizes its speakers in order to validate the law, but . . . promulgates law in order to characterize its speakers."[15]

The use of civil laws to characterize the lawgiver is also known outside the Bible. The Laws of Hammurabi (ca. 1750 B.C.) serve a similar function, as is made clear by its prologue. There Hammurabi boasts that he is a pious provider and protector of the holy city of Nippur, as well as other cities and their gods (Prologue 1.50 – 5.13); and just before the laws he claims that "When the god Marduk commanded me to provide just ways for the people of the land (in order to attain) appropriate behavior, I established truth and justice as the declaration of the land, I enhanced the well-being of the people" (Prologue 5.14-24).[16] After the laws, in the Epilogue, he claims the justice of his laws reflects on his "just" and "able" and "wise" character as a king whose benevolence is for the purpose that "the mighty not wrong the weak, to provide just ways for the waif and the widow" (Epilogue xlvii 9-78). Thus one purpose of the Laws of Hammurabi is to show the reader what a good and righteous king Hammurabi is.

In Exodus 20-23 God is characterized by the narrator through the law-speeches of the Decalogue and the book of the covenant. God introduces his laws by first reminding Israel that he is their redeemer from Egypt and has offered them a personal, covenant relationship with them as "*your* God" (Exod 20:2). He is a God who can dramatically communicate from heaven to his people (Exod 20:22). He seeks to meet with them and bless them in sacrificial worship (Exod 20:24), though he is opposed to all sexual impropriety in worship (exposure of genitals on steps to an altar; Exod 20:26), as he is opposed to sexual impropriety otherwise (adultery, seduction of virgins, bestiality; Exod 20:14; 22:16-17, 19). God declares himself a jealous God who tolerates no other gods as rivals (Exod 20:2, 23; 22:20). He does not even tolerate quasi-religious practices such as sorcery (Exod 22:18).

God claims in the Sabbath law to be the unimaginably powerful and intelligent force that made the universe, and on that basis he claims authority to order the lives of his creatures religiously by decreeing the Sabbath rest after his own creative pattern (Exod 20:11). He also prescribes the other festivals: the Sabbath Year, Unleavened Bread (Passover), the Feast of the Harvest (Weeks), and the Feast of Ingathering (Tabernacles) (Exod 22:29-30; 23:10-19).

---

14. Adele Berlin, *Poetics and Interpretation of Biblical Narratives* (Bible and Literature 9; Sheffield: Almond Press, 1983), 38-39.

15. Watts, *Reading Law,* 90.

16. The translations of the Laws of Hammurabi (or Hammurapi) are from Martha T. Roth, *Law Collections from Mesopotamia and Asia Minor* (SBLWAW 6; Atlanta: Scholars Press, 1995), 80-81, 133.

The law-speeches show God to be a moral, law-giving king[17] who structures not only the religious aspects of his people's lives but also all aspects of their lives. God is so righteous that he punishes iniquity to the third and fourth generations with those who hate him, and he is offended when his name is taken in vain; but to an even greater degree he is a loving God who shows faithful love to the thousandth generation to those who love and obey him (Exod 20:3-6, 23; 22:20; cf. Deut 7:9). He lends respect for parental authority (Exod 20:12; 21:15, 17) and for civil authority (Exod 22:28 "Do not . . . curse a ruler of your people"; Exod 23:1-9 implies a judiciary[18]) without which his own regulations could not be administered. Yet it is clear that his divine law takes precedence over any civil authority (cf. Deut 17:14-20 where even Israel's kings are to be subject to the law of God). God serves as the invisible witness and judge of solemn oaths, such as one made to accept permanent servitude (Exod 21:6; assuming *ĕlohîm* here means "God" rather than "judges"). He also hears exculpatory oaths (Exod 22:11) and as judge can personally declare guilt (Exod 22:10, again assuming that *ĕlohîm* here means "God" rather than "judges").[19] He can also carry out sentences: In Exod 22:23-24 God threatens to send an invasion of marauders to punish those afflicting the poor. Exodus 20:5, 7, 12 also imply direct divine punishment for lawbreakers.

The civil laws show God to be a God of justice. God prohibits perjury and demands complete impartiality in court even if it involves one's enemy (Exod 20:16; 23:1-9). He distinguishes the guilt of intentional murder from that of unintentional manslaughter (Exod 21:12-13). God through his law redresses the wrongs done by manslaughter, abuse of parents, kidnapping, and mayhem (Exod 21:12-27); and he provides remedies to victims of carelessness, negligence, accident, fraud, and devaluation of property (Exod 21:28-36; 22:5-17).

God expects his people to treat each other aright and so gives commands on parents, murder, adultery, theft, false witness and coveting (Exod 20:12-17; cf. the civil laws of Exod 21:2-23:9). He expects them to display holiness in their behavior (Exod 22:31). His laws show God to be concerned with various disadvantaged classes: slaves both male and female (Exod 20:10; 21:2-11, 20-21, 26-27), foreign sojourners, widows, orphans, and the poor (Exod 22:21-27; 23:9). God even shows concern for animals. In Exod 20:10 domestic animals are allowed rest on the Sabbath. In Exod 23:11 the leaving of land fallow is meant to

---

17. Watts, *Reading Law*, 101. As Watts notes, the laws never explicitly call God king, but the character of the laws as decrees clearly implies the kingship of Yahweh.

18. Watts, *Reading Law*, 105.

19. "God" could declare guilt through the oath-taking process: The accused could be found guilty by refusing to make a self-curse. Or the accused could break down under the intense questioning of the oath procedure and confess. On why "God" is more likely than "judges" as the meaning of *ĕlohîm* at both Exod 21:6 and 22:11, see J. M. Sprinkle, *'The Book of the Covenant': A Literary Approach* (JSOTSup 174; Sheffield: Sheffield Academic Press, 1994), 56-60, 145-148. A good case can be made at Exod 21:6 for an alternative view that *ĕlohîm* refers there to ancestral figurines or *terāpîm*.

provide food for wild animals. Exodus 23:4-5, 19 reflect concern for lost and overloaded animals and the perversity of cooking a kid-goat in its mother's milk.

Just as God is gracious towards the poor (Exod 22:27), so he also expects his people to be empathetic to such people. This empathy should be motivated by Israel's own humble national origins as slaves before Yahweh saved them (Exod 22:21; 23:9). Still more surprising and showing the complexity of God's character, God's protection extends also to the life of a thief. Bloodguilt is declared on anyone who kills a thief without mitigating circumstance (Exod 22:2-3).

From the above, it is clear that a great deal can be deduced about the character of God through an analysis of his law-speeches.

3. *Law as God's personal message to Israel gives Israel's law divine authority and motivates obedience.* One purpose of this personal language observed above is to persuade and motivate hearers to obey. Watts states, "When read together, the divine sanctions join the stories and the lists of laws in a rhetoric of persuasion to motivate assent and compliance."[20] The narrative context of the commands of Exodus 20-23 is the exodus story of Exodus 12-18 and the theophany of Exodus 19, so that "Command is rooted in theophany," and thus the commands are impassioned with the motivating emotions of the liberation from Egypt.[21]

For example, the prologue to the Decalogue links the laws with the narratives: "I am Yahweh your God who released you from the land of Egypt, out of the house of slaves. Do not have other gods besides me." (Exod 20:2-3) The first sentence serves functionally as a subordinate clause to the second sentence.[22] The logic of this is probably thus: "Because I Yahweh have delivered you, you are to worship me alone." Thus the emotionally charged reference to who and what God has shown himself to be in the exodus narratives serves to motivate Israel to obey the first and other commandments.

The frequent interjection in the Holiness Code, "I am Yahweh [your God],"[23] has a similar purpose. It says in effect, "It is I, Yahweh your God, who has spoken this, so give heed!" When this expression is attached to promises, it is a way of saying they are sure. When attached to laws, this statement reminds the reader that these rules are not merely the laws of men, but the Law of God.

---

20. Watts, *Reading Law,* 52.

21. Walter Brueggemann, "The Book of Exodus," in *The New Interpreter's Bible* (vol. 1; Nashville: Abingdon, 1994) 1:839.

22. M. Weinfeld, "The Decalogue: Its Significance, Uniqueness, and Place in Israel's Tradition," in *Religion and Law: Biblical Judaic and Islamic Perspectives* (ed. E. B. Firmage, et al.; Winona Lake: Eisenbrauns, 1990), 13 n. 28.

23. Lev 18:2, 4, 5, 6, 21, 30; 19:3, 4, 10, 12, 14, 16, 18, 25, 28, 30, 31, 32, 34, 36, 37; 20:7, 8, 24, 26; 21:8, 12, 15, 23; 22:2, 3, 8, 9, 16, 30, 31, 32, 33; 23:22, 43; 24:22; 25:17, 38, 55; 26:2, 13, 44, 45.

4. *The laws and narratives of Exodus 19-24 intertwine to produce a whole greater than the sum of its parts.* A fourth observation concerning the interrelation of law and narrative is that the literary structure of the laws and narrative serve to convey a greater meaning than would be the case if the laws were independent of the narratives. Chirichigno[24] has demonstrated to my satisfaction that the material of Exodus 19-24 does not follow a strict chronological sequence, but utilizes resumptive repetition instead.[25] According to this view, the laws were given simultaneously with the actions of Exodus 19, and thus Exodus 20-23 represents flashback. If the resumptive-repetition view is correct, then the narrator has abandoned strict chronological arrangement to fulfill topical purposes. This is not unique: A good case can be made that Exodus 18 is out of chronological sequence as well.[26] What we wish to explore is the question of why, in Exodus 19-24, might the author have chosen to do this. A couple of reasons come to mind.

One, this non-chronological style allows the narrator to give a privileged position to the Decalogue, making it first among the law-groups, and arguably thereby preeminent among them. If these laws had been scattered among descriptions of the concurrent actions taking place on the mountain in chapter 19 rather than kept together as a literary unit, the Decalogue's preeminence, its majesty, and its rhetorical power would have been diminished; and it would have been more difficult to study it for didactic purposes. Thus the reader's understanding of the Decalogue's importance is affected by this literary decision.

Second, however, this choice of structure allows the author to convey a deeper message through the structure itself. One way of outlining Exodus 19-24 is chiastically:

---

24. G. C. Chirichigno, "The Narrative Structure of Exodus 19-24," *Bib* 68 (1987): 457-479. Also Sprinkle, 'The Book of the Covenant', 17-34. This synoptic/resumptive analysis of Exodus 19-24 is criticized by Richard Averbeck, "The Form Critical, Literary, and Ritual Unity of Exodus 19:3-24:11" (paper presented to the Biblical Law Group at the annual meeting of Society of Biblical Literature Biblical, Philadelphia, Pennsylvania, 20 Nov 1995), 24 n. 30.

25. On the synoptic/resumptive style, see H. C. Brichto, *Towards a Grammar of Biblical Poetics* (New York: Oxford University Press, 1992), 13-14 (definition) and 16, 19, 75-76, 78-79, 86, 93, 95, 98-99, 165, 227-228 (biblical examples).

26. Watts, *Reading Law*, 85-86. He states, "Even Narrative's time line is affected by atemporal lists in its midst. For example, the introduction to the Sinai legislation suffers chronological confusion for the sake of topical arrangement. The story of Jethro (Exod. 18) presupposes a physical setting (at the mountain) and religious practices (altars and sacrifices) to which the Israelites are introduced only later in the narrative sequences: they reach the mountain in 19.2 and first receive cultic instructions in ch. 20."

A. Narrative: The covenant offered (Exod 19:3-25)
　B. Laws (general): The Decalogue (Exod 20:1-17)
　　C. Narrative: The people's fear (Exod 20:18-21)
　B* Laws (specific): The book of the covenant (Exod 20:22-23:33)
A* Narrative: The covenant accepted (Exod 24:1-11)

This structure arguably conveys some important ideas. For one, the laws are bracketed by narratives that emphasize the covenant offered and accepted (Exodus 19, 24). This bracketing suggests that the overall concept of Exodus 19-24 is covenant, not law, and that the laws are elements subordinate to that covenant. The laws gain importance by virtue of representing stipulations of that covenant. Thus this structure reinforces the conclusion reached earlier that the concept of covenant here is more primary than that of law.

Moreover, at the center of the chiasm is a unit where Israel is told (ironically) "Do not be afraid [*'al tîrā'û*]" but that God has come "so that *the fear of him* [*yirāto*] may remain with you" (Exod 20:20). The same root (Hebrew *yr'*) is used for both terms for fear. So which was it: Were the Israelites supposed to be afraid of God, or not? Well, yes and no. God did not want them to be terrified of him, and yet there is a proper "fear of Yahweh" that the cosmic events at Sinai were meant to instill. In the Wisdom literature, fearing God is associated with turning away from evil (Job 1:8; 28:28; Prov 8:13; 16:6), and elsewhere fearing God is said to make one careful about what one does (2 Chr 17:7). It is also associated with doing God's commandments (Ps 111:10; Eccl 12:13; Gen 22:12 where God knows Abraham fears God because Abraham was willing to obey God's command to sacrifice Isaac) and giving heed to the ethical requirements of heaven (Gen 42:18). The kind of "fear of God" that is appropriate for Israel in Exod 20:20 is the kind that leads them to turn away from evil and to obey God's commandments, specifically the commandments then being given to them. That is the reason why the narrative about fearing God is at the center of the chiasm, for "fearing God" is at the heart of the biblical covenant. This fear is what leads to obedience to God's commandments. Hence the meaning of the whole of Exodus 19-24 is more profound than it would otherwise have been had a strictly chronological structure been chosen.

5. *The narrative context affects the reading of the laws.* A fifth observation concerning the interrelationship between law and narrative is that the narrative context of the laws affect the very way that laws are read and interpreted. Watts states,

First, the narrative context of Pentateuchal law confirms that the Torah is intended to be read as a whole and in order. Unlike law, narrative invites, almost enforces, a strategy of sequential reading, of starting at the beginning and reading the text in order to the end. The placement of law within narrative conforms (at least in part) the reading of law to the conventions of narrative.[27]

Several places show how the existence of the narrative affects the reading of the law.

a. Introductory cultic laws in the Decalogue and book of the covenant. For instance, the narrative context makes sense of the fact that both the Decalogue and the book of the covenant begin with cultic regulations (Exod 20:3-11; 20:23-26). Cultic laws pertain directly to Israel's relating to God. Beginning these two groups of laws with cultic regulations makes perfect sense in the context of Israel's establishing a covenant relationship with God (Exodus 19, 24). The laws about images and altars in Exod 20:22-26 relate to the surrounding narrative by giving important instruction on how God's presence could be experienced within the covenant in the future. It thus prepares for the building of the altar at the consummation of the covenant in the narrative of Exod 24:4.[28]

The narrative context also affects the reading of particulars. Exodus 20:22b states, "You yourselves have seen how from the sky I have spoken with you." This is a double allusion. First there is an allusion to Exod 19:18-19, "Mount Sinai was all in smoke because Yahweh descended upon it in fire. . . . Moses would speak and God would answer him with thunder." There is no contradiction between Exod 20:22's "from the sky" and Exodus 19's indication that God spoke from the mountain, as a simplistic reading might suggest.[29] Rather, "from the sky" means "from the mountain whose top is in the sky." The people at the base of the mountain would be looking skyward when they looked to the top of Sinai. Second, there is probably also an allusion to the Decalogue. As T. D. Alexander observes, the words "I have spoken with you" can be connected with the giving of the Decalogue, for the other cases where the people are addressed by God in Exodus 19-24 are mediated through Moses.[30] Thus, contrary to certain source-critical theories that take the Decalogue as a secondary insertion into the narrative,[31] the author of Exod 20:22 assumes the presence of the Decalogue (Exod 20:1-17).[32]

This connection to the narrative then affects the interpretation of the next verse: "You are not to make in my case either a god of silver, nor even a god of gold are you permitted to make for yourselves" (Exod 20:23). This verse, which expands on the Decalogue's prohibition of images (Exod 20:4-5), makes a logi-

---

27. Watts, *Reading Law*, 29.

28. T. D. Alexander, "The Composition of the Sinai Narrative in Exodus XIX 1-XXIV 11," *VT* 49.1 (1999), 5-6.

29. E.g., J. Philip Hyatt, *Exodus* (NCB; Greenwood, SC: Attic, 1971), 224-225.

30. Alexander, "The Composition of the Sinai Narrative," 9.

31. Cf. A. H. McNeile, *The Book of Exodus* (Westminster Commentaries; London: Methuen, 1908), 114; Hyatt, *Exodus*, 207.

32. Alexander, "The Composition of the Sinai Narrative," 9.

cal connection between how God revealed himself at Sinai and how they are to worship him. The logic between Exod 20:22 and 20:23 is as follows: "Because, as you have seen, I spoke with you as an invisible voice from the sky, I was indicating to you that no earthly image of me is appropriate." This interpretation is implicit here; but it is made explicit in Deut 4:15-16a "Because you saw no form when Yahweh spoke to all of you on Horeb from the midst of the fire, be careful that you not act corruptly and make for yourselves an image."

b. The slave laws. Another way in which the laws of Exodus 20-23 relate to the narrative context is found in the emphasis on slaves. Why, for instance, are the first non-cultic laws of the book of the covenant about slaves (Exod 21:2-11), and why do slaves get mentioned so often elsewhere in the laws (Exod 20:10 [Decalogue]; 21:20-21, 26-27, 32; 23:12)? This is not the case with other ancient Near Eastern law collections. Slave laws end rather than begin the Laws of Hammurabi (§§278-282), and the Laws of Eshnunna place its most substantial slave laws at the end (§§49-52). Middle Assyrian laws only rarely deal with slaves at all. Why then this prominence concerning slaves in the book of the covenant?

The answer lies in the narrative context. Exodus 21 begins with slave laws for the same reason that the prologue of the Decalogue mentions slavery (Exod 20:2): It relates to a central theme of the narratives of the book of Exodus, the release of Israelite slaves from Egyptian servitude.[33]

This connection of slave laws to narrative also bleeds over to the other social justice regulations concerning the poor and especially sojourners. The primarily social-humanitarian regulations of Exod 22:22-23:9, which begin and end with the command not to oppress a sojourner (Heb. *gēr*), are parallel in terms of the literary, chiastic structure with the social-humanitarian laws about slaves in Exod 21:2-11.[34] This is not accidental. The disadvantaged classes of Exod 22:22-27—the sojourner, the widow, the orphan, and the poor—were the very people most subject to becoming enslaved on the basis of unpaid debts.[35] Israel itself had become enslaved in Egypt after entering it as sojourners, as the regulation itself suggests: "Do not oppress a sojourner, for you were sojourners in the land of Egypt" (Exod 23:9). The experience of Israel in Egypt recorded by the narrative is thus the basis for the motive clause promoting legal obedience.

c. The use of the number 7. The narrative of God's resting or ceasing to create on the seventh day of creation (Gen 2:1-4) influences several laws in Exodus 20-23. Exodus' version of the Decalogue (Exod 20:11) finds the basis for the human Sabbath day in the pattern that God rested on his seventh day. The asso-

---

33. U. Cassuto, *A Commentary on the Book of Exodus* (trans. I. Abrahams; Jerusalem: Magnes, 1967), 266; Shalom Paul, *Studies in the Book of the Covenant in the Light of Cuneiform and Biblical Law* (VTSup 18; Leiden: Brill, 1970), 107.

34. Cf. Sprinkle, *'The Book of the Covenant'*, 200.

35. Jackson, "Multiculturalism in Early Biblical Law," 197.

ciation of God's seventh day with "ceasing" or "resting" helps to explain why the Hebrew slave is released on the seventh year (Exod 21:2), not on the third year as in the Laws of Hammurabi (§117) or the fifth or eight year. This is in accord with the symbolism of "ceasing, rest" invested in the number seven through the creation narrative. The symbolism of "ceasing, rest" invested in the number seven also explains why the land is to lie fallow specifically on the seventh year (Exod 23:11). Outside of Exodus 19-24 there are other places where the number seven appears to reflect the symbolism derived from the creation narrative: The Sabbath year occurs every seven years (Lev 25:1-7); the year of Jubilee occurs after seven times seven years (Lev 25:11); and the remission of debts, every seven years (Deut 15:1-3; 31:10).

d. The altar laws. It is well known that the altar of earth law of Exod 20:24-26 is hard to reconcile with the references to the other altars in the Bible (Exod 27:1-8: bronze altar; Lev 17:3-9; Deuteronomy 12). Although there are a variety of ways to approach this problem, one way to explain the differences among these laws is on the basis of their occurrences at differing points in the narratives.

The following reconstruction seems possible: Before the exodus, no explicit regulations about altars are recorded. God did command that one not eat the flesh of an animal "with the blood" (Gen 9:4), but this command may or may not assume the use of altars. The altar law of Exod 20:22-26 limits altars to simple, "natural" and unmanufactured, stone materials, in contrast with the bronze altar of the tabernacle (Exodus 27). This difference of material is probably intended to show the pre-eminence of the tabernacle's altar. At the altars of stone šĕlāmîm (fellowship or peace) offerings for the purpose of obtaining meat to eat were available even for the ceremonially unclean (1 Sam 14:31-35), whereas the unclean were not to eat meat from the tabernacle's altar (Lev 7:20) or other more formally consecrated food (1 Sam 21:4). In the wilderness the pre-eminence of the tabernacle's altar is further underscored by a temporary measure limiting all slaughter to the tabernacle (Lev 17:4-7), a measure meant to counteract the temptation to idolatrous goat-demon worship at that particular occasion in the desert. What Lockshin calls "The standard understanding of most halakhic exegetes"[36] was that the opening verses of Leviticus 17 are limited to the context of the Israelites traveling through the Sinai wilderness. But when Israel came to the land, altars of stone again were permitted and built (Deut 27:4-8; Josh 8:30-35). Deuteronomy 12:5, however, anticipates a day when all sacrifice would be limited to the one "place that Yahweh your God will choose." Although in Moses' day and for a number of generations after Moses, altars after the description of Exod 20:24-26 continued to be allowed; 1 Kgs 3:2 sees this as temporary: "The people, however, were still sacrificing at the high places, because a temple had

---

36. Martin I. Lockshin, trans. and ed., *Rashbam's Commentary on Leviticus and Numbers: An Annotated Translation* (BJS 330; Providence, RI: Brown University, 2001), 93 n. 20.

not yet been built for the name of Yahweh." According to the narrator of this text, there is no condemnation of sacrificing on the high places as such. Nevertheless, it does foresee a day, after the temple is built, when sacrifice at the high places would cease. This prediction came true through Josiah's reforms around 621 BC (2 Kgs 23:15, 19-20).

The above line of interpretation does not resolve all difficulties, and other solutions are defendable and may even be preferable. But it does seem possible to explain the differences among the altar laws on the basis of their placement in the framework of the Bible's narrative chronology. It thus shows the fruitfulness, hermeneutically, of taking narrative into consideration when interpreting law.

e. Firstfruits, firstborn, and holiness. Another place where the narrative affects the interpretation of law is Exod 22:29-31. Here God commands Israelites to give to him the overflow (of wine/oil), the firstborn of their sons, and the firstborn of their livestock; adding that they are to be holy by not eating carrion.

The call for Israel to be "holy men" (Exod 22:31) picks up on Exod 19:6 that Israel was to be a "holy nation." Exod 22:29-31 is also surrounded by social-humanitarian regulations where further allusion to the exodus is explicit (cf. Exod 22:21; 23:9). The command about the firstborn repeats commands given earlier in conjunction with the Passover narratives, that the firstborn of both man and beast belong to God, though as a concession, human sons and more expensive animals were to be redeemed by sacrifice of a lamb (Exod 13:2, 11-19). Firstborn sons in particular play a prominent role in the Passover narrative (Exod 11:3-7; 12:12-13). Thus, in the light of the Passover law/narratives of Exodus 11-13, it would be wrong to read Exod 22:29 as a call for literal human sacrifice. The narrative context precludes that interpretation, even though the words without the earlier narrative might have been taken that way.

Thus the exodus experience alluded to in these laws implicitly motivates obedience and provides the backdrop for correct interpretation.

f. Driving out the Canaanites. The epilogue of the book of the covenant (Exod 23:20-33) is also better understood with reference to biblical narratives. It commands Israel not to worship Canaanite gods, but instead to drive the Canaanites out and obliterate their cultic objects (Exod 23:24). God goes on to say that he would fix their boundaries from the Red Sea to the Sea of the Philistines to the Euphrates (Exod 23:31). This is clearly an allusion to the land promise given to Abraham (Gen 15:18-20) where the dimensions are from the river of Egypt to the Euphrates. God said he would fulfill this promise by bringing Israel from Egypt to Canaan (Exod 6:2-8). Thus the basis for the law to drive out the Canaanites is the narrative promise to the patriarchs and the promise given to Moses in Exodus 6.

6. *The legal context affects the reading of narratives.* Not only do the narratives affect the understanding of the laws, but also the laws affect our reading of

the narratives. This is certainly true of narratives subsequent to the giving of the law and is also true of earlier narratives.

a. *"Do not approach a woman" (Exod 19:15)*. God had Moses admonish the Israelite men in preparation for his manifesting himself on Mount Sinai, "Do not approach a woman" (Exod 19:15). This seems to anticipate the laws of purity in Leviticus 15 where even ordinary sexual intercourse made a person ceremonially unclean (Lev 15:16-18), and contact with a woman in her period would also transfer uncleanness (Lev 15:19). Those who are ceremonially unclean were prohibited from approaching the presence of God in a sanctuary (Num 5:1-3). Viewed in the light of the later laws, this admonition asked the Israelite men, in effect, to avoid contracting ceremonial impurity before coming into the presence of Yahweh. Thus this narrative is best understood when read in conjunction with the laws.

b. *The Creation Accounts (Genesis 1-4)*. Calum Carmichael in his book *The Origins of Biblical Law* argues that the Decalogue has been structured on the basis of the creation narratives. The command to honor parents and the Decalogue's prohibitions against murder, adultery, theft, false witness, and coveting were given, he says, to elaborate on matters found in the narratives of Genesis 2-4: the coveting and theft of the forbidden fruit by Eve; the false witness in trying to pass off the blame to others by Adam and Eve after the partaking of the fruit; the teaching about marriage in the creation narrative; and how Cain dishonored his parents, Adam and Eve, by murdering his brother Abel.[37] Exodus' version of the Sabbath (Exod 20:8-11) could be derived from the narration of God's six days of creation followed by his rest on the seventh day (Gen 1:1-2:4), and also be a response to Aaron's improper declaration of a special day in the Golden Calf narrative (Exod 32:5).[38]

I am unconvinced by Carmichael's thesis that these laws or their structuring are derived from the narratives, but I do think that he shows adequately that these narratives are better understood when read in the light of the laws. This can be justified because the narratives were written by an author who was already familiar with the Mosaic laws and so can assume them in his narrative. Moreover, this author writes for an audience who would also have prior acquaintance with the laws and, therefore, could be expected to have such laws in the back of their minds as the narrator presents his stories to them.

c. *The Golden Calf narrative (Exodus 32)*. The prohibition against making "a god of gold" in Exod 20:23 (see also Exod 20:4-5) provides the framework for reading the Golden Calf story of Exodus 32. In Exodus 32 the calf/bull is called

---

37. Calum M. Carmichael, *The Origins of Biblical Law: The Decalogues and the Book of the Covenant* (Ithaca, New York: Cornell University Press, 1992), 37-45.

38. Carmichael, *The Origins of Biblical Law*, 45-46.

"a god of gold" (Exod 32:31), but it also appears to be identified as an image of Yahweh. The calf stands for the one who brought them from Egypt (Exod 32:4), and upon its construction a feast for Yahweh was declared (Exod 32:5). This indicates that the "calf" was a representation of Yahweh.[39] The narrative must be read in the light of the law, for it calls what Israel did an act of turning away from what God commanded them (Exod 32:8). But the narrative likewise clarifies the law, showing that the prohibitions of images in Exod 20:4-5, 23 include images of Yahweh, not just images of other gods. Thus law and narrative must be read in conjunction with each other to derive the correct meaning.

   d. Joshua and the altar of stone (Josh 8:31-35). Joshua's construction of the altar of unhewn stones on Mount Ebal (Josh 8:31-35) is said to be "as Moses the servant of Yahweh commanded" (v. 32). This is a clear allusion to the earlier altar of stone laws in Deut 27:2-8, which itself draws upon the altar law of Exod 20:24-25. The text assumes that the reader is acquainted with the earlier altar laws to inform the understanding of the narrative event.

   e. Abraham, Laban, Jacob and the slave and brideprice laws. Exod 21:11 says that if the husband of a slave-wife (*'āmâ*) is unwilling to grant to the wife choice food (literally "flesh"), appropriate clothing, and a term that may mean conjugal rights, that she is to be released without payment of money.[40] This passage informs one's reading of God's command for Abraham to "divorce" his slave-wife Hagar (Gen 21:8-14). When Sarah tells Abraham to drive out Hagar (Gen 21:10) and when he sent her away (Gen 21:14), the text uses language associated elsewhere with divorce.[41] The verb "sent away" is the piel of *šālah* that is often used for divorcing wives (Deut 22:19; 24:1, 3; Jer 3:8); and the verb used to "drive her out," the piel of *gāraš*, is also used for divorce (Lev 21:7, 14; 22:13). In this narrative God told Abraham to drive out Hagar as Sarah had requested (Gen 21:12), thus lending divine sanction for this divorce. Arguably the row between Sarah and Hagar (as well as Hagar's unruliness) had made it impossible for Abraham to function as Hagar's and Sarah's husband at the same time. Yet according to Exod 21:11, if a slave-wife ceases to be a wife, she cannot remain on as a slave but is to be released. Read in the light of Exod 21:11, Abraham was in fact following the practice of what later would be Mosaic law. This helps to explain why God was willing to go along with Sarah's request.

   Another place where the law is illuminating for narratives has to do with Jacob's working seven years each for his wives Rachel and Leah (Gen 29:18, 27). The requirement for Jacob to work for Laban in order to obtain a daughter in

---

39. The Decalogue's prohibition of images and of taking God's name in vain in Carmichael's view (*The Origins of Biblical Law*, 28-34) elaborates on the Golden Calf story where Aaron takes God's name in vain by declaring a feast to Yahweh when the calf was made.

40. For exegetical details, see Sprinkle, *'The Book of the Covenant'*, 53-54.

41. G. Wenham, *Genesis 16-50* (WBC 2; Dallas: Word, 1994), 82.

marriage has to do with the widespread cultural phenomenon of brideprice. In the ancient Near East—as in some Third World cultures today—it was customary to give a significant gift to the bride's family (the father if alive) in conjunction with a marriage contract of betrothal. The brideprice, in turn, would be given back in part or whole as a dowry for the bride. The dowry in the Bible is mentioned only in 1 Kgs 9:16 and Mic 1:14, but is well-known from second millennium Mesopotamia and fifth century B.C. and later Jewish marriage contracts. In the Laws of Hammurabi, the dowry belonged to the woman. In the event of her death before bearing children, the dowry went back to her father (cf. LH §§162-164). In a case of divorce, the dowry ordinarily left with the woman unless forfeited though her bad behavior (cf. LH §§138, 141-142, 149), a fact that would discourage divorce. In the book of the covenant, the brideprice (Heb. *mōhar*) is mentioned as a cultural institution in Exod 22:16-17, where it is required of a man who has seduced an unbetrothed maiden regardless of whether the marriage is then allowed to take place. This protected the girl economically, insuring that a seduced woman could have an adequate dowry.

The cultural institution of brideprice and dowry explains Jacob's working for his wives: He was destitute and could not afford to pay a brideprice outright. His time of labor, seven years, is identical with the maximum amount of time that the Hebrew slave could serve according to the book of the covenant (Exod 21:2), suggesting that Jacob was essentially an indentured servant. Carmichael asserts that the seven-year limit for slaves in the book of the covenant may have its backdrop in the seven years of servitude of Jacob.[42] Laban in turn gave Rachel and Leah female slaves as dowries (Gen 29:24-29), as he previously had done for Rebekah (Gen 24:59-61), though they complained that this was inadequate in return for Jacob's years of service (Gen 31:15). The law in the book of the covenant may well explain another aspect of the story. Though promised Rachel, Jacob married Leah on account of Laban's deception (Gen 29:21-25). Presumably he was too drunk to tell the difference between Rachel and Leah! To marry Rachel also, Jacob had to commit himself to another seven years of service as a brideprice for Rachel. Why could Jacob not say that this was a mistake and demand Rachel for his servitude? Well, having "seduced" Leah, the first brideprice was forfeit per the principle of Exod 22:16-17. Or at least this would be Laban's argument.

f. The rape of Dinah and the kidnapping of Joseph (Genesis 34; 37). Another place where the laws illuminate the narrative is the rape (or possibly seduction) of Dinah by Shechem (Gen 34:1-31). This act outrages her brothers. Shechem, by indulging in sex with Dinah without permission of her family, had "humiliated her" (v. 2)[43] and, according to Levi and Simeon, "treated her like a whore"

---

42. Carmichael, *The Origins of Biblical Law*, 80.

43. Heb. ʿānâ "humiliate, violate" is used of enforced marriages, simple adultery, and rape (Deut 21:14; 22:24, 29).

(v. 31). Simeon and Levi responded to their sister's violation by tricking Shechem's clan into being circumcised as a condition of future intermarriage between the clans (Gen 34:22-24). After Shechem's clan complied and were in great pain because of the circumcisions, Simeon and Levi then killed every male with the sword, their opponents being too weak from the circumcision to fight back (Gen 34:25-27). They went on to plunder the city (Gen 34:28-29). Jacob complained that this would make his name odious among the inhabitants (Gen 34:30) and later cursed them for their act (Gen 49:6-7), though his sons insisted that they were justified by what Shechem had done to their sister (Gen 34:31). Who was right?

The laws of seduction and rape clarify the situation. In the book of the covenant, the penalty for seduction of an unbetrothed woman was either payment of brideprice followed by marriage or else forfeiture of the brideprice without marriage if the father objected to the marriage (Exod 22:16-17). Deuteronomy gives a more stringent penalty for rape, setting the brideprice at an extremely high fifty shekels (Deut 22:29), the price of a prime-aged, adult male slave (Lev 27:3). But neither rape nor seduction were capital offenses so long as the girl was unbethrothed. In the light of these laws, Simeon and Levi's killing of Shechem was clearly way out of proportion with the crime that was committed. The Mosaic law, then, supports Jacob's disapproval of the act of his two sons.

The kidnapping and selling of Joseph into slavery (Gen 37:28) is similarly seen in a new light when read in conjunction with the book of the covenant. There kidnapping (literally, "stealing a man") was punishable by death whether or not the victim were sold into slavery (Exod 21:16). This law underscores the heinous nature of what Joseph's brothers did.

g. The two tablets of stone for the Decalogue. In Exod 24:12 Moses is told to receive tablets of stone on which would be written the law and commandments. Later these tablets are said to be two in number that were inscribed front and back (Exod 31:18; 32:15), and upon them were the ten words (Exod 34:18; Heb. *děbārîm*; often here rendered commandments), that is, the Decalogue. Artistic portrayals of the Decalogue have concentrated on the fact that there were two tablets and assumed that the first five "words" (or "commandments") were on the first tablet, whereas remaining laws were on the second tablet. Which commandments are included by an artist depends on whether one is following Jewish, Catholic, or Reformed numbering. In terms of content, it is widely recognized that the Decalogue begins with cultic laws that deal with Israel's relationship with God and then goes on to laws on how they were to relate to other human beings. Could it be that the first tablet contained the religiously oriented laws, whereas the second had the more ethical commandments?

Youngblood may well be correct in thinking all these constructs are wrongheaded, and that the two tablets may have been meant to represent two copies of the Decalogue as a covenant treaty, one for Israel as vassal and one for God as suzerain.[44] Even then, however, one might raise the question of which parts are on the obverse and which are on the reverse. Speculations along these lines have been around since the third century A.D. *Mekhilta*.[45]

Although the question of which commands occur on which tablets (and which on each side) cannot be definitively answered, the nature of that speculation is determined by the structure of the laws. This illustrates how the law can influence the interpretation of the narrative.

III. CONCLUSION

Law and narrative must be read together in order to obtain the fullest and most accurate interpretation of both. The practice of many traditional exegetes and critical scholars of reading laws apart from their narrative context in the final form of the text distorts to some degree the meaning of both law and narrative.

The discussion above has tried to show that the Decalogue and the book of the covenant must be read as part of the narrative in which God graciously establishes a personal relationship with Israel through the covenant. This explains the prevalence of "I-Thou" language in the laws. The laws must also be seen as the narrator's way of painting the merciful but just character of Yahweh for the reader. The fact that the laws are given as speech from Yahweh as a character in the narrative serves to lend authority to these laws and motivate Israelites to obey them as the Law of God, not as laws of men. Moreover, the chiastic and non-chronological structuring of the laws and narratives of Exodus 19-24 produces meanings of the whole greater than the individual parts; in particular, giving a privileged position to the Decalogue, indicating the priority of covenant over law, and placing the concept of fear of Yahweh at the heart of that covenant.

The interaction of law and narrative affect the interpretation of particulars in both. Attention to the narratives provides explanations for why both the Decalogue and the book of the covenant begin with cultic regulations, why the civil laws begin with slaves, and why the number seven is used. The narrative's chronological framework may provide a solution as to how to reconcile the various altar laws. It provides the proper framework for understanding the laws of firstfruits, firstborn, and holiness, and the command to drive out the Canaanites.

Conversely, attention to the laws of Exodus 20-23 helps to explain the seventh day of creation, the nature of the offense in the Golden Calf Story (as well as what the law actually prohibits), the way Joshua constructed his altar on Mount Ebal, and aspects of the stories of Abraham, Jacob, and Joseph. It also is suggestive for interpreting the nature of the two tablets of the Decalogue described in subsequent narratives.

---

44. Ronald Youngblood, "Counting the Ten Commandments," *BRev* 10, no. 6 (December 1994): 34.

45. Jackson, "Multiculturalism in Early Biblical Law," 187.

I have primarily limited myself to matters related to Exodus 19-24, but a fuller application of the conclusions reached here would encourage interpreters to read all Old Testament narratives and laws in the light of each other. Examples could be multiplied where attention to the interaction of law and narrative is exegetically fruitful: the practice of war in the narratives can be compared with the rules of war in Deuteronomy 20, the Sodom narratives of Genesis 19 can be compared with laws on homosexual acts and incest in Leviticus 18 and 20, and references to ceremonial uncleanness in narratives (e.g., Gen 7:8; 1 Sam 20:26; 21:4-5; 2 Sam 11:2, 4) require an understanding of the purity laws. The narratives of both the Pentateuch and subsequent biblical history were written by authors familiar with the laws, and so one seems justified in reading the narratives in the light of the laws. And the laws of the Pentateuch at the least assume the narratives of the Pentateuch, and so one may reasonably suppose that these narratives may illumine the laws at points. Perhaps greater attention to the relationship of laws and narratives will prove a fruitful avenue for future Old Testament research.

Chapter 5

EXODUS 21:22-25 (*LEX TALIONIS*) AND ABORTION

I. INTRODUCTION

W. C. Kaiser, in defending the use of OT law for formulating Christian ethics, argues that many ethical questions of interest to the modern Christian are not addressed in the NT, but only in the Old. "Where," he asks, "will we obtain authoritative materials on the abortion question if the OT is not consulted?"[1]

The passage most directly relevant to the abortion question according to Kaiser is Exod 21:22-25, the case of a pregnant woman struck during a brawl.[2] Key to finding direct relevance in this passage to the abortion question is the interpretation that, contrary to the view exemplified by most commentators and translators,[3] premature birth rather than miscarriage is involved in the first half of this passage where there is no serious injury (Heb. *'asôn*). Only in the second case with serious injury is the death of the fetus and/or the mother contemplated, and there the *lex talionis*, the "law of retaliation," is applied "life for life," implying that the killing of the fetus was regarded as taking human "life" (Heb. *nepeš*). This interpretation, reflected in many recent Evangelical translations (NIV, NASB [1995 updated edition], NKJV, NLT, GOD'S WORD, WORLD ENGLISH BIBLE, HCSB), implies that deliberate, induced abortion of a human fetus is murder.

Many anti-abortion Christian theologians and ethicists adopt this interpretation to bolster their case against abortion.[4] However, this line of interpretation is

---

1. W. C. Kaiser, *Toward Old Testament Ethics* (Grand Rapids: Zondervan, 1983), 34.

2. Kaiser, *Ethics,* 168-172.

3. Kaiser (*Ethics,* 170) lists the RSV, BERKELEY VERSION, NAB, JB, AMPLIFIED BIBLE, DOUAY-RHEIMS, MOFFATT, and GOODSPEED, that take the miscarriage view. NJPS, NEB, REB, NRSV, NASB [1977 edition], TEV, BIBLE IN BASIC ENGLISH, CEV, and THE MESSAGE can be added to the list. The ESV is hyper-literal ("so that her children come out") and is thus neutral.

4. Among them: J. W. Cottrell, "Abortion and the Mosaic Law," *Christianity Today* 17 (March 16, 1973): 6-9; J. M. Frame, "Abortion from a Biblical Perspective," in *Thou Shalt Not Kill* (ed. R. L. Ganz; New Rochelle, NY: Arlington House, 1978), 51-56; J. W. Montgomery, *The Slaughter of the Innocents* (Westchester, IL: Cornerstone, 1981), 98-101; J. J. Davis, *Abortion and the Christian* (Phillipsburg, NJ: Presbyterian and Reformed, 1985), 150-151; P. B. Fowler, *Abortion: Towards an Evangelical Consensus* (Portland: Multnomah, 1987), 147-149; J. K. Hoffmeier, "Abortion and the Old Testament Law," in *Abortion: A Christian Understanding and Response* (ed. J. K. Hoffmeier; Grand Rapids:

subject to criticism on exegetical grounds. It will be my purpose to reexamine the interpretation of this passage and reassess its relevance to the issue of abortion.

II. EXEGETICAL PROBLEMS IN EXODUS 21:22-25

Any interpreter of Exod 21:22-25 should begin by confessing that this passage is extremely difficult due to the large number of exegetical cruxes it contains. The variety of ways in which scholars have resolved these cruxes has resulted in a multitude of specific interpretations of the pericope as a whole.[5] The following is an interpretative translation of Exod 21:22-25 that will facilitate a discussion of its exegetical difficulties. English words in italics have been supplied to fill out the sense.

> (22) If men are in struggle with one another and butt a pregnant woman so that the product of her womb [Heb. *yelādêhā*; lit. "her children"] comes forth *in fatal miscarriage*, but there is no *further* serious injury [Heb. *'āsôn*] *to the woman*, then someone (*the guilty party or a representative of the guilty parties*) will be charged *tort* in accordance with what the woman's husband requires of him, paying the amount for which he is culpable (?) [Heb. *biplilîm*]. (23) But if there is *further* serious injury *to the woman*, then you *O Israelite* will pay out [Heb. *nātattâ*; lit. "give"] *as the guilty party according to the formula:* "the *monetary value of a* life in exchange for *the* life *lost* [Heb. *nepeš taḥat nepeš*], (24) *the value of an* eye in exchange for *the* eye *lost, the value of a* tooth in exchange for *the* tooth *lost, the value of a* hand in exchange for *the* hand *lost, the value of a* foot in exchange for *the* foot *lost*, (25) *the value of an injury caused by* burning in exchange for the burning *inflicted, the value of a* wound in exchange for *the* wound *inflicted, the value of a* stripe in exchange for *the* stripe *inflicted*."

Here are the main exegetical issues in this passage: Did the men strike the woman intentionally or unintentionally, or does intention make a difference in this case? Was the husband involved in the brawl? Was the woman actively involved or merely an innocent bystander? Why is the plural *yelādêhā* ("her children") rather than the singular "her child" used for the fetus? Must the woman's "children" that "come forth" have been born dead, or does the regulation contemplate also the possibility of their being born alive? Related to this, what is the meaning of *'āsôn*: death? serious injury? disaster for which no one can be blamed? What accounts for the change in person and number in this passage in

Baker, 1987), 57-61; R. J. Sider, *Completely Pro-Life* (Downers Grove: InterVarsity, 1987), 46-47; N. Geisler, *Christian Ethics: Options and Issues* (Grand Rapids: Baker, 1989), 145.

    5. For a partial tracing of the history of the interpretation of this passage, cf. B. S. Jackson, "The Problem of Exod 21:22-25 (*Ius Talionis*)," *VT* 23 (1973): 273-304; repr. in *Essays in Jewish and Comparative Legal History* (SJLA 10; Leiden: Brill, 1975), 75-107, and S. Isser, "Two Traditions: The Law of Exod 21:22-23 Revisited," *CBQ* 52 (1990): 30-44.

which "men" struggle, but only one man (the verb is third masc. sing.) pays a tort to the woman's husband in the case without 'āsôn; but if there is 'āsôn, not "he" but "you" pay "life for life"? Why does only one person pay a tort if more than one man were fighting? Who is the "you" who renders "life for life": the same man who pays the fine in the case without 'āsôn or Israel? What is the meaning of *biplilîm*: by judges? by arbitrators? by guardians? by assessment? alone? as the culpable party? Can some of the problems be best explained on the assumption that there are textual corruptions, or that two originally unrelated laws have been awkwardly thrown together? How does the so-called Law of Retaliation relate to the situation described? Was the application of "life for life, eye for eye, tooth for tooth" applied literally in the sense of capital punishment and physical mutilations of the offenders, or does this formulation imply monetary composition ("the value of a life for the life taken," etc.)? If the latter, how would such pecuniary values be determined? How does the regulation relate to other regulations concerning slaves that precede it and follow it? Why is this example addressed at all? What principle(s) does it seek to convey?

The analysis will be simplified a bit by eliminating all views—and these are not uncommon—that suppose the text is so corrupt as to require radical surgery to make sense of it.[6] I operate on the assumption that the text as it stands makes sense if rightly interpreted, an assumption vindicated through exegesis. The key issue for the remaining interpretations of the text as it stands pertains to the question of whether or not the text implies the death of the baby (or babies) both in the case with and the case without 'āsôn, or whether the case without 'āsôn allows for the possibility of the child surviving.

The majority view, both in ancient times among rabbinical interpreters and among modern exegetes, is the "miscarriage view," the view that the death of the child is assumed throughout this case.[7] On the other hand, the view that the death

---

6. E.g., A. S. Diamond ("An Eye for an Eye," *Iraq* 19 [1957]: 153) calls the *lex talionis* "one of the plainest interpolations in the Pentateuch, being inconsistent with its immediate context." S. E. Loewenstamm ("Exod XXI 22-25," *VT* 27 [1977]: 357) thinks that "the text of a law dealing with a blow given to a pregnant woman has become mixed up with the text of another law providing consequences of blows which men dealt upon one another in a brawl." Jackson (*Essays*, 105) claims that Exodus 21:24-25 (the *lex talionis*) is a later interpolation inserted on the basis of the similar language of the slave law of vv. 26-27. H. Cazelles (*Études sur le code de l'alliance* [Paris: Letouzey et Ané, 1946], 56) thinks vv. 24-25 belong after vv. 18-19 rather than in their present position. Similarly A. H. McNeile (*The Book of Exodus* [3rd ed.; London: Methuen, 1931], liii and 129) comments that vv. 23b-25 are irrelevant in their present context. L. Schwienhorst-Schönberger (*Das Bundesbuch (Ex 20,22-23,33)* [BZAW 188; Berlin: Walter de Gruyter, 1990], 81-83) concludes a more complete survey of critical scholarship with the remark that only a few exegetes (R. Westbrook is the only one footnoted) regard Exod 21:22-25 as a unity in the strict sense.

7. Among commentators taking the miscarriage view are the standard commentaries on Exodus by S. R. Driver, M. Noth, B. Childs, J. P. Hyatt, N. Sarna, and P. Enns, as well as S. M. Paul (*Studies in the Book of the Covenant in the Light of Cuneiform and Biblical*

of the fetus is not assumed has existed from ancient times, going back at least to Philo of Alexandria, and continues to be defended today.[8] According to this interpretation, the focus of the passage is on the child's life, not on the woman's, or at least a combination of both the woman and child. The death of the child is not assumed in the expression "her children [yelādêhā] come forth" since premature labor induced by the trauma of the blow could result in a healthy birth and no permanent injury to the mother. Moreover, the verb rendered "come forth" (Heb. yāṣā') can be used of ordinary birth rather than miscarriage.[9] Hence the expression "there is no 'āsôn" could mean that there is not "serious mishap" to either the mother or the child. If there is no deadly and/or serious injury ('āsôn may not always imply death), the offender was still guilty of exposing a pregnant woman and her fetus to unnecessary life-threatening danger, an offense deserving monetary penalty. On the other hand, if the child (or the mother) dies or is seriously injured so that there is 'āsôn, then the so-called talionic formula's "life for life" (nepeš taḥat nepeš) applies, sometimes taken in the sense of capital punishment for murder. The fetus, according to this view, is in any case a "human life" (nepeš).

III. A PROPOSED INTERPRETATION OF EXODUS 21:22-25

What I would like to do is examine the cruxes of interpretation in Exod 21:22-25 and offer an analysis of the passage based on solutions to these cruxes.

1. *Is the blow to the woman intentional?* To begin, was the blow to the pregnant woman intentional or unintentional? A few interpreters have argued that the attack on the pregnant woman was intentional.[10] It is true that the Heb. verb ngp,

---

Law [VTSup 18; Leiden: Brill, 1970], 70-77), and R. Westbrook ("*Lex Talionis* and Exodus 21:22-24," *RB* 93 [1986]: 52-69). Isser ("Two Traditions," 31-38) notes that the majority ancient Jewish tradition followed this interpretation: Josephus, *Ant.* 4.8.33 §278; *Tg. Onq.; Mek.; m. Ketub.* 3:2; *m. B. Qam.* 5:4.

8. Along the lines of this general interpretation are the standard commentaries on Exodus by Cassuto and Durham, as well as J. Weingreen ("The Concepts of Retaliation and Compensation in Biblical Law," *Proceedings of the Royal Irish Academy* 76 [1976]: 1-11), M. G. Kline ("*Lex Talionis* and the Human Fetus," *JETS* 20 [1977]: 193-201), H. W. House ("Miscarriage as Premature Birth: Additional Thoughts on Exodus 21:22-25," *WTJ* 41 [1978]: 108-123), and J. Ellington ("Miscarriage or Premature Birth," *BT* 37 [1986]: 334-337). Several elements of this interpretation are also found in Jackson ("The Problem of Exod. 21:22-25 [*Ius Talionis*]," 273-304). Isser ("Two Traditions," 36-38) notes the minority of ancient Jewish tradition contemplates the possibility that the child might be born alive: Philo, *De spec. leg.* 3.108-9.

9. Cf. "and the first one was born [Heb. root yṣ'] red" (Gen 25:25); "this one was born [root yṣ'] first" (Gen 38:28).

10. D. Daube, *Studies in Biblical Law* (London: Cambridge University Press, 1947), 108, for example, argues from Deut 25:11-12 (where the wife grabs the genitals of a man fighting her husband), that the blow in Exodus "must be regarded as a deliberate,

"butt, push, gore," usually refers to intentional acts. But in this case, given the plural, that "*men* . . . butt a pregnant woman," it seems more likely that the men, while intentionally fighting each other, have flown out of control and unintentionally hit the woman as an innocent bystander.

2. *Is the* lex talionis *literal or figurative?* Next, is the punishment in the so-called *lex talionis* formula literal or figurative? According to the figurative view, the *lex talionis* has to do with "composition" in the legal sense of the satisfaction of a wrong or injury by money payment. This is an old, rabbinic interpretation.[11] Modern scholars, however, frequently understand it to refer solely to literal retaliation involving execution and maiming. In the discussion that follows, the figurative interpretation will be defended.

There are a number of arguments that favor the figurative interpretation.[12] First, the literal application of the so-called *lex talionis* is inconsistent with the principles and legal outcomes of other laws elsewhere in the literary unit of Exod 20:22-23:19. Exod 21:18-19, for example, presents a more serious case, a case of deliberate injury as opposed to the accidental nature of the injury of the pregnant woman described here in Exod 21:22-25. The penalty there, however, is not to strike the offender and injure him in exactly the same way in which he injured the other man as one would expect on a literal understanding of *lex talionis*—which, by the way, would be absurdly impractical—but for the offender to pay money, i.e., to pay for the medical costs and for the lost time of the man he injured.[13] In Exod 21:26-27, the penalty for striking out the eye or tooth of a bondsman likewise does not result in talion against the owner's eye or tooth, but a release of the bondsman, equivalent to forgiveness of the bondsman's debt. Moreover, the literal talion of "life for life" in the case of accidental killing of a

---

malicious attack." But, unlike Deut 25:11-12, the text's silence concerning the relationship between the woman and the men fighting more likely indicates that whether or not her husband was involved is of no relevance to this case. Deut 25:11-12 is a substantially different case of little relevance for comparison. Accordingly, Kaiser's statement (*Ethics*, 102) that this "pregnant woman intervened" in the fight–as if a pregnant woman were likely to jump into a brawl!–and was "perhaps the concerned wife of one of them" is needless speculation. Surely the active "intervening" of the woman would affect the legal outcome inasmuch as the one striking her could with justification plea "self defense."

11. Cf. *b. Sanh.* 79a; *b. B. Qam.* 83b; *b. Ketub.* 33b; Rashi on Exod 21:24; *m. B. Qam.* 8:1.

12. P. Doron, "A New Look at an Old Lex," *Journal of the Near Eastern Society of Columbia University* 1.2 (1969): 21-27; and J. K. Mikliszanski, "The Law of Retaliation and the Pentateuch," *JBL* 66 (1946): 295-303, summarize most of these arguments.

13. Paul (*Studies in the Book of the Covenant,* 67-68) argues that the reason the talionic punishment ("eye for eye, tooth for tooth," understood literally) is not invoked in this case is that there was no original intent to cause injury. But whether or not there was "original intent," the use of a stone shows there was certainly "subsequent intent," and this would have been sufficient, had the man died, to make it a *môt yûmāt* capital offense.

pregnant woman would be in contradiction with the principle expressed in Exod 21:13-14 that indicates that accidental manslaughter is not a capital offense.

It is a general hermentutical principle that one should assume that an author or editor of a literary unit can be expected to be self-consistent. Hence, one regulation of our unit of Exod 20:22-23:33 ought not to be interpreted in ways contradictory to another of its regulations so long as there are other, plausible interpretative possibilities which produce no contradictions. This principle leads to the rejection of literal talion.

Second, Exod 21:29-30 shows that ransom could serve as a substitute for literal talion. A man who does not restrain an ox with a known tendency to gore, so that as a result it gores someone to death, is liable on the principle of "life for life" to give up his own life. Hence, the text says, "also its owner is to be put to death" (Exod 21:29b). But the text immediately allows the possibility of ransom: "If a ransom is laid on him, he will pay the price of redemption for his life [Heb. *nepeš*] whatever is laid upon him" (v. 30). In other words, v. 29 applies the principle of "life for life" [*nepeš taḥat nepeš*]: A man whose negligence has caused the loss of a life forfeits his own life. But v. 30 goes on to show that this operates within a system that permits a payment of money to take the place of the actual execution of the offender. Though in principle such a man forfeits his life, it was possible (and in practice probable)[14] for him to redeem his life by paying the offended party a ransom. A similar principle seems to be implicit elsewhere in this collection. For example, if someone injures another person, as in the case in Exod 21:18-19, the offender on the principle of "wound for wound" deserves to be punished in the same way. But rather than actually injuring him, which does nothing for the victim, the man normally pays a ransom, consisting in the case of Exod 21:18-19 of payment for the inactivity and medical expenses of the man he

---

14. Acceptance of ransom is the probable resolution to the situation here. (1) The death of the negligent owner would give no tangible benefit to the victim's family, whereas ransom would both punish the culprit and benefit the family. Family self-interest dictates the ransom option. (2) Other forms of negligent but unintentional homicide are not capital offenses–cf. Exod 21:12-14; Num 35:9-15; Deut 19:1-13. To make negligence with an ox a capital offense, but negligence with a stone, ax head, or some other inanimate object not a capital offense seems inconsistent. (3) As I read the OT, it seems clear to me that the moral sensitivities of the ancient Israelites were not radically different from those of modern people. Modern people would see capital punishment for unintentional manslaughter as excessive and hence morally objectionable as compared with accepting a ransom. So did the ancient rabbis of the Talmudic period. They concluded that ransom must always be accepted in such cases–cf. J. J. Finkelstein, *The Ox that Gored* (Philadelphia: American Philosophical Society, 1981), 31; *b. B. Qam.* 40b-c; *m. B. Qam.* 4:5. It seems to me probable that the Israelites of the biblical period would also be sensitive to the injustice of making unintentional manslaughter a capital offense, and would ordinarily on that basis be persuaded to accept a ransom. In sum, there is good reason to suppose that the death sentence of Exod 21:29 is mostly hyperbole to underscore the seriousness of negligence that threatens the life of another human being.

injured. By paying this "ransom," the culprit thereby avoids having the same injury imposed on him.

Additional evidence that "life for life" can be related to ransom is provided by 1 Kgs 20:39: "Guard this man! If he is missing it will be your life for his life [Heb. *napšekā taḥat napšô*], or you must weigh out silver." Here "life for life" in the sense of capital punishment has an explicit alternative of monetary substitution, which obviously would be the option chosen by anyone who could afford to pay. There is reason to suppose that this option was available even where not explicitly stated. The availability of ransom seems to have been so prevalent that when biblical law wants to exclude it, as in the case of intentional murder, it must explicitly prohibit it (Num 35:31).[15] The system of ransom means that though the *lex talionis* could in principle be applied literally[16] normally it was not. Rather, monetary composition usually substituted for literal talion.

Third, the use of the Heb. verb *nātan* "to give" in "You will *give* life for life" suggests monetary exchange. The "you" here most plausibly refers to the nation Israel personified as an individual (cf. the same usage in Exod 21:2, 14; 22:18, 21, 23, 25-26, 28-30; 23:1-19). *Nātan* is used here in the sense of making monetary payments: "you, O Israelite, must *pay money* [as the guilty party]."[17] The sense of "pay money" is well attested for *nātan* in the immediate context. This verb is used in the sense of monetary payment immediately before the so-called *lex talionis* when Exod 21:22b states, "and he will *pay* [Heb. *nātan*] by *pelilîm*." A few verses earlier in Exod 21:19b, *nātan* is used to describe payment for the injured man's time of convalescence ("he will *pay* for his inactivity"). A few verses later, three other examples occur: "He will *pay/give* the ransom for his life (Exod 21:30); "He will *give* thirty shekels of silver to his master" (Exod 21:32); and in the context of bailments, "If a man *gives* his fellow silver" (Exod 22:7).

---

15. Num 18:15-17 gives further illustration of the ransom principle. This text specifies that the firstborn son, who was in principle to be sacrificed to God, must in practice be redeemed for five shekels, the "sacrifice" in effect being a legal fiction. The broad availability of "ransom" is also illustrated here, for the text is compelled to prohibit the redemption of firstborn sheep and goats precisely because otherwise the availability of the ransom option would be assumed.

16. Josephus (*Ant.* 4.8.35 §280) seems to suppose that the *lex talionis* was applied literally "unless indeed the maimed man be willing to accept money." Hence he sees the possibility of either literal application or the substitution of a ransom.

17. Another sense of *nātan* is just possible: "You, O Israel, are to *impose (monetary) penalty*" (insofar as you act as judge in such a case). For the sense "impose penalty" for *nātan*, see 2 Kgs 18:14 and 23:23, where the verb is used of Sennacherib's "imposing" tribute and Neco's "imposing" a fine. However, these cases use *nātan* in conjunction with the preposition *ʿal* to designate the one on whom the penalty is imposed, whereas our case does not. Cf. U. Cassuto (*A Commentary on the Book of Exodus* [Jerusalem: Magnes, 1967], 275), who renders "You, O judge (or you, O Israel, though the judge who represents you) shall adopt the principle of 'life for life', etc."; Schwienhorst-Schönberger (*Das Bundesbuch*, 126) who renders, "you are to utilize [the principle]."

Hence, the general employment of *nātan* in the verses surrounding Exod 21:23-25 suggests the giving of money is a probable meaning in v. 23 as well.[18]

Fourth, the usage of the word translated "for" (Heb. *taḥat*) is consistent with the monetary interpretation. The meaning here can be taken as "instead of, in place of," that is, substitutionary compensation—"eye *in compensation for* an eye." This usage is illustrated in Exod 21:26b, 27b where a bondsman whose master has struck out his eye or tooth is freed *in compensation for/in place of* the eye or tooth he lost. Likewise, in Exod 21:36, if an ox is known to be a gorer and yet it was permitted to gore to death another man's ox, its owner is negligent and must make restitution "ox for [*taḥat*] ox." That is, he must provide compensation either by giving the monetary value of an ox or by providing the live animal itself as a substitute for the dead one. In Exod 22:1 a thief makes restitution "five members of the herd *in place of* [*taḥat*] the ox" he stole and "four members of the flock *in place of* [*taḥat*] the sheep." That is, he compensates for his stealing not only by restoring a replacement for the ox or sheep he stole but also by providing additional oxen or sheep (or their monetary value) as a penalty for the act. This monetary understanding of *taḥat* is further supported by the parallel in Deut 19:21 where *taḥat* is replaced by preposition *bĕ*, the *beth pretii*, "of price."

Some arguments can be raised in support of taking the *lex talionis* as literal retaliation. One argument is from comparative Near Eastern laws. A. S. Diamond,[19] for example, argues that the *lex talionis* was applied literally by comparing with LH (Laws of Hammurabi) §§229-230:

> If a builder has constructed a house for a seignior but did not make his work strong, with the result that the house which he built collapsed and so has caused the death of the owner of the house, that builder shall be put to death. If it has caused the death of a son of the owner of the house, they shall put the son of that builder to death.[20]

Diamond also cites LH §§196-197, 200 that says if a gentleman destroys the eye or breaks the bone or knocks out the tooth of another gentleman, they will destroy his eye or break his bone or knock out his tooth. Similarly, LH §218 states that a physician whose patient dies in surgery or is blinded by surgery is to have his hand cut off. If literal talion applied in these cuneiform laws, then it lends plausibility to the view that it also applied in Israel's laws.

J. J. Finkelstein, however, argues that such laws were hyperbolic rather than to be taken literally. He remarks concerning LH §218, "it is inconceivable that

---

18. Compare the frequent employment of the Akkadian cognate *nadanu* in economic texts for the payment of money (*CAD* N 1:45-46). Schwienhorst-Schönberger (*Das Bundesbuch*, 102) thinks the Akkadian expression "X *kima* X *nadanu*" corresponds with the Hebrew expression "X *taḥat* X *nātan*," both meaning "to pay a sum of money corresponding to the value of X."

19. Diamond, "Eye for an Eye," 151-155.

20. Translations of ancient Near Eastern laws here are from *ANET*.

any sane person in ancient Mesopotamia would have been willing to enter the surgeon's profession" if such a law were literally enforced. Finkelstein concludes that such laws were from the beginning hyperbolic, having more of an admonitory than a legal function, saying in effect, "Woe to contractors and physicians who because of negligence, greed, laziness, or any other reason endanger the life and limb of others." [21]

R. Westbrook[22] goes on to argue that the system of ransom seen in the Bible is also assumed in the ancient Near Eastern laws, so that laws that seem to imply literal mutilation allowed monetary substitution for literal talion. He uses this to resolve contradictions between LH §§196-97, 200 that demands talion, and the culturally, geographically and chronologically similar Laws of Eshnunna §42 where it is not: "If a man bites the nose of a(nother) man and severs it, he shall pay one mina of silver; for a tooth, one-half mina; (for) a ear, one-half mina; (for) a slap in the face, 10 shekels of silver." The latter (in agreement with yet earlier Laws of Ur-Nammu) specifies monetary payment for such offenses. Westbrook concludes that in practice both had similar outcomes since ransom could substitute for talion. If Westbrook is right, neither biblical nor cuneiform law absolutely demanded literal talion.

E. Otto,[23] however, is not convinced by Westbrook's arguments. Otto argues instead that the Laws of Eshnunna and those of Hammurabi differed in legal outcomes. The Laws of Hammurabi, according to Otto, reflect a legal reform taking into consideration the class structure of society in which talion was applied to upper classes, but Eshnunna's monetary compensation continued to apply to lower classes and slaves (see LH §§198, 199, 201, 211-14).

If Otto is right, ancient Near Eastern law provides no confirmation of Westbrook's ransom theory. But in showing inconsistencies among Mesopotamian laws, Otto also weakens the case that the *lex talionis* in the Bible must be taken literally because it was taken that way in the ancient Near East, for Mesopotamian laws are not entirely consistent in this area. In any case, biblical law and cuneiform law do not always follow the same legal reasoning, so the argument for literal talion from comparative ancient Near Eastern law is not as conclusive as the biblical evidence against it.

It has also been argued that literal talion was practiced in the Bible. One passage cited in this regard is Judg 1:6-7. This text records the cutting off of thumbs and big toes of King Adoni-Bezek, who himself had previously done the same to seventy kings. Although this is often taken as a literal application of the principle

21. Finkelstein, *The Ox that Gored,* 34-35.

22. R. Westbrook, *Studies in Biblical and Cuneiform Law* (CahRB 26; Paris: J. Gabalda, 1988), 45, 47-55.

23. E. Otto, "Aspects of Legal Reforms and Reformations in Ancient Cuneiform and Israelite Law," in *Theory and Method in Biblical and Cuneiform Law* (ed. B. M. Levinson; JSOTSup 181; Sheffield: Sheffield Academic Press, 1994), 168-175 (especially note 47).

of *lex talionis*, it may be more "poetic justice" than an application of the original, intended legal principle of this law.

Lev 24:19-20 also sounds like a literal application of talion: "If anyone maims his fellow, as he has done, so it shall be done to him: fracture for fracture, eye for eye, tooth for tooth. The injury which he inflicted on another shall be inflicted on him." This prima facie seems to imply literal talion, but such language does not do so necessarily. Lev 24:17-18 applies the principle of "life for life" to cover not only homicide but also the destruction of a beast. In the case of an animal, surely monetary payment would be acceptable. In addition, literal sounding language is not always literal. As Ibn Ezra pointed out, Samson in Judg 15:11 says, "as they have done to me, so I did to them," yet he had not done *exactly* what the Philistines had done to him. They burned to death his wife and father-in-law (Judg 15:6), but he simply slaughtered a great many of them (Judg 15:8).[24] In a similar way, in Lev 24:20 the "injury which he inflicted upon another" could be "inflicted upon him" not by *exact* duplication of the injury, but figuratively though a ransom that serves as a substitute for that injury. Moreover, in Deut 19:15-21, the so-called *lex talionis* is applied to the case of a false witness, with the judgment that whatever verdict would have been carried out against the falsely accused should be carried out against the false witness. Here the talionic formula "life for life, eye for eye, tooth for tooth, hand for hand, foot for foot" is not applied literally, but merely means that the punishment varies with the severity of the accusation. On the basis of these arguments, a strong case can be made that the *lex talionis* did not have to be carried out literally but could have been applied figuratively through payment of ransom to achieve composition.

The *lex talionis* was never meant to justify personal revenge, as some in Jesus' day evidently were applying it (cf. Matt 5:38-42 where Jesus corrects this misuse of the *lex talionis*). But it was meant to express the legal principle that the (monetary) penalty one can demand for an injury must be proportional to the degree of injury involved so that the less the injury, the less should be the penalty. It thus limits the penalty to the monetary equivalent of the injury caused, excluding punitive damages (e.g., "two eyes for an eye").

As for the formulation, "life for life, eye for eye, tooth for tooth," which has a poetic ring to it, there is clear organization in three sections: (1) "life for life" representing the most serious, i.e., deadly injuries; (2) "eye for eye, tooth for tooth, hand for hand, foot for foot" representing various parts of the body injured, working progressively down from the head to the foot; (3) "burning for burning, wound for wound, stripe for stripe" representing various types of injuries.[25] In this regard, categories (2) and (3) overlap—one can have a "wound" to a "foot" or a "hand." It can also be noted that at least one element of this formula, e.g.,

---

24. Cited by Doron, "A New Look at an Old Lex," 25-26.

25. After H. J. Boecker, *Law and the Administration of Justice in the Old Testament and the Ancient East* (Minneapolis: Augsburg, 1980), 173.

"burning for burning," is an unlikely injury in the context of a blow to a pregnant woman. This confirms that this formula is broader than the present context, expressing a general principle in a poetic/proverbial manner, a conclusion supported by the partial repeating of the formulation in Lev 24:18b, 20 (where "breaking for breaking" is added before "eye for eye" and the formula ends with "tooth for tooth") and Deut 19:21 (where only "life for life" though "foot for foot" is quoted, and the preposition *bĕ* replaces *taḥat*, "for"). In the present context, the *lex talionis* is saying that if there is any further injury, no set rule can be given; but the extent of the (monetary) penalties paid to the aggrieved family should correspond to the extent of the injuries.

As for the specific amount of payment for a specific injury, Exod 21:22 and 21:30 suggest that this was a matter of tort for the family and the offender. As a practical matter, judges could well become involved should the parties fail to agree on a price (cf. Deut 21:18-21 where elders confirm that a son is incorrigible before allowing the parents to have him executed), though not necessarily otherwise. If judges became involved, guidelines such as those at Eshnunna (cf. LE §42 above) could well have been utilized, though presumably with enough flexibility to allow the judge to take into account individual circumstances.

The conclusion that the *lex talionis* in Exod 21:22-25 has to do with composition is important since it undermines one line of argument that draws a distinction between the death of the fetus, in which money is paid, and the death of the mother, which is said to be a capital offense where "life for life" is exacted in terms of literal execution. On the contrary, the above argumentation has attempted to show that "life for life" in the present context probably does not imply capital punishment, but rather alludes to a system where composition is achieved through ransom where money substitutes for literal talion. If so, there is no distinction in the *quality* or kind of punishment between the death of the mother and the death of the child whether or not one sees miscarriage in the case without *ʾāsôn*.

3. *What is the Meaning of* ʾāsôn? The key term *ʾāsôn* is a rare one, used but five times in the OT, twice in Exod 21:22-25, and three more times in the Joseph Story (Gen 42:4, 38; 44:29). It is also used in the Apocrypha (Sir 31:22 [34:22]; 38:18; 41:9). Most interpreters have felt the general interpretation offered by BDB, "mischief, evil, harm," to be more or less correct. A few interpreters[26] assert that this word more specifically implies "deadly calamity" or the like, support for which can be derived from the occurrences in Genesis where *ʾāsôn* is used for Joseph's alleged death by the attack of a wild animal.

A quite different view of *ʾāsôn* has been offered by R. Westbrook.[27] He claims *ʾāsôn* does not mean "deadly calamity" but refers to "cases where re-

---

26. Among the rabbis, the *Mek.* states, "*ʾāsôn* here only means death" (cited by Paul, *Studies in the Book of the Covenant*, 72 n. 3). Similarly *HALOT* 1:73 defines it as "fatal accident."

27. Westbrook, "*Lex Talionis*," 52-69.

sponsibility cannot be located." This new meaning radically affects the overall interpretation. The woman, according to Westbrook, has a miscarriage after being struck in a brawl; but in the first instance there is not '*āsôn*, that is, there is not a case of "perpetrator unknown," but rather the culprit is known. In that case the culprit pays the fine "alone" (*biplilîm*).[28] But if there is a case of '*āsôn*, so that responsibility among the men (more than two being involved) cannot be established, the "you" pay "life for life, eye for eye, tooth for tooth," the "you" referring to Israel as a whole as elsewhere in the book of the covenant. The second half of this regulation is thus an example of a humanitarian principle that the Israelite community as a whole (through its representatives) should compensate persons who suffer a loss where individual responsibility cannot be established.

Westbrook claims to find this meaning of '*āsôn* in Gen 42:4, 38; 44:29, the only other OT occurrences of this word; but his interpretation seems suspect. Jacob is not so much worried about "a disaster for which no one can be blamed" as he is about a disaster, namely, losing the last remaining son of his favorite, deceased wife, Rachel. Westbrook's technical, legal meaning for '*āsôn* seems out of place in a private, family conversation; such is much more appropriate in a courtroom setting. Also, "disaster for which no one can be blamed" fails in another way. In Gen 42:38 Jacob fears lest '*āsôn* befall Benjamin immediately after Reuben volunteers to take responsibility for the safety of Benjamin (Gen 42:37). This could not be a case of '*āsôn* as Westbrook defines it, for Jacob had someone to blame were Benjamin not to return.[29] The usage in Sirah also contradicts Westbrook's proposed meaning: The LXX renders '*āsôn* in Sir 31:22 [34:22] as Gk. *arrōstēma* "sickness"; 38:18 renders it as *thanatos* "death," and 41:9 renders it *katara* "curse." In none of these cases does the inability to blame someone have any relevance. Nor does Westbrook's definition work very well in Exod 21:22-25. Striking a pregnant woman during a brawl seems an unlikely circumstance for having a "perpetrator unknown." One would expect plenty of witnesses: the woman, other brawlers, and gawking bystanders. Anonymity in the close-knit society of ancient Israel would be uncommon. Thus the "perpetrator unknown" interpretation seems farfetched.

The etymology of the word '*āsôn* is not certain, though one plausible etymology brings us back to the traditional view. Heb. '*āsôn* could be derived from the root '*āsâ* meaning "to heal, be unhappy." That would make it related to the noun '*āsēy* "physician" in Talmudic Aramaic (and Syriac) which is derived from *asū* "physician" in Akkadian which itself is a loan word from Sumerian A.ZU (traditionally "knower of the waters").[30] Denominative verbs have been

---

28. Westbrook, "*Lex Talonis*," 58-61.

29. Schwienhorst-Schönberger, *Das Bundesbuch*, 91.

30. S. A. Kaufman (*Akkadian Influences on Aramaic* [Assyriological Studies 19; Chicago: University of Chicago Press, 1974], 37) provides some of this information, though he in fact rejects association of Akk. *asū* with Heb. '*āsôn*. *CAD* A 2:347 rejects that A.ZU means "knower of the waters."

derived secondarily from this non-Semitic noun in Aramaic (Aphel "to cure"; Ithpaal "be cured, recover). If Heb. '*āsôn* is cognate with these words for physician and healing, it would be expected to have a medical rather than a legal orientation, meaning originally something like "injury requiring attention of a physician, serious injury" or the like. From that the meaning "deadly injury" could have developed.

In the context of Exod 21:22-25, '*āsôn* is not limited to "deadly injury"—even though that is the sense in Genesis—but "serious injury/medical calamity," encompassing injuries up to and including death. This seems clear from the talionic formula after the case with '*āsôn* which does not end with "life for life," but contemplates various lesser injuries as well.

4. *What is the meaning of* biplilîm? The philologically difficult term *biplilîm* cannot be pinned down with certainty. Traditionally it has been understood to mean "by judges/arbitrators" (to keep the husband from demanding too much; so *Tg. Onq.*), but this meaning is doubtful. Although the verb of the root *pll* does seem to have the meaning "to judge,"[31] the lexical meaning of "judge" for the noun *pālîl* is not well established from its only other occurrences in Deut 32:31 and Job 31:11. Moreover, the context of Exod 20:22-23:33 makes the interpretation "judges" suspect. If one excludes the philologically and contextually far-fetched view that '*ĕlohîm* means "judges" in Exod 21:6 and 22:7-11[32] and lay aside *biplilîm* in Exod 21:22, then we find no direct reference to judges in the entire legal unit of Exod 20:22-23:33. Indeed, it seems that even among those regulations of the book of the covenant that might not inappropriately be called "laws," those laws regularly lack administrative details such as who decides a case, who carries out a sentence, and how the sentence is to be carried out. All this suggests that these so-called laws might be better characterized as giving "religious and ethical instructions in judicial matters" (Cassuto)[33] than as a complete law-code. This context casts doubt on the traditional rendering.

If *biplilîm* does not refer to judges, then to what does it refer? There has long been a conjectural emendation that replaces the term with *bannepālîm*, meaning "the price of the miscarriage."[34] I am normally reluctant to accept conjectural emendation, but this reading cannot be altogether ruled out.

---

31. Heb. for "to pray" (*hitpallēl*) can be understood as the HtD stem of *pālal* with the meaning "to seek a judgment for oneself"; cf. M. Greenburg, *Biblical Prose Prayer* (Berkeley: University of California Press, 1983), 21-22.

32. For why '*ĕlohîm* is unlikely to mean "judges" in Exod 21:6 and 22:8-9, see Joe M. Sprinkle, '*The Book of the Covenant': A Literary Approach* (JSOTSup 174; Sheffield: Sheffield Academic Press, 1994), 56-60, 145-148.

33. Cassuto, *Exodus, 262*.

34. S. R. Driver, *The Book of Exodus* (Cambridge: Cambridge University Press, 1911), 219; BDB 813.

Another interpretation of *biplilîm* has been offered by E. Speiser.[35] He argues that the root has to do with "reckoning, assessing" and that *biplilîm* means "by assessment/reckoning." Hence the penalty paid is assessed on the basis of the stage of development of the dead fetus. The rationale for this view is that the later the stage of the pregnancy, the more time lost to the woman, the greater the grief at the loss of the child, and the more difficult the miscarriage. This may have been the view of the LXX which paraphrases *lo' yihĕyê 'āsôn* as "imperfectly formed child" and translates *biplilîm* as "with valuation."[36] Furthermore, Speiser's view gains credibility in that penalties for causing miscarriage actually do vary with the age of the dead fetus in the parallel Hittite Law §17, which states, "If someone causes a free woman to miscarry—if (it is) the tenth month, he shall give ten shekels of silver [a later version reads twenty shekels], if (it is) the fifth month, he shall give five shekels of silver and pledge his estate as security."

Speiser makes a good case for his interpretation of *biplilîm*. Those who oppose abortion are understandably uncomfortable with this view because the life of a young fetus is credited with less worth than an older one. This might be used to justify first trimester abortions when the fetus is less valuable. This is not a necessary deduction from Speiser's view, however.

Lev 27:1-8 gives monetary values for redeeming persons who have been given as a votive offering to the sanctuary. It is interesting to note that the monetary values assigned to people for their redemption varies according to age and sex, from a low of three shekels for a girl between one month and five years, to a high of 50 shekels for a male aged twenty to sixty. Yet despite these differing monetary valuations, probably reflecting the market value of slaves, the intentional killing of any one of them would be considered murder. The same could be true of the fetus, having a lower economic value to the family early in pregnancy and a higher economic value later on, but perhaps being considered equally human throughout. Note also Exod 21:32 where a monetary value of thirty shekels is assigned to a male or female slave gored to death by an ox, but the transcendent life value of the slave is nonetheless affirmed by the execution of the ox as a murderer for taking a human life in violation of Gen 9:5. This stoning of the ox is in contrast with the case where an ox gores an ox to death in which the goring ox need not be dispatched because human life is not involved.

There is another view on the meaning of *biplilîm* that is neutral on the question of whether or not the fetus dies. Westbrook, as we have seen, understands the root *pll* to imply the sense of "sole responsibility" and that *biplilîm* means "[he pays] alone." He argues that *pll* in the basic Qal stem mean "take sole re-

---

35. E. A. Speiser, "The Stem *PLL* in Hebrew," *JBL* 82 (1963): 536-541.

36. Weingreen ("The Concepts of Retaliation and Compensation in Biblical Law," 9-10) argues that the LXX rendering, which may imply that an "imperfectly formed" fetus is not a human person, was influenced by the debate among Greek thinkers as to whether or not an embryo is to be considered a living entity.

sponsibility" and in the Piel stem means "shift responsibility (to subject or object of verb)."[37]

E. Otto rejects Westbrook's view, arguing that *biplilim* is instead derived from Akkadian *pālilu(m)* meaning "guardian."[38] Otto's view could bring us back to a version of the traditional view "judges," though it might refer to the leaders of the family.

A. Berlin also criticizes Westbrook's view, rightly questioning Westbrook's emphasis on "sole/alone." Instead she makes a good case that this root simply has to do with "responsibility, accountability." According to her, *biplilim* means "as the culpable party."[39]

Berlin's view could be slightly modified by taking the *bĕ* as a "*beth* of price" and the plural as that of abstraction. In that case the text translates, "he pays *the amount for which he is culpable*" (lit. "amount of culpable ones/culpability"). If taken this way, the expression could refer to some customary set amount (perhaps varying according to the development of the fetus as in the Hittite Laws) or an amount that takes into account any extenuating circumstances. My translation above tentatively adopts this view.

In sum, the meaning of *biplilim* is the most difficult exegetical crux of this passage and is not yet resolved. There are too many uncertainties to make any firm conclusions on this expression, though fortunately this does not affect the overall interpretation very much.

5. *Is there miscarriage in the case without 'āsôn?* Does the case without *'āsôn* imply the death of the fetus? My answer is yes, and several lines of argument support this conclusion: there are medical reasons for thinking this view likely; the use of the plural form *yelādêhā* (lit. "her children") gives support to it; and comparison with similar ancient Near Eastern laws suggests this line of interpretation.

First are the medical reasons. In the days before modern medical science, most premature births under these circumstances would result in the death of the fetus. R. N. Congdon, writing as a physician, remarks on this passage by reviewing modern medical statistics concerning premature births following physical trauma (usually automobile related) to a pregnant mother. He points out that only in the last six weeks (of a normal forty weeks) of pregnancy would an infant's lungs be sufficiently developed for it to survive outside the womb. Apart from modern medical technology, any premature birth before that time would result in fetal death. But not even premature birth in the last six weeks would

---

37. Westbrook, "*Lex Talionis*," 58-61.

38. Otto, "Aspects of Legal Reforms," 185 n. 79.

39. A. Berlin, "On the Meaning of *PLL* in the Bible," *RB* 96 (1989): 345-51. Kline ("*Lex Talionis* and the Human Fetus," 195-196) earlier came to a similar view that *pālil* has to do with incurring guilt, though he exceeds the evidence by claiming it could mean "liability to death." I doubt Kline's view that the final *mem* is an emphatic enclitic since this is both rare and limited to archaizing texts.

necessarily result in a live birth. A blunt blow severe enough to induce premature labor frequently causes such damage as fetal skull fracture, disruption of the oxygen supply though the umbilical cord, uterine rupture, and overt disruption of the connection between the placenta and the uterus, each of which is fatal to the fetus. Even less severe disruptions of the placenta creating an impaired oxygen supply, if not repaired, typically result in labor or in fetal death within forty-eight hours.[40] Congdon concludes: "There are only a few instances, in a non-technological era, in which blunt trauma serious enough to cause abortion of the fetus would result in a viable birth. If medical data has anything to say about Exodus 21:22, it indicates that the overwhelming probability for such a situation is an outcome of trauma-induced abortion with fetal demise."[41]

A second argument in favor of assuming the death of the fetus comes from the use of the plural *yelādêhā* (lit. "her children"). One of the arguments used by W. Kaiser against assuming the death of the child is that if the author wanted to denote a miscarriage, he should have used the verb *šākal* (a verb used of miscarriages; cf. Exod 23:26) along with *yelādêhā*.[42] This argument from silence is not particularly strong, however. It can also be turned on its head by posing an equally weak argument from silence: Why did the author not use the ordinary word for a live birth, namely *yālad*, if he had that in mind, rather than the more ambiguous *yāsā'* ("came out")? The better answer to Kaiser, however, is to observe that the author does not need to use the term for miscarriage because the plural form *yelādêhā* is a plural of abstraction with the sense "the product of her womb," an apt term for an inadequately developed baby.[43]

Other explanations for this plural are unconvincing. Keil supposed the plural was used "because there might possibly be more than one child in the womb."[44] This seems far-fetched, however, since the possibility of twins introduces an unneeded complication to the point being made by the case. Kaiser adds that the plural "allows for . . . either sex,"[45] but this suggestion too is an irrelevant complication. Moreover, such a plural is not the way the book of the covenant expresses the idea that a regulation applies regardless of gender. For that one expect something like *yeled 'ô yaldâ* ("a boy or a girl"; cf. Exod 21:15, 17, 28, 31, 32).

---

40. R. N. Congdon, "Exodus 21:22-25 and the Abortion Debate," *BSac* 146 (1989): 140-142.

41. Congdon, "Exodus 21:22-25," 142.

42. Kaiser, *Ethics*, 170 n. 22.

43. Schwienhorst-Schönberger (*Das Bundesbuch*, 97-98) has come independently to similar conclusions.

44. C. F. Keil, *Pentateuch* (1864; Commentary on the Old Testament by C. F. Keil and F. Delitzsch; repr., Grand Rapids: Eerdmans, 1978), 135.

45. Kaiser, *Ethics*, 103.

More plausible is the view that the plural refers to a not fully developed fetus that is not viable when born, and that the plural of abstraction,[46] "the product of her womb," is used proleptically in anticipation of, or foreshadowing, the fatal outcome (note the situation described would usually result in a stillbirth). This interpretation, by the way, need not imply that a live, unaborted fetus is sub-human. It merely implies that a corpse is subhuman.

Finally, the comparison with ancient Near Eastern laws confirms the view that the fetus is assumed to have died. When the case laws of the Bible are compared with those of the ancient Near East, it is clear that in broad terms they come out of the same cultural milieu. Indeed, that one biblical law is identical with a Mesopotamian one (cf. Exod 21:35 with Laws of Eshunna §53) suggests some degree of literary dependence. While biblical laws are essentially making moral comment on legal matters rather than producing a comprehensive law-code, their wording nonetheless draws upon legal traditions that would have been known to the Israelites, though modifying those laws to express a uniquely Israelite ideology. But since Mesopotamian legal traditions (probably via the Canaanites) are being drawn upon, it is not irrelevant to make comparisons (and contrasts) with cuneiform laws that deal with similar subject matters, as has been the universal practice of modern scholars of biblical law.

When this is done, it is discovered that not only Hittite Laws §17 but also Laws of Lipit-Ishtar §§d-f, a Sumerian Laws Exercise Tablet §§1'-2 ' (c.a. 1800 B.C.), Laws of Hammurabi §§209-214, and Middle Assyrian Laws A §§21, 50-53 all refer to causing miscarriage by striking a pregnant woman, sometimes discussing the penalty for killing her in the process; but none of them contemplates the possibility of a birth of a viable baby.[47] Surely this evidence suggests that our case, where the language is a bit ambiguous and is set in a corpus of laws that are drawing upon contemporary legal traditions influenced by Mesopotamia, probably does not contemplate a viable birth either.[48]

We conclude that the death of the fetus is to be assumed so that the question of *'āsôn* ("serious injury") applies solely to the mother.

6. *How are the changes in person and number in Exod 21:22-25 to be explained?* We may now review our conclusions, paying particular attention to the changes in person and number in Exod 21:22-25. If there is no *'āsôn* after the

---

46. For the plural of abstraction, see B. Waltke and M. O'Connor, *IBHS* 120-121, §7.4.2; Joüon 502-503, §136g-i.

47. For translations, see Martha T. Roth, *Law Collections from Mesopotamia and Asia Minor* (SBLWAW 6; Atlanta: Scholars Press, 1995).

48. S. Paul (*Studies in the Book of the Covenant*, 71 n.1) correctly observes, "The fact that so many of the legal corpora specifically refer to [causing a miscarriage], which apparently was not too common, may be due to the literary dependence of one corpus upon another." That the Bible refers to it suggests some sort of literary dependence here too. Kaiser (*Ethics*, 103) states, "We cannot agree that these laws are the proper background for [Exod 21:22-25]." To this I can only ask, "Why not?"

miscarriage, that is, no serious injury to the woman, then somebody ought to pay the father for the economic loss to the family of the child. The purpose of the plurals (*men* brawl, *men* strike a pregnant woman) is to indicate the unintentional nature of the injury—they are fighting each other, not the woman, and are out of control.[49] The switch to the singular, "*he* pays," reflects an indefinite use of the singular.[50] That is, someone pays, whether the most negligent party in the brawl (Berlin's view that *biplilîm* means "as the culpable party" would go along with this view) or a representative of the men who brawled. The point is that the accidental, negligent taking of the life of an embryo has resulted in great loss for the woman's family, and someone should compensate monetarily for the damage done by paying the father as head of the family.

As for the other half of the regulation, if there is serious injury (*'āsôn*) to the woman up to and including death, then the so-called *lex talionis* applies which states that the penalty, in this case monetary, should vary according to the degree of injury caused. The "you" (sing.) who pays according to this principle is Israel represented by an individual. Westbrook, as seen above, also argues that the "you" is Israel, but in his view Israel pays only if the guilty party cannot be determined. In my view, in contrast, the "you" is Israel personified as the guilty party and is not a different entity from the one who pays the fine to the husband.[51] This use of the second person serves to remind the reader that this is Yahweh's personal address to Israel, not an impersonal law-code.

IV. EXODUS 21:22-25 AND THE SURROUNDING SLAVE LAWS

The case of the pregnant woman struck during a brawl breaks a sequence between two bondsman laws: Exod 21:20-21 having to do with striking a bondsman to death and Exod 21:26-27 having to do with injuring a bondsman. Why the case of the pregnant woman should come between these two has puzzled commentators.

---

49. Kline (*Lex Talionis and the Human Fetus*," 198) suggests this plural may be "the indefinite plural active used as a passive, signifying 'a pregnant woman is struck.'" But the ready antecedent of *'ănāšîm* ("men") speaks against this interpretation.

50. On the indefinite singular, cf. F. E. König, *Historisch-comparative Syntax der hebräischen Sprache* (Leipzig: Hinrichs, 1897), 354-55, §324d; Waltke and O'Connor, *IBHS* 70-71, §4.4.2. Examples: Gen 19:17; 38:28; 48:1; 50:26; Exod 10:5, 21b; Lev 2:8.

51. The singular "you" in biblical law flows easily between Israel as a whole (personified as the original patriarch) and a particular Israelite within Israel. Compare the use of the second person singular elsewhere: the "you" of Exod 21:2 ("If *you* acquire a Hebrew slave") is Israel represented by an individual Israelite who happens to be a slaveholder; the "you" of Exod 21:14 ("from my altar *you* may take him") is Israel as represented through those responsible for executing murderers; the "you" of the Decalogue is Israel, and hence individual Israelites; "*your* poor" in Exod 23:6 is Israel's poor. For a more complete discussion, see Dale Patrick, "I and Thou in the Covenant Code," *SBLSP* (1978): 1:71-86.

According to D. Patrick, Exod 21:22-25's link with Exod 21:26-27 is only superficial. The case of the injured bondsman came to the lawgiver's mind because, like the *lex talionis*, it deals with "eye" and "tooth" and uses the term *taḥat*.[52] Others less graciously suggest scribal misadventure.

My own view, suggested to me orally by H. C. Brichto, is that Exod 21:20-27 as a group is fundamentally about injuries to bondsmen, specifically debt slaves as in Exod 21:2-5. This is a natural sequel to the discussion of injury to the full citizen in Exod 21:18-19. Exod 21:22-25 on the pregnant woman is parenthetical, though necessary to further the author's discussion of bondsmen.

What the case of the pregnant woman introduces is the principle that one should, as a rule, pay the exact monetary equivalent for mayhem that one has caused even if the mayhem was unintentional, as the striking of a pregnant woman during a brawl among men would be. This principle was introduced, however, to form a contrast with the case of injury to a bondsman that follows. The case of injury to a bondsman by using similar language but drawing a quite different conclusion indicates that this principle does not apply in the case of a beating of a bondsman in which the beating is intentional (this is the master's right if for the purpose of making him work), but the maiming (in all likelihood) was unintentional. In this case, and unlike the talionic formula, the penalty does not vary according to the degree of injury; but maiming of any sort—as great as the loss of an eye, as little as the loss of a tooth—results in the bondsman's freedom and loss of the master's investment; i.e., the master loses the time owed by the bondsman in lieu of the bondsman's unpaid debt.

The reason why the talionic formula does not apply, but that any maiming results in the slave's freedom, is that this bondsman (being actually a "distrainee" or an "indentured servant" rather than a "slave"—cf. Exod 21:2-4) must be treated as a human being despite his reduced social status. The master has the right to the bondsman's time and to a limited extent can use force to make him work, but the master has no right to the bondsman's person. If he murders the bondsman, he is subject to "vengeance" (Exod 21:20-21) as with the murder of any other human being. If he maims him, he loses all rights as master (Exod 21:26-27) since he has no right to treat another human being that way, even a servant. Hence the biblical author has artfully expressed a philosophical concept concerning the humanity of a bondsman by this juxtaposition of the case of a pregnant woman and the cases of killing and maiming a bondsman.

If this view is correct, the case of the pregnant woman was introduced not to prove or disprove the humanity of the fetus—a point on which it is ambiguous—but rather to prove the humanity of slaves.

---

52. D. Patrick, *Old Testament Law* (Atlanta: John Knox, 1985), 77.

V. CONCLUSION

Although one might like to find definitive answers to the abortion question from Exod 21:22-25, it is not possible to do so. The detailed exegetical analysis of Exod 21:22-25 (*lex talionis*) given above shows the passage to be ill suited for establishing a biblical ethic concerning abortion.

On the one hand, the case of the pregnant woman does not disprove the humanity of the fetus. The killing of the fetus and the killing of the mother are treated alike: in both cases composition is achieved though payment of money. The text talks only about accidental killing; and exegetically from this passage alone, we have no way of knowing whether the intentional killing of the fetus by its mother would have been considered murder. What is clear here is that the accidental killing of the unborn is punished. What about the intentional killing of the unborn? Would it go unpunished? Exod 21:22-25 does not exclude the possibility that the intentional killing of the mother and the intentional killing of the fetus would also have been treated alike, that is, as murder.

On the other hand, the case of the pregnant woman cannot be used to prove the humanity of the fetus either. Contrary to the exegesis common among certain anti-abortion Christian theologians, the most likely view is that the death of the fetus is to be assumed throughout the entire case. It cannot be proven whether the formula "life for life" applies to the fetus since it occurs in the instance with ʾāsôn ("serious injury") that deals exclusively with injuries to the mother. The wording of this case does not rule out the possibility that the fetus was considered subhuman. Rather than proving the humanity of the unborn, the passage instead serves (by its contrast with the subsequent case) to demonstrate the humanity of slaves.

VI. POSTSCRIPT: THE REST OF THE OT AND ABORTION

If Exod 21:22-25 does not give us much data concerning abortion, what does the rest of the OT and its laws have to say about that subject? The answer, unfortunately, is that it does not address the topic directly at all. To approach this matter, one must seek the principles found in the OT relevant to the question of abortion and try to deduce from them what it would have said about abortion had it addressed the subject.

The OT first of all condemns the taking of innocent human life: "Do not commit murder" (Exod 20:13). This does not preclude all taking of human life. Exceptions are made for punishing the guilty in the various capital offenses and for taking human life during times of war. But it gives an orientation towards preserving life.

Does the OT consider the fetus to be human life? Or to put it differently, at what point is a developing human considered a human person protected by the Decalogue's prohibition of murder?

Some, in attempting to answer this question, have fallen into the etymological fallacy: One word for human "life" is the Heb. *nepeš*, derived from a root meaning "to breathe." So, it is argued, until persons breathe, they cannot be a *nepeš* or a human person (cf. Gen 2:7, "God breathed into [Adam's] nostrils the breath of life and he became a living *nepeš*"). However, even if this were the right etymology for *nepeš* (the verb occurs but 3 times in the Hebrew Bible), usage rather than root meaning determines what a word means. It turns out that *nepeš* is used of fish that breathe no air (e.g., Gen 1:20 where "living creatures" that teem in the waters is identical in Hebrew with the description of man as a "living being"—both translate the same Heb. expression *nepeš hayyâ*). If a fish in water can be a *nepeš* without breathing air, then presumably a living fetus in the amniotic fluids of the womb could also be a *nepeš* without breathing air.

More promising are descriptions of unborn fetuses that might suggest they are persons. For example, before Esau and Jacob are born, they are described as "sons" striving with each other in their mother's womb (Gen 25:22; cf. Luke 1:41-44 where John has joy in womb). Their activity in the womb anticipates their struggle in life and suggests they are already persons expressing human personalities before birth. Ps 139:13, 16 says, "You wove me in my mother's womb . . . your eyes saw my embryo [Heb. *gōlem*]." This suggests that the psalmist considers his person ("me") to have been in the womb before birth (cf. also Jer 1:5). The development of his embryo was considered more than biology; it was an act of creation by God. The text does not specify, however, at what stage the human person is there: fertilization, implantation, heartbeat, quickening, brain waves, viability outside the womb, or what.

The evidence, it seems to me, clearly indicates that according to the OT the fetus late in pregnancy is a person; and so in principle the OT precludes late term abortions. It may preclude all abortions, though that is not entirely clear. In any case, caution seems prudent: One does not blow up a building if one thinks it is possible that a person is in it. The Bible's positive attitude towards having children ("be fruitful and multiply" Gen 1:28; "children are a heritage from the LORD" Ps 127:3) and the evidence above that the formation of the embryo was considered a creative act by God, an act that one should presumably be reluctant to undo, make it hard for me to imagine biblical writers accepting as moral elective abortions of convenience whether or not it was considered murder.

Even if the Bible in general seems to discourage the practice of abortion, are there exceptions? Perhaps. Biblical law arguably acknowledges the concept of self-defense: If someone kills a thief who has broken into the house at night, no blood guilt is upon the person killing the thief (Exod 22:1-4). This killing is probably justified on grounds of self-defense, for it was uncertain whether the thief had come to steal or come to murder. By analogy, it may be justified to take the life of a fetus if a continued pregnancy threatens the life of the mother. This logic was followed in Jewish interpretation that allows dismemberment of a fetus to save the mother, though prohibits it once the baby is partially born "since the claim of one life cannot override the claim of another life" (Mishnah *'Ohalot*

7:6).[53] In the former case, the baby is treated as if he/she were a pursuer trying to kill its mother. So in those rare medical conditions where a choice must be made between mother and fetus, the self-defense argument might justify an abortion. Medical necessity for abortion is rather rare today, though an ectopic pregnancy, where the fetus implants outside the uterus, is such a situation. Other so-called exceptions, such as for rape and incest, are more difficult to justify on biblical grounds.

The above remarks no doubt go too far for some readers and not far enough for others. It does represent an attempt to examine briefly OT evidence apart from Exod 21:22-25 related to the morality of abortion.

---

53. Translation by H. Danby, *The Mishnah* (Oxford: Oxford University Press, 1933), 660. This rabbinic ruling seems to indicate that the fetus does not have full and equal rights with the mother until it begins to be born.

Chapter 6

"DO NOT STEAL": BIBLICAL LAWS ABOUT THEFT

Biblical law attempts to protect individuals from the unwarranted removal or destruction of their property. To that end, pentateuchal laws specified various punishments for acts that, whether intentionally or unintentionally, unlawfully deprived one member of the community from his or her own legal property. Even beyond that, these laws sought to create a certain ethos in Israel, one that discouraged the inward attitude of heart that leads to theft. In addition, it promoted through these laws the value of human life over property and encouraged a right relationship with God and one's neighbor. By thus promoting and balancing justice and fairness, the biblical laws concerning theft and deprivation of property were intended to enable Israel to enjoy the harmony and material well-being intended by God.

I. CATEGORIES OF THEFT AND DEPRIVATION OF PROPERTY

Our discussion of the laws of theft will begin by defining a number of categories. Most of these categories are related to particular Hebrew roots, so our study will largely consist of short analyses of these key terms.

1. *Theft, stealing, burglary (Heb.* gnb*).* The most frequent Hebrew root in the general semantic range of theft—the one used in the Decalogue's prohibition (Exod 20:15; Deut 5:19)—is *gnb*. Rabbinic tradition[1] holds that this root has the connotation of taking by stealth and deception, as opposed to "robbery" which is done openly using threat of violence (see below). This analysis generally holds true for the occurrences of *gnb* in the Pentateuch except for kidnapping (lit. "stealing a person"), which presumably does involve use of force (Exod 21:16; Deut 24:7). There are a number of examples of the use of this root where deception is involved: Rachel stole the *terāphîm* when Laban was away shearing sheep (Gen 31:19). Jacob *stole the heart of* Laban, and Absalom *stole the hearts of* the Israelites in the metaphorical sense of *deceiving* them (Gen 31:21, 30; 2 Sam 15:6). Predatory animals steal sheep when a shepherd sleeps (Gen 31:29). Jacob tried to preclude the possibility of accusation of theft by keeping in his flock only animals of specific colors different from Laban's, making chicanery seemingly impossible (Gen 30:32-33). Burglars try to break into houses either

---

1. Raymond Westbrook, *Studies in Biblical and Cuneiform Law* (CahRB 26; Paris: Gabalda, 1988), 15.

when no one is home or when the residents are asleep (Exod 22:2-3 [MT 1-2]), and Joseph's brothers feared accusation of stealing in the sense of stealthily carrying away silver (Gen 44:8).

2. *Robbery (Heb.* gzl*).* The Hebrew root *gzl*, on the other hand, appears to be a stronger term than *gnb*. Traditionally it has been understood to refer to an open act involving threat or use of violence. B. S. Jackson[2] qualifies this rabbinic view, arguing that *gnb* is used for an individual within the community whereas *gzl* refers to a group act of outsiders. R. Westbrook[3] rejects Jackson's "insider-outsider" dichotomy but argues that the essence of *gzl* is "abuse of authority," as when the influential *seize* the houses of the poor (Job 20:19; Micah 2:2). An example of *gzl* in the sense of robbery is the time that certain men of Shechem sat in ambush to *rob* those that came along the road (Judg 9:25). Other examples of *gzl* that illustrate the use of force include Abimelech's servants *seizing* a well belonging to Abraham (Gen 21:25), Laban and his posse threatening to *take by force* his two daughters whom Jacob had married (Gen 31:31), and the Benjaminites *seizing* and carrying away girls from Shilo to become their wives (Judg 21:23).

3. *Confiscation, withholding (Heb.* ʿšq*).* The Hebrew root *ʿšq* is often translated generally with the notion of "oppress" or "exploit," but Milgrom[4] argues the meaning is more explicit, referring to such actions as *withholding* of wages (Lev 19:13; Deut 24:14-15; Mal 3:5) and *confiscating* pledges in the case of loan default (Ezek 18:7; cf. Deut 24:6, 10-14). It is used in parallel with *gzl* as an act of abuse of power ("Do not confiscate [*ʿšq*] from your neighbor nor rob [*gzl*] him," Lev 19:13; "oppressed [*ʿšq*] and robbed [*gzl*]," Deut 28:29; "they covet fields, then rob [*gzl*] . . . and they confiscate [*ʿšq*] a man and his house" Mic 2:2). Like *gzl*, *ʿšq* can involve the use of open force (to confiscating houses, lands, pledges, and persons), but *gzl* is usually an act of the lawless; whereas, *ʿšq* is an act by the rich or the powerful that is either technically legal or else is an abuse of power tolerated by (even perpetuated by) legal authorities. Whether or not legal, *ʿšq* is always pitiless and can amount to legally sanctioned robbery.

4. *Spoil, plunder (Heb.* bzz, šll*).* Jacob's sons *looted* (*bzz*) Shechem for the rape of their sister Dinah, taking livestock, wives, and children (Gen 34:27-29). The kings of the East *looted* (*bzz*) Sodom and Gomorrah, taking Lot and his possessions as plunder (Gen 14:11-12). Israelites in the desert feared becoming plunder (*baz*, Num 14:3), though they themselves were sometimes allowed to plunder (Num 31:9-47 [*bzz*, *šll*]; Deut 2:35 [*šālāl*]; 20:14 [*bzz*, *šll*]).

---

2. Bernard S. Jackson, *Theft in Early Jewish Law* (Oxford: Oxford University Press, 1972), 8.

3. Westbrook, *Studies*, 17, 23-30.

4. Jacob Milgrom, *Leviticus 1-16* (AB 3; New York: Doubleday, 1991), 337.

5. *Fraud.* Fradulent acts include using dishonest scales (Lev 19:35-36; Deut 25:15), sending one's cattle to graze another man's field (Exod 22:5 [MT 4]), refusing to return an item that was lost and found or else left in bailment with another (Exod 22:7-13 [MT 6-12]), and moving a boundary stone (Deut 19:14).

6. *Usury (Heb.* nešek, m/tarbît*).* OT laws seek to protect the poor Israelites from economic exploitation ensuing from loans to them at interest (Exod 22:25; Lev 25:35-38). Terms for interest are *nešek,* literally "bite," perhaps referring to the interest paid up front to the lender at the beginning of a loan (like points on a house loan), and *m/tarbît,* literally "increase," which may refer to interest paid subsequently. Another view is that the former is interest on money; the latter, on produce.[5] The Laws of Eshnunna §§18a-21 (c. 1800 B.C. Babylonia) limited interest rates to 20 percent for money and 33.3 percent for grain, exorbitant rates by modern standards that could easily lead to default, forfeiture, and enslavement (Neh 5:3-5; 2 Kgs 4:1).

Deuteronomy 23:19-20 appears to condemn interest-taking altogether (except to foreigners), not just for the poor, a view put into practice by the medieval Church. However, in view of Exod 22:25 and Lev 25:35-38, which refer explicitly to the poor, the poor may also be in mind in Deut 23:19-20 (so Calvin).[6] Proverbs condemns the exploitation of the poor via interest-taking (Prov 28:8) and warns that the borrower is a slave to the lender (Prov 22:7), but it extols one who lends without interest as lending to God who will reward such a person (Prov 19:17). Lending without interest is described as a virtue (Pss 15:5; 37:26; 112:5; Ezek 18:7-8, 17). Failure to address the needs of debtors could spawn civil unrest (cf. the defaulting debtors among David's disenfranchised, early followers; 1 Sam 22:2).

7. *Coveting (Heb.* ḥmd*).* The Decalogue admonishes, "Do not covet . . . anything that belongs to your neighbor" (Exod 20:17; Deut 5:21). To "covet" (Heb. *ḥmd*) something is to have a strong desire for that thing. There is thus a close relationship between this tenth commandment of the Decalogue and the eighth commandment against theft (Exod 20:15; Deut 5:19) since strong desire to have something can lead to robbery or theft ("They covet [*ḥmd*] fields and they rob [*gzl*] them; houses and they take them away" [Micah 2:2]; Achan's confession, "I coveted [precious items under the ban] and I took them" [Josh 7:21]; cf. Prov 12:12). It is also closely related to the seventh commandment against adultery since coveting can also lead to that (Prov 6:25). Because the other commandments of the Decalogue refer to concrete acts rather than subjective feelings, some scholars have tried to make this commandment more than internal thoughts, but rather "intrigues that lead to the taking of possession that which is

5. S. E. Loewenstamm, *"Nešek and M/tarbît,"* *JBL* 88 (1969): 78-80.

6. John R. Sutherland, "The Debate Concerning Usury in the Christian Church," *Crux* 22.2 (June 1986): 3-9.

coveted,"[7] such as plotting and scheming. However, the niphal passive participle of this root simply means "desirable" as when God's commandments are described as more *desirable* than gold or of a tree *desirable* [*pleasant*] to look at (Ps 19:10 [MT 11]; Gen 2:9). Moreover, the parallel in Deut 5:21 uses *ḥmd* only for coveting one's neighbor's wife, but switches to another word for desire (Hithpael of *'wh*) for the other items of the neighbor's household, emphasizing the subjective and internal nature of coveting.

II. PENALTIES FOR THEFT AND DEPRIVATION OF PROPERTY

Penalties for various forms of theft and deprivation of property varied according to the seriousness of the crime The discussion below is in the order of most severe punishments to least severe punishments for offenses related to the concept of theft.

1. *Kidnapping: execution.* Kidnapping, literally "stealing a person" (Exod 21:16; Deut 24:7), was punishable by death. Kidnapping is generally related to the slave trade (Gen 40:15; cf. Gen 37:18-36 and 1 Tim 1:10 where "kidnapper" [Gk *andrapoistes*] is a term for slave dealers). It was a capital offense whether the victim was found in the thief's possession or whether the victim had been sold into slavery. This law's penalty is thus unlike the penalty for theft of animals (see below) where a distinction is made between cases where the goods were disposed of and cases where they were not disposed of, with a lesser penalty for the latter offense. Because transcendent life value is involved in stealing a human being, that made it unlike a case merely involving animals. Thus kidnapping was subject to the maximum penalty regardless of whether the kidnapper disposed of the person stolen.

2. *Animal theft with disposal of goods: fourfold or fivefold restitution (possible slavery).* Exodus 22:1 (MT 21:37) indicates that a stealer of an ox or sheep which he has slaughtered or sold must return fivefold for the ox, fourfold for the sheep. Multiple restitution for animal theft is probably a result of the importance of animals to an agricultural/pastoral society, for they were not only the herdsman's property but also his livelihood. Stealing these was akin to stealing a carpenter's tools or a fisherman's nets, depriving one of future as well as present benefits. Also the greater multiple for an ox probably represents its comparatively greater importance within the ancient economy.[8]

If the thief were too poor to pay full restitution, he could be sold into slavery for up to six years (Exod 22:3 [MT 2]; cf. Exod 21:2), the proceeds of his sale going for the restitution. In the ancient Near East, an ox was worth more than

7. Johann J. Stamm and Maurice E. Andrew, *The Ten Commandments in Recent Research* (SBT; Naperville, IL: Allenson, 1967), 103.

8. Joe M. Sprinkle, *'The Book of the Covenant': A Literary Approach* (JSOTSup 175; Sheffield: Sheffield Academic Press, 1994), 134-135.

half the value of a typical slave—in fifth century BC Babylonia, forty shekels as compared with sixty shekels[9]—so the owner who had an ox stolen by a poor man would receive less than full multiple restitution. Poor thieves were deterred by potential loss of freedom; rich thieves, by the multiple restitutions.

3. *Animal theft without disposal of goods: twofold restitution.* Unlike stealing a person, a distinction of penalty is made between theft where the animal has been disposed of and where it has not. Only twofold restitution is required where the goods were not disposed of. The rationale for this is puzzling since, as B. S. Jackson puts it, a thief caught with the goods is not less guilty, only less successful.[10] One possibility is that moral rather than strictly legal considerations come into play: the thief, until he has disposed of the goods, is not yet "rooted in sin" (Rabbi Akiva, *t. B. Qam.* 7) and still has the possibility of repentance. Perhaps the lower penalty reflects the hope that this might lead to repentance (see below).[11]

4. *Theft of personal property: twofold restitution.* When household goods were stolen and the thief is found, twofold restitution was required (Exod 22:7, 9 [MT 6, 8]); that is, the object or its value was returned plus one hundred percent.

5. *A thief who repents: reparation/guilt offering and restitution plus twenty percent.* The priestly law (Lev 6:1-7 [MT 5:20-26]) deals with the case of sacrilege (Heb. *m'l*) caused by swearing falsely concerning a deposit, an investment(?), something robbed (*gzl*), something withheld (*'šq*), or something lost. In this case, the culprit pronounces the self-curse of an oath (see below) that he or she has not done this, but subsequently "feels guilty."[12] The thief then is to make restitution to the person defrauded, adding one-fifth to it as a penalty. Reduction from the usual twofold restitution for theft takes into account his repentance (see above). Besides restitution, which provides satisfaction to the person defrauded, the culprit is to offer a guilt/reparation offering to atone for the offense against God.

6. *"Theft" of crops by one's animals: more than one hundred percent restitution.* When one's animals have grazed a neighbor's fields (Exod 22:5 [MT 4])—a form of theft if deliberately driven into the field, but in any case negligence—restitution must be made from the "best" (or highest value) of the victim's field, resulting in one hundred percent plus compensation for the loss. By replacing the damaged crop at the maximum yield the field could be expected to

---

9. Sprinkle, *'The Book of the Covenant'*, 133.
10. Jackson, *Theft in Early Jewish Law*, 134.
11. For other views, see Sprinkle, *'The Book of the Covenant'*, 135-137.
12. After Milgrom, *Leviticus 1-16*, 338-345. Contrast the other interpretations: "becomes guilty" [RSV, NASB]; "realize guilt" [NJPS].

produce (more than it might actually have produced), the owner of the field has no grounds for complaint even if he suspects the act were deliberate.

7. *Damages to animals or property due to negligence: simple restitution.* Related to the theft laws are laws concerning damages due to negligence, all of which require exact replacement of the loss, with no windfall to the victim. Hence the owner of an ox with a tendency to gore who fails to take precautions to control his ox must make restitution "ox for ox" (Exod 21:36) if it kills another man's ox, though the owner is allowed to salvage the value of the carcass. A similar rule applies in the case of an animal dying due to negligence regarding an open pit (Exod 21:33-34). When fire ravages a neighbor's field, in which case, unlike the case of grazing his field, the negligent party receives no benefit (see above); simple restitution (rather than restitution from the "best" of the field) is prescribed (Exod 22:6 [MT 5]).

8. *Damages to another's animal without negligence: share the loss.* In Exodus 21:35 two oxen owned by different owners share the same field, and one gores the other to death unexpectedly. No one was at fault; either ox could have been killed. In this case, rather than making one man bear the whole loss, the law demands splitting the loss between the two parties (a ruling identical with Laws of Eshnunna §53). J. J. Finkelstein[13] terms this a primitive form of shared-risk accident insurance following a principle of loss distribution.

9. *Suspected theft with no proof: an oath but no restitution.* Where evidence is lacking, justice could be left to God through oaths. When a bailee claimed the item left with him was stolen, but the bailor suspected it was actually expropriated by the bailee but had no proof, the bailor could force the bailee to swear an oath; that is, to make a conditional self-curse that he did not trespass his neighbor's property (Exod 22:7-8, 11 [MT 6-7, 10]). Without solid evidence, the plaintiff could not demand any restitution.

A similar outcome occurs in the next case: A lost or stolen item is found by the original owner, but the owner cannot prove that the found item is actually his or her property (Exod 22:9 [MT 8]). The owner cannot force the current possessor of the item to return it nor demand multiple restitution, for the real owner has no proof. The owner can, however, force the possessor to come to "God"[14] and can force the accused to swear that he did not trespass his neighbor's property (Exod 22:11 [MT 22:10]). The accuser also must swear that he or she is not making false accusation in an attempt to expropriate the property of the accused.

---

13. J. J. Finkelstein, *The Ox that Gored* (Philadelphia: The American Philosophical Society, 1981), 23, 36.

14. "God" is the rendering of the Hebrew term *hā'elōhîm*, the common OT term for God. It is rendered "the judges" in many EVV of this verse, but this is philologically dubious; see Sprinkle, *'The Book of the Covenant'*, 145-148.

The use of the oath assumes that even where human courts fail, the divine Judge can punish wrongdoers and is especially inclined to do so in cases of false oaths (cf. Zech 5:2-4). In the process of oath taking, the accused may, under fear of divine wrath, break down and confess the crime or else show guilt by refusing to pronounce the self-curse. In either case this could be interpreted as "God declaring him guilty" (Exod 22:9 [MT 8]), in which case he must pay twofold (see above). Oaths operated similarly in ancient Mesopotamia.[15]

Other cases were also enforced by God, not the state. Even without an oath, threat of divine intervention remains, as when Deut 25:15 admonishes Israelites to keep honest scales "so that your days may be prolonged in the land." Similarly, one who moves a boundary stone is declared "cursed" by God (Deut 27:17). Oppressive usury-taking and pledge-seizing from the poor may lead to imprecatory prayers against the lender and judgment from God (Exod 22:25-27 [MT 24-26]), preventing the lender from receiving God's full blessings (Deut 23:19-20 [MT 20-21]). Apparently the usury "laws" served as moral admonitions rather than state-enforced statutes, since Nehemiah the governor has to cajole rather than command rich Israelites to stop taking interest from poor Israelites, this despite Ezra's having made the Mosaic law the law of the land (Neh 5:1-13; cf. Ezra 7:25-26). Laws enforced by God rather than the state are not "laws" in the ordinary, modern sense.

10. *Accusation of theft with proof to the contrary: no restitution, no oath.* If the accused can show some exculpatory evidence—as in the case of a bailee suspected of wrongdoing with an animal left in his care who produces evidence of depredation beyond his control (Exod 22:13 [MT 12]—then the plaintiff could demand neither restitution nor the taking of an oath. The oath was reserved for cases where evidence was lacking.

11. *Coveting: no human penalties.* If (as argued above) coveting is an internal feeling and thought rather than an action, the commandment against it is by nature incapable of being enforced by the state as a law, and thus there can be no human penalties imposed at the violation of this commandment until and unless the thought of coveting leads to illicit actions. Indeed, the fact that none of the commandments in the Decalogue have penalty clauses suggests that all of them are to be understood as moral precepts rather than laws, taking many things regarded as crimes against people (theft, adultery, etc.) and now showing them to be sins against God. This last commandment against coveting shows that OT law was meant to be a spiritual and internal thing rather than merely an external norm. It is meant to sanctify the heart, the thought life. According to the tenth commandment, it is not only wrong to steal but it is also wrong to foster the

---

15. K. van der Toorn, *Sin and Sanction in Israel and Mesopotamia* (SSN 22; Assen: Van Gorcum, 1985), 45-49.

desires that lead to stealing. However, penalties for this offense are for God to determine and mete out on his own. They are not mediated through the judiciary.

III. THEOLOGY, IDEOLOGY, AND MORALITY IN THE THEFT LAWS

Every society has condemned theft as disruptive of the social order, and there are many similarities between Israel's laws/morality and its neighbors.[16] Nonetheless, the Pentateuch, by placing theft in the Decalogue (Exod 20:15; Deut 5:19) as one of the kinds of behavior fundamentally incompatible with a covenant relationship with Yahweh, as well as coveting that can lead to it (Exod 20:17; Deut 5:21), underscores that theft is not only a "crime" but is also a "sin" against God. From the theological perspective, unjustly depriving others of goods is to deprive them of the blessings and tangible benefits that God meant for his people to enjoy and is therefore an undermining of divine purposes.[17] Even where deprivation comes legally as a result of economic ups and downs, it was the divine purpose that on the Sabbatical Year (Deut 15:1-3; 31:10) there be a remission of debts and that in addition on the Year of Jubilee (Lev 25:39-55) there be a release from slavery and a restoration of ancestral land to the original owners. Permanent deprivation was thus contrary to the divine will.

In some ways the Bible seems lenient concerning theft. In the ancient Near East, theft of an animal could require up to thirtyfold restitution and the death of the thief who could not pay (Laws of Hammurabi §§8, 265; Hittite Laws §§57-59, 63, 67, 69). The Laws of Eshnunna (§13) require the execution of the housebreaker at night, and the Laws of Hammurabi (§21) require any housebreaker to be executed. Biblical law, as M. Greenberg[18] points out, differs from ANE laws in limiting restitution to at most fivefold and not allowing a death penalty for property crimes. Only "stealing a person" and taking an item under the ban (Deut 7:26; 13:17; cf. Josh 6:18; 7:15) are capital offenses, never ordinary theft of property. Indeed biblical law, unlike cuneiform law, protects the life of the housebreaking thief (Exod 22:1-4 [MT 21:37-22:3]) by pronouncing bloodguilt upon anyone who murders the thief except in what might be termed an act of self-defense at night. Hence biblical law values human life above property to a greater degree than cuneiform law.

Similarly, other laws show the value of human life over property. Unlike similar cuneiform laws, biblical law sharply distinguishes between the case where an ox gores an ox (Exod 21:35-36), involving mere property, and where an ox gores a human (21:28-31), involving transcendent live value. The latter requires the execution of the goring ox; whereas, the former does not. Moreover, if negligence is involved in an ox goring a person to death, the owner must

---

16. See van der Toorn, *Sin and Sanction, passim.*

17. Christopher J. H. Wright, *God's People in God's Land: Family, Land, and Property in the Old Testament* (Grand Rapids: Eerdmans, 1990), 136-138.

18. Moshe Greenberg, "Some Postulates of Biblical Criminal Law," *Yehezkel Kaufmann Jubilee Volume* (ed. M. Haran; Jerusalem: Detus Goldman, 1960), pp. 3-28.

ransom his life in order to avoid execution. He thus could possibly give an economic windfall to the victim's family—he will give all he has to save his life. In contrast, negligence resulting in the death of a neighbor's ox results in replacement value of the animal and no more, with the owner of the goring ox even keeping the carcass. Similarly, as discussed above, kidnapping without disposing of the person kidnapped (Exod 21:16) follows a different legal principle from stealing an animal and not disposing of it (Exod 22:4 [MT 3]) precisely because the first case involves a human being. These differences underscore the supreme value of human life over property in biblical law.

Moral and religious admonition is wedded with legal procedure in these laws. Creditors were admonished to respect the dignity and property rights of debtors by not barging into the house to seize a debtor's pledge but were to wait outside for the debtor to bring it out (Deut 24:10-11). Out of compassion, creditors are encouraged not to seize as pledge a person's only cloak needed to keep one warm nor a person's only millstone for preparing the flour essential for subsistence (Exod 22:26-27 [MT 25-26]; Deut 24:6, 12-13). Biblical law provides for the possibility of repentance and placating both persons and God, and it threatens wrongdoers with divine punishment even where they escape human justice.

By promoting a sense of justice and fairness—punishing thieves both rich and poor, tempering legality with compassion, encouraging repentance by reducing penalties when it occurred, compensating those who suffer loss by negligence, endorsing the sharing of losses when no one was at fault, and placing wrongs in the hands of God when beyond human courts—these laws were meant to assure harmony and material well-being in Israel.

Chapter 7

UNDERSTANDING LAWS OF CLEAN AND UNCLEAN

Ritual cleanness and uncleanness (associated with the Heb. roots *ṭāhēr* and *ṭāmē'*) represents a major theme of the Pentateuch. Purity rules describe the rituals, varying according to the "severity" of the impurity contracted, for ceremonial uncleanness due to skin disease, bodily discharges, touching unclean things, and eating unclean foods. The rationale for these laws is never clearly spelled out, but several explanations probably have some validity, including hygiene, the need to dissociate oneself from disgusting or pagan things, various other ethical lessons, the association of Yahweh with life and wholeness rather than death or disorder, the separation of worship from expressions of sexuality, and the need for Israel to be separated from the Gentiles. However, the most important message conveyed by these laws is that God is holy; and mankind, conversely, is contaminated and unfit, in and of themselves, to approach a holy God. All this, in turn, served to inculcate in the mind of the ancient Israelite the sacredness of the tabernacle/temple space within the conceptual "cultic topography" produced by the clean and unclean system.

I. HOW UNCLEANNESS WAS CONTRACTED

According to the laws of the Pentateuch, the Israelite was to regard most things as "clean," but a person or thing could contract uncleanness in a variety of ways. Several broad categories are found in Num 5:2: "Command the Israelites that they are to send away from the camp anyone with scale disease [Heb. *ṣārû'*], anyone with a discharge, or anyone unclean due to a corpse." This gives three broad causes of uncleanness:

- Diseases of the skin (scale disease)
- Discharges of bodily fluids
- Contact with something unclean such as a dead body

A fourth cause of uncleanness is given in Leviticus 11 and Deuteronomy 14:

- Use of unclean animals and foods

These categories will now be explained.

1. *Diseases of the skin.* Anyone with a scale-like skin disease (Heb. ṣārû‘) was regarded as unclean (cf. Leviticus 13-14). The term ṣāra‘at has been traditionally translated "leprosy," but the consensus of scholars is that the term is not limited to modern clinical leprosy (Hansen's disease); instead, this term covers a variety of skin diseases.[1] A garment or leather object in a household or the house itself that contracts mold or fungus that looks like scale disease was likewise deemed unclean (Lev 13:47-59; 14:33-57).

2. *Discharge of bodily fluids.* Bodily discharge refers primarily to natural and unnatural genital flows, but not to open wounds from accidents.[2] Childbirth, via its association with the discharge of the bloody placenta from the vagina, rendered a woman unclean for forty days for a male child, eighty days for a female child (Lev 12:1-8). Onset of menstruation rendered a woman unclean for seven days (15:19-24; compare Ezek 36:17), and any unnatural genital flow of blood rendered her unclean until seven days after that flow of blood ceased (15:25-30). Ordinary marital intercourse rendered the couple unclean till evening (15:18; cf. Exod 19:15), while inadvertent intercourse with a menstruating woman rendered the man unclean for seven days (Lev 15:24), and deliberate intercourse with such a woman—a practice Ezekiel lists as a sin (Ezek 18:6; 22:10)—made both subject to divine "cutting off" (Lev 20:18).

Given that a case of intercourse with a menstruating woman is difficult to detect and prosecute in a human court, "cutting off from their people" in Lev 20:18 likely denotes neither banishment nor human execution but death and extirpation of descendants by divine intervention. Milgrom believes "cutting off from one's people" may also involve separation from the relatives in the afterlife, a view that explains why some cases involved both "execution" and divine "cutting off" (Lev 20:2-3; Exod 31:14).[3] Alternatively, Levine understands such verses to imply that "if the community failed to punish the offender or failed to uncover the offense, God would mete out punishment in His own way and in His own good time."[4] In any case "cutting off" reflects punishments at the hand of God.

Ejaculation of sperm outside of intercourse (wet dreams, etc.) rendered a man and his bedding unclean till evening (Lev 15:16); and other flow from his genital (15:2-3), such as from gonorrhea or a urinary infection, rendered him unclean until seven days after the flow ceased (15:13).

---

1. Gordon J. Wenham, *The Book of Leviticus* (NICOT; Grand Rapids: Eerdmans, 1979), 195; R. K. Harrison, *Leviticus* (TOTC; Downers Grove: InterVarsity, 1980), 136-139; John E. Hartley, *Leviticus* (WBC 4; Dallas: Word, 1992), 187-189; Jacob Milgrom, *Leviticus 1-16* (AB 3; New York: Doubleday, 1991), 816-826.

2. Richard Whitekettle, "Levitical Thought and the Female Reproductive Cycle: Wombs, Wellsprings, and the Primeval World," *VT* 46 (1996): 377.

3. Jacob Milgrom, *Leviticus 1-16* (AB 3; New York: Doubleday, 1991), 457-460.

4. Baruch A. Levine, *Leviticus* (JPS Torah Commentary; Philadelphia: Jewish Publication Society, 1989), 242.

Discharge from the "flesh" (Heb. *bāsār*) in Lev 15:2-3 is to be understood as synecdoche for the sexual organ as in 15:19 rather than taken more generally for the body (cf. NIV "bodily discharge") since the other cases contextually refer to sexual emissions. R. L. Harris,[5] in contrast, argues from Deut 23:10-11 that abnormal bodily discharges such as diarrhea are also included here and ties this to a hygienic explanation of these laws as a whole. While it is true that Deuteronomy requires soldiers at war to defecate outside the camp because "YHWH your God goes in the midst of your camp," thereby implying defecation could ceremonially defile (Deut 23:12-14; cf. Ezek 4:12-13), both Deut 23:10-11 and Leviticus 15 seem to refer specifically to genital discharges. Perhaps the close proximity of the organs of excrement and the organs of reproduction make Deuteronomy's extension possible.

Priests were required to marry virgins since any women previously sexually active (the immoral, divorced, for the high priests even a widow) brought with them elevated levels of sexual impurity (Lev 21:7, 14). Whereas elsewhere the penalty for non-adulterous sexual immorality was (possible) marriage (Exod 22:16-17), a priest's daughter who brought elevated sexual impurity into her father's house through sexual immorality was subject to being "burned" (Lev 21:9).[6]

3. *Contact with unclean things.* Uncleanness conveyed by touch usually lasted until evening, though touching a human corpse made one unclean for seven days (Num 19:11). The following conveyed uncleanness till evening: touching the carcasses of unclean animals (Lev 5:1-3; 7:19, 21; 11:24-28, 44); or the unwashed person, contaminated chair, or bedding of a menstruating woman or of a man with an unnatural genital flow conveyed uncleanness till evening (Lev 15:4-11, 19-24). An unclean man could transfer uncleanness onto a clay pot by touch (15:12) and onto a person by spitting (15:7). Objects touching a carcass became impure (15:32), though certain objects—springs, cisterns, plant seeds—were immune from impurity by touch (11:36-38). The contents of an unclean vessel and anything touched by water from an unclean vessel were rendered ritually unclean (11:33-34). Hosea states that "mourner's bread," i.e., food contaminated by being in the house with a corpse, defiles (Hos 9:4); and Haggai affirms that a man contaminated by a corpse transmits uncleanness via touch (Hag 2:13).

A priest was not to be involved in the burial of any corpse except that of an immediate relative (mother, father, son, daughter, brother; Lev 21:10-12) since touching the corpse would lead to defilement and exclusion from his duties in the

---

5. R. L. Harris, "Leviticus," *The Expositor's Bible Commentary*, vol. 2 (ed. F. Gaebelein; Grand Rapids: Zondervan, 1990), 586.

6. "Burned" is ordinarily taken to mean cremated after execution. Another possibility is that this is a reference to branding, a practice known from Egyptian law: see David Lorton, "The Treatment of Criminals in Ancient Egypt though the New Kingdom," *JESHO* 20.1 (1977): 15.

sanctuary. Some close relatives were excluded: He could not bury in-laws nor a non-virgin sister. In both these cases others could take that responsibility; and in the case of a non-virgin sister, her sexual impurity heightened her corpse contamination (Lev 21:3-4). The high priest was not to be in the same room as a corpse even for a close relative (Lev 21:11-12). Isaiah reminds priests and Levites not to touch what is "unclean" (Isa 52:11). Nazirites, who like priests were holy, were to avoid corpse contamination, not even being allowed to bury a parent (Num 6:6-7).

The purification (sin) offering (Heb. *ḥaṭṭā'ṭ*), itself used as a purifying agent, ironically could also convey impurity by touch.[7] The carcass of the Day of Atonement *ḥaṭṭā'ṭ* had to be burned, and its handler evidently became ceremonially unclean since he had to wash his clothes and body before returning to the camp (Lev 16:27-28). Similarly, vessels in which the *ḥaṭṭā'ṭ* was cooked evidently also became unclean since they must be broken if earthenware and scoured if copper (Lev 6:28). The ashes of the red heifer *ḥaṭṭā'ṭ*-offering[8] also conveyed uncleanness on its handlers so that it had to be taken outside the camp; and both the priest conducting the sacrifice and the one who burned it into ashes were unclean, as was the one who applied the ashes. Hence all these had to bathe and wait until evening to return to a state of purity (Num 19:3, 7-8, 10, 21). Leviticus 7:7 suggests that the guilt/compensation (*'āšām*) offering was disposed of in the same way as the *ḥaṭṭā'ṭ* offering and so probably likewise conveyed uncleanness. The bodies of clean animals properly slaughtered for the fellowship (well-being, peace) offering (*zebaḥ šelāmîm*) and other offerings did not convey uncleanness at first, though it was best to eat the sacrifice on the day of the sacrifice; and by the third day any sacrificial carcass must be burned (Exod 12:10; 29:34; Lev 7:17, 31-32; 19:6), perhaps related to carcass uncleanness.

4. *Use of unclean animals and food.* Animals were either "clean" or "unclean," a distinction first made in the account of Noah's flood (Gen 7:2) but elaborated in detail in Leviticus 11 and Deuteronomy 14.[9] Some among the unclean animals are designated *šeqeṣ* "cultic abomination" or *tô'ēbâ* "abomination, abhorrence." These transmitted an especially loathsome form of uncleanness

---

7. David P. Wright, *The Disposal of Impurity* (SBLDS 101; Atlanta: Scholars Press, 1987), 129-146.

8. Jacob Milgrom (*Numbers* [JPS Torah Commentary; Philadelphia: Jewish Publication Society, 1989] 160, 438-43), argues convincingly that Num 19:9 should be rendered, "It is a *ḥaṭṭā'ṭ* [i.e., a purification offering]" (cf. NRSV, REB). Many EVV regularly render misleadingly "for removal of sin" or the like (e.g., RSV, NIV, NASB), but rendering the word "sin" is unacceptable since contamination by removing a corpse from a tent (Num 19:14) involves no sin. Rather, this is a purification offering for ceremonial uncleanness.

9. A monograph on this topic is: Walter Houston, *Purity and Monotheism: Clean and Unclean Animals in Biblical Law* (JSOTSup 140; Sheffield: Sheffield Academic Press, 1993).

(Lev 11:10, 11, 12, 13, 20, 23, 41; Deut 14:3). Eating an unclean animal rendered a person unclean, in this case till evening, whether it be flesh from an inherently unclean animal, flesh of a clean animal rendered unclean by death from natural causes (Lev 11:39-40; 17:15), or any food rendered unclean by contact with something else unclean (cf. Hag 2:10-13). Nazirites like Samson were to take special care to avoid eating anything unclean (Judg 13:4, 7, 13; compare Num 6:5-8). Pious Israelites such as Daniel would refuse to defile (*gā'al*) themselves by eating non-"kosher" foods (Dan 1:8), whereas eating unclean food such as swine and mice was an act of impiety condemned by Isaiah (Isa 65:4; 66:17).

It was only the *dead* unclean animals that polluted by touch (Lev 5:1-3; 7:19, 21; 11:24-28, 44), perhaps for the practical reason that otherwise one would be unclean every time one rode a donkey or a camel.[10] As discussed above, touching or eating a clean animal properly slaughtered as a fellowship/peace offering did not convey uncleanness on the day it was slaughtered, but even a clean animal that died of natural causes conveyed uncleanness by touch (Ezek 44:31).

An animal that was lame, blind, or with other defect was not unclean; hence both the clean and the unclean may eat of it, but it could not be rendered "holy" so as to offer it and/or partake of it in the central sanctuary (Deut 15:19-23). It is thus rendered no more than "common." However, to offer a "common" blemished animal to God is to offer what Malachi terms "defiled" (*gā'al*) food, and such an act did ritually defile (*gā'al*) the table of the LORD (Mal 1:7-8, 12).[11]

These regulations imply that one should avoid ceremonial impurity; but the nature of the rules given above shows that this, even by natural biological processes, was not always possible. Everyone became unclean from time to time. Periodic states of uncleanness were unavoidable.

II. WHAT WAS TO BE DONE ABOUT UNCLEANNESS

Where contraction of impurity occurred, it was obligatory that the unclean person avoid that which is holy and take steps, involving the rituals for disposal

---

10. Houston, *Purity and Monotheism*, 51.

11. In addition to these "unclean foods," consumption of fat and blood were prohibited (Lev 7:22-27), violation of which put a person under threat of being "cut off." In the ritual of sacrifice, all the fat was burnt in offering to God even when (as in "peace/fellowship" offerings) most of the animal was eaten by the worshiper. Suet for animals permitted for the altar (cattle, sheep, goats) was not to be used at all when the animal was sacrificed to God. That is, none was to be saved for private use. Also the fat was not to be eaten even if the animal became ineligible for the altar by dying of itself or being killed by predators, though (in an economic concession) the fat in the latter case could be used for other purposes (lamp, etc). Though it is less clear, the fat of wild game (i.e., clean animals ineligible for the altar) probably could be eaten (cf. Lev 17:13-14 where blood requirement is repeated for wild game, but not the fat; so Milgrom, *Leviticus, 1-16,* 427). The prohibition against eating the fat of sheep, goats, and cattle reminded Israel that certain clean animals were set apart to God for sacrificial worship and for making blood atonement.

of impurity, to return to a state of cleanness. Uncleanness placed a person in a "dangerous" condition under threat of divine retribution, even death (Lev 15:31), especially if the person were to approach the sanctuary. Indeed, the largest body of laws of clean and unclean, Leviticus 11-15, is bracketed (forming an inclusio)[12] first by the account of the death of the two sons of Aaron, Nadab and Abihu, for improperly approaching the sanctuary (Leviticus 10) and second by the Day of Atonement ritual (Leviticus 16) where reference to the death of Aaron's two sons (v. 1) is part of a warning against arbitrary entrance into the sanctuary (v. 2). That in turn leads to a prescription to conduct an elaborate sacrificial ritual to cleanse the priest first and then to remove sin and uncleanness from both the sanctuary and people (vv. 3-19). The community's uncleanness imperiled the whole nation because uncleanness defiles the LORD's tabernacle, God's dwelling place in their midst (Lev 16:16; Num 19:13, 20), as well as the land itself (Lev 18:27), and could make God's continued dwelling in their midst impossible (Ezek 43:7-9; cf. 9:7). If unpurged, uncleanness could lead to a general outbreak of divine wrath and ultimately the expulsion of the land's inhabitants (Lev 18:25), as did in fact happen in the Babylonian exile. Consequently, through the various sacrifices there must be a purging of uncleanness from the altar and the sanctuary (Ezek 43:19-27; 45:19) to remove the contamination of both sin and ceremonial impurity. Uncleanness and the danger pertaining to it lingered upon those who did not take the necessary steps to be purified (Num 19:12-13; Lev 17:16).

Priests, as ministers in the sanctuary, were to take special care to avoid becoming ritually defiled. If defiled—as everyone from time to time must be—the priest was to abstain from his sacred duties. Failure to do this could result in the priest's being "cut off from [God's] presence" (Lev 22:3-9) by divine punishment (e.g. Nadab and Abihu, Leviticus 10). To remove any vestige of uncleanness, priests and Levites would purify themselves with a ritual sprinkling of water and washing their clothes in preparation for service in the sanctuary and offer for themselves a purification offering (Lev 16:3-4; Num 8:7-8).

Ordinary laymen who became unclean were not to eat consecrated meat sacrificed to God in the sanctuary (Lev 7:20-21; so Saul supposed of David in 1 Sam 20:26; compare 1 Sam 21:4). Nor were they even to tithe consecrated food to the Levites while unclean (Deut 26:14). However, the ceremonially unclean could eat wild game and meat slaughtered outside of the central sanctuary (Deut 12:15, 22). An unclean person could not celebrate the Passover while unclean (Num 9:6-13), though provision was made for celebrating Passover after a month's delay. In the context of the sojourn in the wilderness, an Israelite who became unclean was to go "outside the camp," that is, away from the tabernacle where the LORD dwelt among them (Num 5:3).

The way in which a ceremonially unclean person became clean varied in accord with the severity of the uncleanness. Judging from the purification proce-

---

12. Richard E. Averbeck, "Clean and Unclean," *NIDOTTE* 4:480.

dure, Milgrom[13] has categorized types of impurity from the most serious to least serious cases as follows:

1) Skin disease (Leviticus 13-14)
2) Childbirth (Leviticus 12)
3) Abnormal genital discharges (Lev 15:3-15, 28-30)
4) The corpse-contaminated priest (Ezek 44:25-27)
5) The corpse-contaminated Nazirite (Num 6:9-12)
6) One whose impurity is prolonged (Lev 5:1-13)
7) The corpse contaminated lay person (Num 5:2-4; 19:1-20)
8) The menstruating woman (Lev 15:19-24)
9) The handling of the ashes of the red cow or the Day of Atonement offerings including the scapegoat and the purification [sin] offering which was burnt to ashes (Num 19:7-10; Lev 16:26, 28)
10) Emission of semen (Lev 15:16-18)
11) Contamination by a carcass (Lev 11:24-40; 22:5)
12) Secondary contamination (Leviticus 15, 22:4-7, Num 19:21-22)

The most serious case of uncleanness was the person with a skin disease (Leviticus 13) since such a one remained permanently unclean unless healed. One with a skin disease was to wear rent clothes, have disheveled hair, call out "unclean, unclean" as a warning to others, and live apart from others outside the camp (Lev 13:45-46). If the skin disease healed, the person could undergo a purification ritual over eight days to return to full cleanness (Lev 14:1-32).[14] On day one the person meets outside the camp with a priest who performs a ritual involving two birds, cedar wood, crimson yarn, hyssop, and spring (or "river"; literally "living") water. The priest sacrifices one bird and dips the live bird in the blood mixed with the other items. He then releases the live bird. This ritual, by analogy with the Day of Atonement sacrifice (Leviticus 16), probably symbolizes purification via sacrifice (the killed bird whose purifying blood is sprinkled by hyssop seven times onto the person designates the man or woman as "clean") and removal of uncleanness (the live bird having symbolically absorbed uncleanness flying to an open country). The person then washes his or her clothes, shaves all hair, and bathes his or her body. At that point the person may enter the camp but is not to sleep in their tent until the ritual of the seventh day, for the

---

13. Jacob Milgrom, "Rationale for Cultic Law: The Case of Impurity," *Semeia* 45 (1989): 104.

14. Although it does not precisely follow the prescribed procedure for Israelites healed from scale disease, Naaman the Syrian was told by Elisha to follow a ritual reminiscent of it: washing seven times in the Jordan after which his flesh was restored and he became ritually "clean" (2 Kings 5:10-14). In poetic justice, Gehazi the servant of Elisha contracted Naaman's leprosy as punishment for his greed, showing again the close relationship between sin and uncleanness, and that impurity could be transferred (5:15-27).

person is only partially purified. On the seventh day the person again shaves his or her hair and washes his or her clothes and bathes the body to remove symbolically another level of impurity. The person is now considered sufficiently clean to enter their tent. On the eighth day the person brings to the sanctuary oil and offers a reparation/compensation/guilt offering, a purification/sin offering, and a whole burnt offering in which blood from the reparation/compensation/guilt offering and some of the oil is placed on the right ear, right thumb, and right big toe of the person. The person is then anointed with the remainder of the oil, symbolizing that the whole person has been cleansed and elevated to the status of fully "clean." He or she is thus fully restored to the community and free to approach the sanctuary. In the New Testament, Jesus required the lepers he had cleansed to show themselves to the priest in accord with this Mosaic law (Luke 17:11-17).

The second most serious "uncleanness" is childbirth. At childbirth (Lev 12:1-8) a woman who bore a son became highly unclean (as with menstruation) for seven days. On the eight day the son was to be circumcised. Afterwards the mother remained somewhat unclean and unable to touch (i.e. "eat") that which is holy for another 33 days, after which her purification is completed (total of 40 days). If she bore a daughter the numbers double: She became most unclean for two weeks and somewhat unclean for 66 days beyond that (total of 80 days). The reason for the numbers 7 and 40 is not explained in the text, though a case can be made for them being numbers symbolizing "wholeness, completeness."[15] Seven days represents the completion of the period of greatest impurity, and forty days represents completion of all impurity. Moreover, forty days is about the period of time necessary for the womb to undergo the process of devolution and destruction followed by regeneration during which it goes from being uninhabitable/dysfunctional (for reproduction) to being once again restored to "wholeness" and full sexual function.[16]

At the end of her impurity, the post-partum woman is to bring a lamb (a bird will do if she is poor) for a burnt offering and a pigeon or turtledove for a purification offering to be offered by the priest. Mary, the mother of Jesus, underwent this ritual after the birth of Jesus (Luke 2:22-27).

The reason for the distinction between the sexes in post-partum uncleanness is not stated. Among the speculations (listed more or less in the order of least to most likely in my judgment) are these: that women are supposedly subject to stronger attacks by demons;[17] that it reflects the female's role as first in transgression in the garden of Eden;[18] that it is a provision for the care of baby girls who being less desired than boys might otherwise receive inferior care from

---

15. Whitekettle, "Levitical Thought and the Female Reproductive Cycle," 381.

16. Whitekettle, "Levitical Thought and the Female Reproductive Cycle," 390.

17. A. Noordtzij, *Leviticus* (Grand Rapids: Zondervan, 1982), 131.

18. A. A. Bonar, *A Commentary on Leviticus* (London: Banner of Truth, 1966 [1852]), 229; S. Kellogg, *The Book of Leviticus* (Minneapolis: Klock & Klock, 1978 [1899]), 229.

thoughtless husbands;[19] that circumcising the boy baby on the 8th day somehow reduces the attendant uncleanness;[20] that the distinction reflects the lower social status of women in ancient Israel;[21] that girls are destined to become a source of menstrual and maternal uncleanness in the future;[22] and that the longer maternal discharges after the birth of a girl as compared with that of a boy and the periodic vaginal bleeding of baby girls demands a longer period of uncleanness.[23] More than one of these explanations may be true.

Abnormal genital discharge (Lev 15:3-15, 25-30) is the third most serious "uncleanness." A man or a woman who had an abnormal genital discharge, which might be due to a venereal disease or a urinary tract infection, was to wait seven days after healing, launder his or her clothes, and bathe the body in spring ("living") water to obtain one degree of purification. On the eighth day he or she was to take two turtledoves or pigeons and offer up one as a purification offering and one as a burnt offering to effect full purgation of uncleanness.

The fourth and fifth most serious cases are those of the corpse-contaminated priest and the corpse-contaminated Nazirite. Regulations in the Pentateuch regarding such priests have already been addressed (see above). Ezekiel 44:25-27 adds that the corpse-contaminated priest must offer a purification offering after seven days for his offense. Numbers 6:9-12 discusses the corpse contamination of a Nazirite. During the period of their vow Nazirites were to abstain from grapes and wine, refrain from cutting their hair, and avoid contact all with corpses even if a parent or sibling (Num 6:1-8). If a Nazirite touched a corpse, he or she violated the Nazirite vow. The remedy for the contaminated Nazirite was to shave his or her head on the first and seventh days after the period of uncleanness had passed and offer two turtledoves or pigeons, one as a purification offering and one as a burnt offering (these were required to end the vow anyway;

---

19. Harris, "Leviticus," 574.

20. Harris, "Leviticus," 254; Bonar, *Leviticus,* 229.

21. Hartley, *Leviticus,* 168.

22. Harrison, *Leviticus,* 135; Levine, *Leviticus* 250.

23. Ramban cited by Levine, *Leviticus,* 250; C. F. Keil, *The Pentateuch* (Commentary on the Old Testament by C. F. Keil and F. Delitzsch; Grand Rapids: Eerdmans, 1978), 376 with citations affirming that the ancients believed a mother's discharge to be greater after the birth of a girl; D. I. Macht, "A Scientific Appreciation of Leviticus 12:1-15," *JBL* 52 (1933): 253-60, a physician, shows that a somewhat longer discharge (not double) after the birth of a girl is a scientifically confirmed phenomenon. Jonathan Magonet, "'But if it is a Girl She is Unclean for Twice Seven Days . . .' The Riddle of Leviticus 12.5," *Reading Leviticus* (JSOTSup 227; ed. J. F. A. Sawyer; Sheffield: Sheffield Academic Press, 1996), 144-152, points out that the withdrawal of maternal hormones at birth causes roughly one in ten female babies to experience vaginal bleeding, a fact that is regularly communicated to beginning midwives so they would not be overly concerned. Hence, a double period of purification could be a result of not infrequently having two females (mother and baby) producing impurity through vaginal discharges, with the baby's impurity being reckoned to the mother with whom she had been united.

Num 6:13-16), as well as a lamb for a compensation/guilt offering for having violated the vow (see Lev 5:14-6:7).

Sixth, anyone whose impurity was prolonged by failing to go through the proper purification rite within prescribed time limits was to offer a compensation/guilt offering (Lev 5:1-13).

Seventh, any layman unclean due to touching a human corpse (Num 5:2-4; 19:1-20) was unclean for seven days and had to go though a ritual involving the ashes of a red heifer. A red heifer (red a symbol of blood and life) was burned to ashes that could be mixed with water whenever needed. The corpse-contaminated layman was then sprinkled with water mixed with these ashes on the third and seventh days, and on the seventh day he laundered his clothes and bathed himself to become clean. Numbers 31:19-24 elaborates on the regulation: In war soldiers involved in killing and who touched corpses, as well as the captives returning from war, were unclean for seven days. On the third and seventh days they themselves, their captives, their garments, and whatever was made of leather, goat hair, or wood were to be purified with water; and items of metal, purified with fire.

Eighth is the menstruating woman (Lev 15:16-24). Normal genital discharge (see below) only required waiting till evening and a ritual bath, but seven days of uncleanness are prescribed for a menstruating woman (or a man having intercourse with such a woman) with ritual washing not stated but probably implied.

Bathsheba in her bathing within eyeshot of the palace rooftop (2 Sam 11:2-4) was arguably undergoing some sort of ritual purification, probably for menstrual uncleanness. If the bath were for menstrual uncleanness, it would fit perfectly with the story: The ritual bath for the end of her menstrual impurity would then be public proof that the child Bathsheba conceived after adultery with David could not have been fathered by her husband Uriah. The Bathsheba story can thus be taken as evidence that by David's day it was assumed that Leviticus 15 required a bath for the menstruating woman even though the text does not say this explicitly. After having sex with David, Bathsheba left, but only after "having purified herself from her uncleanness" (2 Sam 11:4). This expression (*mitqaddešet miṭṭum'ātāh*) is probably a reference to ritual washing after sexual intercourse.

The remaining cases are minor ones: handling a purification offering or handling the Day of Atonement (purification/sin) offerings or the handling of the ashes of the red cow (Lev 6:27-28; 16:26, 28; Num 19:7-10), emission of semen (Lev 15:16-18) which includes the ejaculating man and his inseminated wife, touching a carcass (Lev 11:24-40; 22:5), and secondary contamination by touch (Leviticus 15; 22:4-7; Num 19:21-22). In each of these cases persons simply washed their bodies and clothes (in some cases washing is not stated but is probably implied) and waited till evening to be considered clean.

Depending on the material (Lev 11:32-35; Num 31:21-23), objects that became unclean either had to be washed in water (wood, cloth, hide, sackcloth) or purified by fire (metals) or destroyed (clay pots, earthen oven, or clay cooking pot).

III. THE RATIONALE OF THE PURITY LAWS

Complex religious and theological symbolism is conveyed by the system of purity and impurity, though unfortunately in most cases the symbolism is implicit rather than explicit. The interpreter must take the rules given in the laws and what explanations the texts do provide as the basis for reconstructing the conceptual world of the purity/impurity system.[24]

The following discussion surveys interpretations of the rationale behind these laws from the least to the most important. These interpretations are not necessarily mutually exclusive. Several categories may be simultaneously valid.

1. *Hygiene.* The explanation that I heard as a new Christian for the laws of clean and unclean was that they had to do with health and hygiene.[25] There is, to be sure, an incidental contribution made by the laws of purity/impurity to hygiene. Certainly the exclusion from the camp of those with possible symptoms of leprosy and gonorrhea (Leviticus 13-14; 15:2-15) in effect quarantined these dangerous diseases and contributed to public health. The avoidance of touching carcasses, or eating animals which died of natural causes, or contacting human sputum and discharges would do the same. The ritual baths associated with returning to cleanness would also contribute to hygiene. Certain unclean animals are known to transfer diseases to humans: The pig bears trichinosis (tapeworm) and the hare tularemia; carrion eating birds harbor disease; and fish without fins and scales attract disease because they are mud burrowers. Eating animal suet is now known to lead to heart disease.

Hygiene, however, is at most a secondary explanation. Some animals that are excluded have no association with disease. The camel, for example, is a delicacy for Arabs to this day, and there is no evidence that the camel passes disease to humans.[26] Wild boars rarely have trichinosis and proper cooking of pork, in any case, generally makes its transmission to humans rare.[27] Pork was a staple of Israel's neighbors, so evidently they had learned to prepare the meat in such a way as to avoid most ill effects. Poisonous plants are not mentioned, though inclusion of "clean and unclean" plants would be expected were hygiene the purpose of these laws. Furthermore, some of the clean animals present health haz-

---

24. The following analysis leans heavily on works of Jewish scholar Jacob Milgrom who has spent a lifetime of research in the area of cultic law. I have also found the works of evangelical scholar Gordon Wenham of help in this area. Milgrom has provided the most satisfactory reconstruction of the symbolism of the ceremonial laws to date.

25. A popular version of the theory is found in S. I. McMillen, *None of these Diseases* (Westwood: Revell, 1963).

26. Milgrom, *Leviticus 1-16,* 719.

27. Hartley, *Leviticus,* 142.

ards: The ruminants of "clean" cud-chewing animals are host for a number of parasitic organisms.[28] Although "leprosy" is treated, other infectious diseases well known in antiquity are ignored in the biblical regulations, a fact inexplicable if hygiene were the primarily motive. Moreover, absolutions through ritual baths for one with a skin disease occurred after his healing; whereas, for purpose of hygiene it should occur before healing.[29] Finally—and especially important for the Christian—it is inconceivable that Christ would have abolished the distinction between clean and unclean foods (Mark 7:19) if hygiene were the purpose of this distinction.[30] These data lead to the conclusion that ritual symbolism is more central to the purpose of these laws than hygiene.

2. *Association with disgusting or pagan or demonic things.* Perhaps some unclean things were condemned because of an association with disgusting things and/or paganism. For example snakes (Lev 11:42) and camels (Lev 11:4; Deut 14:7) and certain predatory or slimy or creeping animals may have been declared unclean because they awaken a natural aversion in the minds of people.[31] With snakes, this aversion may go back to the curse of the fall (Gen 3:14-15).

The disgusting behavior of pigs (Lev 11:7; Deut 14:8) and dogs (cf. Lev 11:24) was proverbial: "Do not give what is holy to dogs, and do not throw your pearls before swine, or they will trample them under their feet, and turn and tear you to pieces" (Matt 7:6 NASB). These may have been considered unclean because they are scavengers that feed on refuse, including corpses.[32] Rodents such as the mouse (Lev 11:29) invoke disgust as they infest and destroy human stockpiles of grain.

However, certain observations argue against this theory. Although it explains why some animals might be clean or unclean, it does not adequately explain all animals. There seems no natural aversion to the hyrax or hare; whereas, the goat, an animal declared clean, can be disgusting in its omnivorousness.[33] Some animals, perhaps even the camel, may have been excluded to keep the classification system simple and without many exceptions (e.g., hoofs having clefs and animals chewing the cud) rather than because of disgust.

---

28. Hartley, *Leviticus,* 142.

29. Milgrom, *Leviticus 1-16,* 963.

30. G. J. Wenham, "Christ's Healing Ministry and His Attitude to the Law," *Christ the Lord* (ed. H. H. Rowdon; Leicester: Inter-Varsity, 1982), 117; *idem* "The Theology of Unclean Food," *EvQ* 53 (Jan./Mar 1981): 7.

31. J. Barton Payne, *Theology of the Older Testament* (Grand Rapids: Zondervan, 1962), 370.

32. Houston, *Purity and Monotheism,* 189-191. He notes that the LXX of 1 Kgs 21:19 and 22:38 reads *"pigs and* dogs licked the blood of Naboth" and *"pigs and* dogs licked up the blood, and the prostitutes will wash in your blood." The MT lacks "pigs" in both cases, but the LXX Vorlage's reading may well be original.

33. Houston, *Purity and Monotheism,* 76-78.

Association with pagan religious practices could be a rationale for declaring certain animals unclean, and yet against this notion is the fact that the animals commonly used by Israel's pagan neighbors for sacrifice and worship (e.g., the bull) were the very same animals commonly used by Israel itself.[34] It is often supposed that "cooking a kid in its mother's milk" was condemned because it was a pagan practice. However, there is no evidence of such a pagan practice.[35] Moreover, if God wished for Israel to avoid the appearance of pagan practices, he should have condemned the use of the bull for sacrifices since the bull was a favorite sacrificial animal among Canaanites, and gods in the form of bulls were worshiped both in Egypt and Canaan.[36]

Since it is clear that Israel's sacrificial worship shared much in common with her pagan neighbors, this line of interpretation seems doubtful. However, cooking a kid goat in its own mother's milk might be considered a disgusting, unbecoming thing to do, even if it were not specifically pagan.

3. *Ethical lessons.* More plausible than the first two categories is that some laws of purity are meant to promote ethical behavior. All the laws of purity, even where arbitrary, cultivated in the Israelite the virtue of self-control, an indispensable first step in the attainment of holiness.[37] Other regulations seem to have more specific ethical concerns. Eating meat torn by wild beasts not only defiles ritually, but it is contrary to ethical holiness by its dehumanizing effect, reducing human beings to the level of a scavenger dog (Exod 22:31).[38] It is possible, though no text explicitly states this, that predatory animals—most unclean animals are predatory—are regularly unclean because we are not to be like them morally, that is, destructive and murderous.[39] A similar moral explanation could apply to some specific, repulsive species (pigs, snakes). Some rabbinic interpreters (Philo, Ibn Ezra, Rashbam) understood cooking a kid goat in its mother's milk (Exod 23:19; 34:26; Deut 14:21) to be a perverse, savage act on the part of those who take delight in creating such an ironic circumstance.[40] Leaving a corpse of an executed man exposed on a tree overnight defiles the land (Deut 21:23) perhaps because it represents an attitude of excessive vindictiveness and barbarism. That those involved in the slaughter of war (Num 31:19-24), even for

---

34. Wenham, "The Theology of Unclean Food," 7.

35. R. Ratner and B. Zuckerman, "'A Kid in Milk'?: New Photographs of KTU 1.23, line 14," *HUCA* 57 (1986): 15-16; Peter C. Craigie, *Ugarit and the Old Testament* (Grand Rapids: Eerdmans, 1983), 74-76. Ratner and Zuckerman show that a text from Ugarit once used as evidence of such a practice (CTA 23.14) is now to be interpreted otherwise.

36. Wenham, "Christ's Healing Ministry," 118.

37. Epstein, cited by Mary Douglas, *Purity and Danger* (London: Routledge & Kegan Paul, 1966), 44.

38. Joe M. Sprinkle, *'The Book of the Covenant': A Literary Approach* (JSOTSup 174; Sheffield: Sheffield Academic Press, 1994), 176.

39. Wenham, *Leviticus,* 184.

40. Sprinkle, *'The Book of the Covenant',* 195.

legitimate reasons (in this case at the command of God), became unclean hints at the *moral* defilement of war. Laws concerning sexual emissions encouraged restraint and sexual self-control (e.g., avoiding sex during menstruation) and would rightly stigmatize violators such as prostitutes as social outcasts.[41]

The command not to eat the flesh with the blood not only reminded the Israelite of God's use of blood for atoning sacrifice but also inculcated respect for animal life.[42] The blood, symbolic of the life, had to be poured back to God even for non-atoning slaughter to symbolize that only by divine permission could even animal life be taken. Hence, the blood prohibition (Gen 9:3-6) taught the Israelite respect for animal life and for the Author of life whose permission was required to shed any blood, whether animal or human. This leads to a further moral implication: If taking mere animal life is not trivial, how much more serious is shedding human blood.

Milgrom adds that the food laws, in accord with the ethical purpose to inculcate reverence for animal life, limited the slaughtering of animals: only for food, only certain species, and only certain procedures.[43] The practical effect of the kosher laws (which are even more complex than the biblical injunctions) has indeed been that many modern observant Jews become vegetarians due to the complications of obtaining kosher meat.

Wright[44] criticizes Milgrom's view, noting it is doubtful that these laws actually reduced the *quantity* of meat consumed by ancient Israel since one may compensate for the limitations by breeding more animals. Moreover, as Houston observes, designating certain species as "unclean, abhorrent, or abominable" rather than "holy" seems an odd way of inculcating "reverence for life."[45] The laws do, nonetheless, discourage indiscriminate killing of animals, such as recreational hunting that leaves the flesh to rot.

4. *Association of Yahweh with life and wholeness rather than death and disorder.* The purity system arguably conveys in a symbolic way that Yahweh is the God of life (order) and is separated from that which has to do with death (disorder). Corpses and carcasses rendered a person unclean because they obviously have to do with death. Most (though not all) of the unclean animals are

---

41. Wenham, *Leviticus* 222-225.

42. Milgrom (*Leviticus 1-16*, 154-155) argues that concern for humane treatment of animals is found even in the way an animal was to be dispatched. An Israelite was to slaughter an animal in the most painless of ways: slitting the throat. "Slaughter" (Heb. *šaḥaṭ*) arguably means specifically "to slit the throat" as in 2 Kgs 10:7.

43. Jacob Milgrom, "Ethics and Ritual: The Biblical Foundations of the Dietary Laws," *Religion and Law: Biblical-Judaic and Islamic Perspectives* (ed. E. Firmage, et al.; Winona Lake: Eisenbrauns, 1989), 159-91.

44. David P. Wright, "Observations on the Ethical Foundations of the Biblical Dietary Laws," *Religion and Law: Biblical-Judaic and Islamic Perspectives* (ed. E. Firmage, et al.; Winona Lake: Eisenbrauns, 1989), 197.

45. Houston, *Purity and Monotheism*, 77.

somehow associated with death, either being predators/scavengers (animals with paws rather than hoofs) or living in tomb-like caves (rock badgers). The pig, in particular, in addition to being a scavenger, was associated with the worship of chthonic or underworld deities and/or demons among the Hittites, Egyptians, and Mesopotamians.[46] The scale disease rendered a person unclean because it made a person waste away like a corpse (cf. Num 12:12: "Let her not be like a corpse," referring to Miriam's skin disease).[47]

Bodily discharges (blood for women, semen for men—blood and semen both being symbols of life) may represent a temporary loss of strength and life and movement towards death. Whitekettle advocates an alternative view that bodily discharges represent lack of wholeness and sexual dysfunction, a womb undergoing self destruction during menstruation or post-partum during which time conception is unlikely.[48] Similarly men, after ejaculation typically need some time to regenerate before being fully sexually functional as well. Because decaying corpses discharge, so natural bodily discharges are reminders of sin and death.[49] Purification rituals symbolize movement from death towards life and accordingly involved blood, the color red, and spring (literal "living") water, all of which are symbols of life (Lev 17:11; 14:5, 50; Num 19:2, 17, etc.).

Even some food laws can be explained on this basis. Why was Israel not to cook a kid in its mother's milk (Exod 23:19; 34:26; Deut 14:21)? Perhaps it was because it was inappropriate to combine that which is a symbol of life (mother's milk) with the death of the kid whose life it was supposed sustain,[50] especially in the context of the festival of Tabernacles (so the context of Exod 23:19) celebrating the life-giving power of Yahweh.[51]

Mary Douglas has shown the connection between cleanness/holiness and such concepts as "wholeness," "physical perfection," and "completeness."[52] Hence, priests and animals with the same physical imperfections were ineligible for the sanctuary (Lev 21:17-21; 22:20-24). Physical imperfections, representing a movement from "life" towards "death," moved a person ritually away from God, who is to be associated with life.

This symbolic system served to separate Yahweh worship from necromancy, spiritualism, and ancestor veneration since dealings with the dead rendered a

---

46. Milgrom, *Leviticus 1-16,* 651.

47. Milgrom, *Leviticus 1-16,* 819.

48. Whitekettle, "Levitical Thought and the Female Reproductive Cycle," 376-391. He observes against Milgrom's view that menstruation represents movement towards death that "no woman has ever menstruated to death" (p. 377), a generality that, though it no doubt has exceptions, is nonetheless well taken.

49. Wenham, *Leviticus,* 188.

50. O. Keel, cited by E. A. Knauf, "Zur Herhunft und Sozialgeschichte Israels," *Bib* 69 (1988): 153-154.

51. Sprinkle, `Book of the Covenant',* 194-195.

52. Mary Douglas, *Purity and Danger* (New York: Praeger, 1966), 51-57.

person unclean (cf. Lev 19:31 where consulting spiritualists renders one "unclean" morally). Even sitting among the graves (Isa 65:4) is condemned.

5. *Separation of holiness from expressions of sexuality.* In certain pagan cults, sexual acts were sometimes performed as part of the worshiper's devotion to deity. For example, there was in Corinth the famous brothel of Aphrodite; and in Babylon (and similarly at Cyprus), according to Herodotus (*Hist.* 1.199)—though perhaps significantly not confirmed by cuneiform sources—every woman was obligated to prostitute herself once at the temple of a goddess (Ishtar?). A once common but more recently doubted[53] scholarly reconstruction is the hypothesized practice of sacred prostitution. According to this reconstruction, pagans in OT times attempted to convey fertility to the land by a form of sympathetic magic involving ritualized sexual intercourse at a cultus. But for anyone following Israel's laws of purity, this practice would be unthinkable. According to those laws, all expressions of sexuality rendered a person unclean and hence unfit to approach a sanctuary. Priests were to wear breeches, and altars were to be made without stairs to avoid even the hint of sexual impropriety in worship (Exod 28:42; 20:26). Since sexual acts rendered a person "unclean," the observant Israelite would have found the whole idea of sacred prostitution repugnant.

Designating sexual activity as "unclean" does not mean that sex was considered inherently evil. However, it does clearly separate sexuality from the holy, relegating it to the sphere of the common, the earthly.[54] It is therefore probably no coincidence that in the resurrection there is no marriage (Matt 22:30). Moreover, making all sexual acts "unclean" may relate to the Fall, which resulted in the perversion of human sexuality: sexual shame (fig leaves), multiplied pain in childbirth, and the man's lust for and domination of the woman (Gen 3:7, 10-11, 16, 19).[55]

6. *Separation from the Gentiles.* One clear purpose of the laws of purity was to separate Israel from the Gentiles. The separation of sexuality from any form of worship just mentioned would have the effect of separating Israel from at least some of her pagan neighbors. More directly, the clean/unclean system divided animals, people, and land into three categories. In the animal realm are clean animals which could be sacrificed on an altar, clean animals (wild game, fish) which could be eaten but not sacrificed on an altar, and unclean animals which ritually defiled the eater and could not be sacrificed (and some among the unclean animals are further called *šeqeṣ* "cultic abomination" or *tôʿēbâ* "abomi-

---

53. Among those questioning whether "sacred prostitution" in the sense of ritualized sexual intercourse to give fertility to the land ever really existed in the Ancient Near East are Jeffrey Tigay (*Deuteronomy* [JPS Torah Commentary; Philadelphia: Jewish Publication Society, 1996], 480-481), and K. van der Toorn (*ABD* 5:510-512). Chapter 10 below discusses this question further.

54. Hartley, *Leviticus,* 214.

55. Payne, *Theology of the Older Testament,* 371.

nation, abhorrence"; Lev 11:10-13, 20, 23, 41; Deut 14:3). This separation among animals parallels that of people.[56] Priests were "holy" and separated from other Israelites for service in the sanctuary; ordinary Israelites are "clean" and separated from non-Israelites, leaving non-Israelites as "unclean" (and some, such as Canaanites, with especially wicked idolatrous practices are called an abomination; Lev 18:26-30; Deut 7:1-5, 25-26; 20:17-18). There is a similar system of separation of space: The tabernacle (associated with priests) is holy; the land (associated with the Israelites) is clean; and the rest of the world (associated with Gentiles) is unclean.[57] Thus the purity system symbolically reinforced teaching elsewhere that Israel was a "holy nation" (Exod 19:6) set apart from all others.[58] In keeping the food laws, the Israelites were thus acknowledging that God had chosen and saved them from the nations.

Moreover, the food laws discouraged table fellowship with the Canaanites, whose diet would ordinarily include the pig and other items condemned as unclean. These laws were thus a practical means of maintaining Israel as a holy people. The connection between the food laws and separation from the nations is stated explicitly:

> You must therefore make a distinction between the clean and the unclean animals and between unclean and clean birds. Do not defile yourself by any animal or bird or anything that moves along the ground—those which I have set apart as unclean for you. You are to be holy to me because I the LORD am holy, *and I have set you apart from the nations to be my own.* (Lev 20:25-26 NIV, italics mine)

Thus these laws, like modern kosher laws for modern Jews, helped maintain the Israelites as a separate and distinct people. The other laws by creating distinctive customs—even where such customs were arbitrary and without any inherent moral value, e.g., Lev 19:19, not wearing garment made of two types of material—nonetheless inculcated Israel with the concept of "holiness" and served as "object lessons" that created in Israel a sense of self identity as a "separated" people.

The abolition of the food laws in the New Testament (Mark 7:19; Acts 10:15 with 11:9; Rom 14:14) conveys deep theological significance. As argued above, the division of animals into clean and unclean symbolized the separation between Israelites and Gentiles. Accordingly, the abolition of the kosher laws must sym-

---

56. Cf. Lev 21:18-21 and 22:20-24 where the symbolic parallelism is seen in that defects which bar a priest from service are the same defects which keep an animal from being offered to God

57. The idea that the nations are unclean, not only ritually but also morally, finds expression in the historical books (Josh 22:19; Ezra 6:19-22; 9:11; 2 Chr 36:14; Neh 13:30). Likewise the prophets imply that foreign land and foreign peoples are associated with uncleanness (Isa 52:1, 11; Amos 1:17; Hos 9:3-4; Ezek 4:9-17; 22:15; 24:11, 13; 36:25, 29).

58. Milgrom, *Leviticus 1-16,* 720-726.

bolize a breaking down of the barrier between Jews and Gentiles.[59] That this is the correct understanding of the symbolism is seen in God's lesson to Peter in Acts 10-11: God now declares the Gentiles "clean," and Peter is not to continue to think of them as inherently unclean. In the new Messianic Age, the principle that God's people are to be separate (holy) from the world remains, but the lines drawn are no longer ethnic in character.

7. *Holiness of God versus the contamination of humans.* The most important explanation of the rules of purity is that they teach the concept of the holiness of God. The account that forms the preface to the laws of purity in Leviticus 11-15 is that of the death of Nadab and Abihu, the sons of Aaron, who were struck dead for improperly approaching the sanctuary (Leviticus 10). God explains that through this incident, "I will show myself holy among those who are near me, and before all the people I will be glorified" (10:3, RSV). Likewise at the end of the food laws, God comments that the Israelites were to be holy and show that holiness by not eating unclean "swarming things" (11:44). God had brought them out of Egypt; and therefore he tells them, "You shall therefore be holy, for I am holy" (11:45). At the end of the purity laws comes the Day of Atonement ritual. In reference to the death of the two sons of Aaron, God warns against coming into the "most holy place" (Lev 16:1-2). This bracketing of the laws of clean and unclean with the death of Aaron's two sons and the idea of the sanctuary's holiness suggest that the most important lesson conveyed by this system is that God is holy (i.e. "set apart").

Conversely, these laws suggest that people, in contrast with the holiness of God, are contaminated and corrupt. Those who approach God must therefore be sanctified or purified. The unclean are excluded from the tabernacle, the symbolic dwelling place of God (Num 5:3; Lev 15:31); and everyone by biology inevitably contracts uncleanness from time to time. Although the texts are notoriously sparse in explanations, when taken in conjunction with biblical teaching as a whole it seems reasonable to deduce from these laws the following lesson: that human beings, by nature of being part of this sin-cursed, fallen world, are "unclean" or "contaminated" and are not automatically eligible to approach God. In any case, the purity system, by emphasizing the holiness of God and the impurity of man, teaches that humans must prepare themselves both ritually and morally before approaching a holy God.

Ceremonial "uncleanness/impurity" cannot simply be equated with "sin" since natural bodily functions and other factors beyond human control could (and periodically did) cause a person to be unclean. Nonetheless, there is a strong analogy between "uncleanness" and "sin." Hence the "sin" or "purification" offering (the *ḥaṭṭāʼt*), including the special "sin offering" on the Day of Atonement, served to cleanse both sin and ritual impurity (Lev 5:1-5; 16:16-22). That uncleanness is also used metaphorically of deviations of morality hints at this sym-

---

59. Wenham, "Christ's Healing Ministry," 122; Milgrom, *Leviticus 1-16,* 726.

bolic connection. In the Pentateuch, rape (Gen 34:5, 13, 27), adultery (Lev 18:20; Num 5:19), bestiality (Lev 18:23), all the various "sins" which led God to remove the Canaanites (Lev 18:24-26), remarriage to a first husband after divorce and remarriage to a second husband (Deut 24:4), consultation with mediums (Lev 19:31), child sacrifice to Molech (Lev 20:3), and murder (Num 35:33-34) are all described using the language of "uncleanness" (*ṭāmēʾ*), showing the symbolic link between ceremonial uncleanness and moral/ethical uncleanness.

Poetical and prophetic writers also use the language of ritual purity for ethical purity, showing that they too recognized the symbolic connection. That the person with the skin disease is analogous to a sinner was evident in Psalm 51 that applied the imagery associated with the purification of lepers to cleansing from sins such as David's sin of murder and adultery (Ps 51:7 "Purify me with hyssop and I will be clean"; cf. Psalm 51's superscript; similarly Lam 4:13, 15). Such examples from the poetic books can be multiplied.[60] Similarly, various prophets (especially the priest Ezekiel) use the language of "clean" and "unclean" metaphorically in the ethical sense. Isaiah states that he and his people have "unclean lips"; that is, they are *morally* impure and unfit to speak for God or to be in his presence (Isa 6:5). However, in the Messianic Age no one (morally) unclean will travel on God's highway of holiness (Isa 35:8). Ezekiel states that transgressions defiled Israel (Ezek 14:11) so that Israel is "unclean of name," that is, has a reputation for (ethical) impurity (Ezek 22:5). Moreover, Ezekiel compares Israel's wicked deeds with the uncleanness of a menstruating woman (Ezek 36:17), and he adds that the exile was due to Israel's (moral) uncleanness and transgressions (Ezek 39:24). Again, in the prophets examples of using the language of ceremonial impurity as metaphors for ethical impurity can be multiplied.[61]

---

60. "Clean" and "unclean" can be used in the sense of "righteous" and "wicked" as shown by the parallelism (Ecc 9:2; Job 17:11). Several acts are cited as producing ethical impurity: repudiation of parents (Prov 30:11-12), shedding the blood of the righteous (Lam 4:13-15), idolatry and child sacrifice (Ps 106:36-39), as well as murder and adultery (Ps 51:2, 7, 10; cf. superscript and 2 Samuel 11). The destruction of (or perhaps plundering of) the temple by the nations defiled it both ethically and ritually (Ps 79:1). The poetical books, moreover, affirm the doctrine of the sinful nature of man, that is, that human beings are (ethically) "unclean" by nature and cannot stand "pure" before a holy God (Prov 20:9; Job 4:17; 14:4). Since only one "who has (ethically) clean (*nāqî*) hands and a pure (*bar*) heart (i.e., the "mind, inward self"; *lēb*)" was eligible to ascend the temple mount to be in God's presence (Ps 24:3-4), moral cleansing of the heart like unto outward ritual purification was required for the sinner (Ps 51:10-11a). The attitude of heart required to produce such "clean" or righteous acts is "the fear of the LORD" (Ps 19:9).

61. Isaiah states all of his people have become "like one who is unclean," and that their righteous deeds were like a filthy garment (*begged ʿiddîm*, literally "a menstrual cloth"; Isa 64:6). See also Isa 59:2-3; Zeph 3:1-4. Various sins are said by various prophets to "defile" morally: adultery (Ezek 18:6, 11, 15; 33:26), incest (Ezek 22:11), idolatry [often under the metaphor of harlotry] (Isa 30:22; Jer 2:23; 7:30; 32:34; Ezek 5:11; 20:7, 8, 18; 22:3-4; 23:7, 13, 30; 36:18, 25; 37:23; 43:8; Hos 5:3; 6:10), child

IV. THE PURITY SYSTEM AND SACRED SPACE

From the foregoing, it may be deduced that the purity system is central to creating a sense of sacred space for ancient Israel. Houston[62] points out that the whole system of purity is concerned with protection of the sanctuary, even where it is not immediately apparent (Lev 12:4; 15:31; Num 19:13, 20); for the sanctuary as God's residence was the source of holiness, blessing, and order; and it was threatened on every side by the pollution that surrounded it. The special holiness of the tabernacle, being incompatible with the condition of uncleanness and with idolatry, was a reminder of the sacredness of tabernacle space, setting it apart from Canaanite sanctuaries that were instead to be profaned. Hence the rules of clean and unclean impressed in the mind of every Israelite that a special holiness was associated with Yahweh's sanctuaries and no others. As Wright[63] points out, the object of ritual cleansing with the purification offering's blood is primarily the sanctuary and not so much the worshiper. That the sanctuary needs this constant cleansing from human impurities and sins shows the sanctuary to be set apart, sacred. Thus the holiness and sacredness of that sacred space is emphasized.

It was the sense of the sacredness of the tabernacle and temple space that made purification from moral and ritual impurity essential. Nehemiah showed the sense of sacred space when he evicted wicked Tobiah's possessions from his chamber in the temple precincts. This defilement had been allowed by the priest Eliashib. Nehemiah then ordered ritual purification (Piel of *ṭāhēr*) of both the room and the priesthood which had been defiled (*gōʾal*) by the association of the temple with things foreign (Neh 13:7-9, 29-30). To protect the sacredness of tabernacle space, laymen, laymen-slaves of a priest, and daughters of priests married to laymen could not eat of the sacred donations to the sanctuary (Lev 22:10-13).[64]

Wright observes,

> . . . the Priestly writings' concern [was] to put impurity in its proper place. When this corpus is studied further, one finds that there is a similar concern about the proper place for holiness and purity. The information about places of holiness, purity, and impurity, as a whole, reveals a larger system of what may be called "cultic topography."[65]

---

sacrifice (Ezek 20:26, 31), bloodshed (Ezek 22:3-4), political intrigues with foreign nations (Ezek 23:17), working on the Sabbath (Ezek 20:12-13, 21; 22:26), violations of laws and covenants (Isa 24:5), and miscellaneous evil deeds (Jer 2:7; Ezek 20:43). The post-exilic prophets use ritual purity to illustrate moral and religious points (Hag 2:10-11; Zech 3:5-11; 13:1-2; Mal 1:7-8, 12-14).

62. Houston, *Purity and Monotheism,* 245.

63. Wright, *Disposal of Impurity,* 18, 130.

64. Layman is the rendering of *gēr,* usually of foreign sojourners, but contextually here of those not of priestly descent dwelling among the priests. See NRSV, NASB.

65. Wright, *The Disposal of Impurity,* 231.

This "cultic topography" serves to distinguish "sacred space" from non-sacred "common space" and defiled "unclean" space. Because the tabernacle (and later the temple) was the "Holy Place," one needed to be very careful not to approach it in a condition of ceremonial impurity. The various rules of holy and clean and unclean raised in the consciousness of the Israelite worshiper the sense that the sanctuary was "sacred space." Some activities must occur only in "a holy place" within the sanctuary precincts, including the consumption of the most holy purification/sin offerings, the guilt/compensation offerings, and the cereal offerings (Lev 6:16, 26-27 [MT 6:9, 19-20]; 7:6; 10:12-14, 17; 14:13; 16:24; 24:9; Exod 29:31); whereas, the fellowship/peace offerings, though they could be eaten in the sanctuary, could also be consumed in a "pure place" outside the sanctuary (Lev 10:14).[66] The carcass of the purification offering also had to be burned and disposed in a "pure place" (Lev 4:11-12, 21; 6:4, 23 [MT]; 8:17; 9:11; 16:27; Exod 29:14; Num 19:9); whereas, the fungus-infected building materials that resemble scale disease were to be deposed in an "impure place" (Lev 14:40-41, 45).[67] Thus these rules underscore three kinds of space: sacred, pure, and impure.

In contrast with the sacredness of the tabernacle, biblical law demanded the desecration of pagan "sacred spaces." Israel was commanded to destroy Canaanite sacred objects and places, putting them under the ban (ḥērem; Exod 23:24; 34:13; Deut 7:5). This represented a desacralization of the Canaanite cultic spaces. Idolatrous practices and objects are never labeled "unclean," and no impurity ritual is prescribed even in places that foreign cult practices are mentioned and where one might expect prescription of such rituals (e.g. Lev 19:4; 26:1-2). Nonetheless, idolatrous things "defile" in the moral sense (rather than ritual) both Israelites and their sanctuary (Lev 18:24, 30; 20:3), implying that idolatry is akin to uncleanness. Moreover, like the transmission of impurity, the status of being ḥērem [dedicated to destruction] was transferable from the idol to the idolater (Deut 7:25-26).[68] For this reason Josiah "defiled" (Piel of ṭāmeʾ), that is, "destroyed," the ritually impure high places and altars of pagan gods which Manasseh his father had allowed to flourish in Jerusalem (2 Kgs 23:8-16; cf. Jer 19:13 where "to defile" houses polluted by idolatry also means "to destroy" them).

In a sense, the whole land of Israel was somewhat sacred space, in contrast with the defiled space of Gentile lands. Nonetheless, Gentile sojourners (gērîm) are allowed to share the semi-sacred space of land, and they could even partake of holy things such as the Passover meal (provided that they followed the law of circumcision) and the Feast of Weeks (Exod 12:48; Deut 16:14). Like Israelites, they had to undergo ritual purification when they contracted carcass impurity (Lev 17:15).

---

66. Wright, *The Disposal of Impurity*, 232-236.
67. Wright, *The Disposal of Impurity*, 243.
68. Wright, *The Disposal of Impurity*, 283-285.

All this is done because the sanctuary, Israel's sacred space, was holy.

V. NEW TESTAMENT IMPLICATIONS

As one approaches the new covenant, in one sense the idea of sacred space has been abolished along with the purity laws. The temple, though still utilized in the book of Acts by the early Christians (Acts 2:46; 3:1; 5:21, etc.), was doomed to destruction (Matt 24:2), a fact that anticipates a new day in which emphasis on that sacred space would by necessity be abolished. Similarly, Jesus tells the Samaritan woman that what is essential for worship will henceforth not be a particular sacred space, but a sacred heart attitude, worshiping God "in spirit and in truth" (John 4:21-24). Instead of a tabernacle in the wilderness symbolizing God's dwelling among his people, under the new covenant Christ tabernacles among us (John 1:14), so wherever two or three gather in his name, there he is in our midst (Matt 18:20). Whereas the purity/impurity laws symbolized both sacred space (land, temple) and sacred community (Israelites, priests), under the new covenant sacred space has been supplanted by sacred community.[69] The sharp division between "clean" Israelites and "unclean" Gentiles has broken down as indicated by the breakdown under the new covenant of the clean/unclean system for food, persons, and space that had symbolized separation from the Gentiles.

Nevertheless, arguably some principles of the purity laws and sacred space are still applicable. Even in the OT cleanness and uncleanness metaphorically symbolized moral purity and impurity, and moral purity is still a Christian ideal. Moreover, the "place" where two or more gather in Christ's name becomes, by that fact, "holy ground." That holy ground can be defiled, not by ceremonial impurity, but by ethical impurity. It remains true that those who would metaphorically ascend the hill of the LORD at the sacred places where believers gather must have ethically "clean hands and a pure heart" (Ps 24:3-4) lest that sacred time and place be defiled.

Evangelical Christians would benefit if they devoted more attention to themes underscored in the laws of clean and unclean. Christians should still disassociate themselves from that which is disgusting, deadly, or dehumanizing. Instead they should affirm self-control, especially sexual self-control, and that which is wholesome and life-promoting. Though separation from Gentiles is obsolete for Christians, separation from the world is not. Though the sacred space of the temple is no more, the very fact that we build churches with "sanctuaries" is an indication that we sense the need psychologically of having sacred spaces even today. But if, by analogy, we, like Israel of old, produce sacred spaces for our sacred communities to gather, ought we not by that same analogy guard the

---

69. Richard Averbeck, "Sacred Space and Sacred Community in the Old Testament and the New Testament," paper read at the Evangelical Theological Society Annual Meeting, Danvers, MA, November 18, 1999.

sacredness of such spaces from all defilements or improprieties that could profane that place for worship? Perhaps the low level of "sacredness" associated with Evangelical sanctuaries comes not so much from Christian liberty as our failure to reflect in our worship truths found in the laws of clean and unclean: the great holiness of God and its incompatibility with the defilement of man.

Chapter 8

THE RED HEIFER

The red heifer is associated with a corpse-decontamination ritual performed by Eliezer, Aaron's son. This ritual involved the ashes of a red heifer (or cow) that were mixed with spring ("living") water and sprinkled upon persons or objects to be purified. This ritual is described in Numbers 19:1-22, and it is applied in the narrative of Numbers 31:19-24 in the case of soldiers and captives returning from war. This ritual allowed a corpse-contaminated layperson to be brought back to a state of purity and so restored to full participation in the religious life of the community. Nazirites and priests required separate purification offerings for corpse contamination (Num 6:9-12; Ezek 44:25-27).

I. DESCRIPTION OF THE RED HEIFER RITUAL

1. *Animal requirements.* The red cow had to be without blemish and, being dedicated to God, never previously yoked for profane use (Num 19:2). This implies it was a young animal. "Red" presumably refers to the hair rather than the skin, although the latter has been suggested.[1] The exact shade of red and its significance is debated. A common interpretation is that red (Heb. *'ădummâ*) is the color of blood (Heb. *dām* ["blood"]) and anticipates the ritual use of blood (Num 19:4) essential for purification. Or red could anticipate its being burned in the reddish fire (Num 19:5-6).[2] The Mishnah, which dedicates tractates *Para* and *'Ohalot* to the red heifer and corpse contamination, emphasizes the rareness of a totally red cow: "If it had two black or white hairs [growing] from within a single hole, it is invalid" (*m. Parah* 2:5). Accordingly, certain modern Jews interested in restoration of sacrificial worship are attempting to breed pure red cows.[3] Brenner,[4] on the other hand, argues that the color here is bay or reddish brown, a more common color. She discounts the rabbinic sophistry on black and white hairs and, due to the text's silence, any symbolic connection with either blood or

---

1. Athalya Brenner, *Color Terms in the Old Testament* (JSOTSup 21; Sheffield: JSOT Press, 1982), 63.
2. Heb. *dām* ["blood"] is possibly cognate with *'ădummâ* ["red"], an observation that lends support to the view that the lawgiver is associating the cow's red color with the blood involved in the ritual.
3. Serge Schemann, "A Red Heifer or Not?" *New York Times International*, June 14, 1997.
4. Brenner, *Colour Terms*, 64-65.

fire. But why then specify the color? Connecting the color with blood, symbolically adding more "blood" to the ashes (J. Milgrom),[5] appears the more acceptable interpretation. The crimson yarn and the [red] cedar (Num 19:6) serve the same symbolic function,[6] as well as adding bulk to the ashes. The blood in the ashes contains the cleansing power.

2. *Nature of the sacrifice.* Does this ritual involve sacrifice or only profane slaughter, and if a sacrifice, what kind?[7] Milgrom argues correctly that Num 19:9 should be rendered, "It is a *ḥaṭṭā't* [i.e., a purification offering]" (cf. NRSV, REB). The Hebrew word *ḥaṭṭā't* can mean both "sin" and "purification [sin][8] offering," so this produces some confusion among translators. Many English versions render this phrase "for removal of sin" or the like (e.g., RSV, NIV, NASB). But rendering *ḥaṭṭā't* here as "sin" is problematic, for contamination by removing a corpse from a tent (Num 19:14) involves no "sin," only ceremonial uncleanness. That the red heifer ritual is profane slaughter is also problematic because the ritual is supervised by Eliezer the priest. Part of the confusion lies in this *ḥaṭṭā't*-offering being completely burned to ashes—skin, flesh, blood, dung—whereas elsewhere it is the *'ôlâ* ("burnt offering") that is so burned. Moreover, unlike other sacrifices, it is slaughtered outside the camp (Num 19:3) rather than at the altar. Nonetheless, it appears that this was neither profane slaughter nor an *'ôlâ*-offering, but in fact a special kind of *ḥaṭṭā't*-offering.

3. *Why a female?* Why does this ritual specify a cow? Milgrom[9] plausibly suggests a bull cannot be used because that was the purification offering for the high priests (Lev 4:1-12; 16:11) or the community (Lev 4:13-21) rather than individual Israelites.

4. *How the ashes cleanse and defile.* Like the Day of Atonement *ḥaṭṭā't*-offering, any priest who handled the red heifer *ḥaṭṭā't*-offering became unclean (Num 19:7-10a, 21; cf. Lev 16:28), even as it purified its recipients. It is as if the impurity that was being absorbed into the cow contaminated the cow's handler.[10] Touching or even being in the same room as a corpse (Num 19:11, 14), handling human bones (rearranging bones in a tomb was common practice), or touching a grave transmitted uncleanness. Being contaminated by war killings, the whole

---

5. Jacob Milgrom, *Numbers* (JPS Torah Commentary; Philadelphia: Jewish Publication Society, 1990), 158.

6. Jacob Milgrom, "The Paradox of the Red Cow," *VT* 31 (1981): 65. Reprinted in *Studies in Cultic Theology and Terminology* (Leiden: Brill, 1983), 85-95.

7. David Wright, "Heifer, Red," *ABD* 3:115.

8. The *ḥaṭṭā't*-offering is in general better rendered "purification offering" (per J. Milgrom) than "sin offering" because it was used not only to purify sin but also to purify ceremonial uncleanness (see Lev 16:15-16).

9. Milgrom, "The Paradox of the Red Cow (Num xix)," 65.

10. Milgrom, *Numbers*, 441.

army (not just ones who actually touched corpses) and its war captives also required purification after battle (Num 31:19-24). The purification ritual took seven days in which the purifying waters mixed with the cow's ashes were sprinkled onto the contaminated person using hyssop branches on the third and seventh days (Num 19:12, 19; 31:19). Hyssop—a small bushy plant used to sprinkle water or blood in other purification rituals—was also considered a purifying agent, burnt and mixed with ashes of other purifying agents: the cow, the cedar, and the scarlet thread (19:6). Ritual cleansing applied also to objects contaminated by a corpse: unsealed vessels in the same room, the tent, its furnishings (Num 19:15, 18), clothing, hides, goat's hair, wooden objects (Num 31:20). All objects that could not be destroyed were cleansed with fire (Num 31:22-23); but the rest, with the waters of purification. The ritual ended with washing clothes and bathing with water on the seventh day (Num 19:19; 31:24). Those who refused to undergo the rite were "cut off" (Num 19:13, 20). The meaning of "cut off" is debated. It may mean excommunication from the community and Yahweh's sanctuary, which their uncleanness could defile; but the more likely view is that it refers to a divine punishment of separation from descendants either in this life (they have no descendants) or the afterlife (not permitted to join their deceased ancestors).[11]

II. THE SIGNIFICANCE OF THE RED HEIFER RITUAL

1. *Relationship with the purity laws.* This regulation fits into the larger matrix of laws of purity and impurity which required anyone contracting uncleanness to avoid that which was holy and take steps to return to a state of purity lest the sanctuary be defiled (Num 19:13; cf. 5:2-4; 31:19). This system symbolically conveys the extreme holiness of God and the unavoidable contamination of human beings, probably symbolic of human sinfulness ("uncleanness" can be used metaphorically for sin); and so those who approach God must be ritually and morally cleansed. It also shows that Yahweh is to be associated with life and is separated from anything associated with death. Minor lessons include showing that war, even under Yahweh's command, nonetheless brings uncleanness and that necromancy and ancestor worship are incompatible with Yahweh worship.

2. *Typology and New Testament.* According to the writer of Hebrews, purging "uncleanness" though the ashes of the red heifer foreshadows the spiritual cleansing of Christian consciences from dead works through the high priestly work of Christ (Heb 9:13-14). The sacrifice of the heifer and the sacrifice of Christ have several similarities: The heifer was "unblemished" (Num 19:2), and Christ was also "without blemish" (Heb 9:14), though Christ in the more profound sense of sinless. Both Christ and the heifer shed their blood, the

---

11. For a discussion, see Milgrom, *Numbers*, 405-408.

heifer's blood being sprinkled seven times towards the presence of God at the tent of meeting (Num 19:4); and the blood of Christ likewise being offered to God (Heb 9:14). The sacrifice of the heifer takes place "outside the camp" (Num 19:3); and the sacrifice of Christ is also "outside the camp," though in his case in the sense of outside the gate of Jerusalem (Heb 13:11-13). And finally both provide purification of the flesh: the heifer in the sense of the body defiled by death, Christ in the more profound sense of purifying the sinful nature and conscience (Heb 9:13-14).

T. Dozeman suggests further, eschatological symbolism: The purging death from the camp arguably anticipates purging death itself from the coming messianic kingdom.[12]

---

12. Thomas B. Dozeman, "The Book of Numbers," *New Interpreter's Bible* (Nashville: Abingdon, 1998) 2:152.

Chapter 9

OLD TESTAMENT PERSPECTIVES ON DIVORCE

I. INTRODUCTION

Old Testament laws and the rest of the OT have much to say about divorce. Unfortunately, theologians reconstructing a biblical ethic of divorce have often ignored many of the relevant passages. This chapter tries to fill this gap by emphasizing these neglected texts in the OT where divorce is either allowed—or sometimes even commanded—and where God's estranged relationship with Israel is described by using divorce imagery. From this data I seek to formulate a systemized OT rationale for the cases that permit or command divorce within the concept of marriage as covenant. This will then be compared with NT teaching about divorce.

It will be observed that the OT permits divorce for a variety of fundamental violations of the marriage covenant. In addition, I will attempt to show that the OT teaching on this topic is compatible with the NT teachings about divorce, and that both together are required for a complete biblical divorce ethic. Only such an approach, it will be claimed, avoids the Marcionite heresy by fully acknowledging the divine authority of the OT teaching on this subject. And only this view is practical in our current, fallen world.

There is no question that OT law allows for divorce. What is less well recognized is that under some circumstances, God commands divorce. I start with evidence that shows that OT law allowed divorce, and then I will go on to look at places where God commanded people to divorce.

II. DIVORCE ALLOWED UNDER SOME CIRCUMSTANCES

A number of passages support the notion that, though divorce was not encouraged, it was assumed that Israelites under the old covenant could in fact under some circumstances divorce their wives. In addition, where divorce occurred, the right to remarry was assumed.

1. *Deuteronomy 24:1-4.* Because of its prominence in the discussion between Jesus and his opponents in the NT, Deut 24:1-4 is the best-known passage in the OT concerning divorce. Unfortunately, it is a text riddled with exegetical difficulties.

One problem is that of syntax. The KJV of Deut 24:1 reads, "When a man hath taken a wife, and married her, and it come to pass that she find no favor in his eyes, because he hath found some uncleanness in her; then let him write her a bill of divorcement, and give it in her hand, and send her out of his house." This interpretation sees v. 1 as having both a protasis and an apodosis in which the apodosis actually adjures that the man divorce his wife if some "uncleanness" is found in her. It is, to be sure, not impossible grammatically to take the Hebrew this way. It is also possible to understand this line as giving permission to divorce rather than commanding divorce. Thus the HCSB translates, "If . . . he finds something improper about her, he may write her a divorce certificate." Most modern exegetes, however, conclude that the second half of v. 1 should be taken as the continuation of the protasis that continues through v. 3, followed by the apodosis in verse 4. Hence, the NASB reads, "When a man takes a wife and marries her, and it happens that she finds no favor in his eyes because he has found some indecency in her, and he writes her a certificate of divorce and puts it in her hand and sends her out from his house, and she leaves his house and goes and becomes another man's wife, and if the latter husband turns against her and writes her a certificate of divorce and puts it in her hand and sends her out from his house, or if the latter husband dies who took her to be his wife, then her former husband who sent her away is not allowed to take her again to be his wife, since she has been defiled." Taken this way, the text does not "command" divorce at all. Assuming a divorce has taken place, it prohibits the remarriage of the wife to her original husband if she subsequently married another man. This is the usual interpretation among modern commentators and translations (e.g., Keil, Craigie, Thompson, Mayes, Kalland, Merrill, McConville, NASB, NRSV, NJPS, NIV, ESV). I have not run across any modern interpreter who defends the KJV's rendering as a command.

Deuteronomy 24:1 does not "command" divorce, but it does under certain circumstances acknowledge divorce as a cultural institution. The giving of a certificate of divorce implies not only a legal permission for divorce, but it also presumes the legal permission for the woman to remarry. After all, what use is a certificate of divorce if not primarily for the allowing of remarriage without the woman being accused of the capital offense of adultery?[1] That in fact is what the woman in this case does: She remarries another man who, as it turns out, also divorces her.

The reason for the divorce is that "something indecent" (NIV) was found in her. The key expression, literally "a nakedness of a thing" (*'erwat dābār*), is never defined. Is it literal nakedness, or is it metaphorical for shameful behavior of whatever sort? The word *'erwâ* is used elsewhere metaphorically of the "nakedness" of Egypt, meaning the "private parts" of Egypt that spies would seek out for weaknesses in her defenses (Gen 42:9, 12). It is used literally in reference to the shameful or immoral exposure of the genitals. For example, steps were

---

1. It could, of course, also be a legal document to affirm, with witnesses, that her dowry had been returned. Permission to remarry is not required for the man since in a polygamous society the man could take a second wife whether or not he divorced his first one.

prohibited for altars that Israelites would build since their use could lead to the indecent and inappropriate exposure of the worshiper's private parts (Exod 20:26). "Nakedness" is used figuratively of Jerusalem's nakedness being exposed in the sense of Jerusalem's being disgraced and humiliated by exposure (Lam 1:8; Ezek 16:37).

The 1997 version of this chapter asserted, "The 'nakedness of a thing' certainly cannot mean adultery, since adultery was a capital offense, not a grounds for divorce."[2] Subsequently, however, I have come to change my mind. "Nakedness of a thing" cannot be interpreted loosely for anything a husband dislikes. A reasonable interpretation, adopted by the lexicons, is that the term should be taken broadly and figuratively of "improper behavior" (BDB) or "what is unseemly, unbecoming" (*HALOT*). This meaning is seen in Deut 23:15 where *'erwâ* is used of what is unbecoming.[3] I accept this view, so far as it goes. Certainly this term cannot refer to trivial matters: Even the Laws of Lipit-Ishtar condemn divorcing a wife because "she loses her attractiveness" or "becomes a paralytic" (§28). One would not expect a lower standard from Scripture.

But can we be more specific? The word "nakedness" (*'erwâ*) is used frequently in an idiom for sexual intercourse ("to uncover the nakedness of someone"; Lev 18:6, 7, 8, 9, 10, etc.), so sexual connotations are not implausible. Could it refer to adultery even though adultery was a capital offence? Yes. As Otto observes, no one could be executed without having two or three witnesses (Deut 17:6-7). A man could know that his wife committed adultery but not be able to prove it. In such a case, the man might instead choose to divorce her for this "something indecent."[4] Moreover, a man might, like Joseph in the NT (Matt. 1:19), choose not to press capital charges but choose divorce instead.

Bruce Wells[5] has made a good case that "nakedness of a thing" might include adultery as grounds for divorce. First, Jer 3:1-8 cites Deut 24:1-4 and applies it to the relationship between God and Israel. But God did not execute Israel for her adulteries. Instead, God sent her away into Assyrian exile with a "certificate of divorce" (Jer 3:8). Hence, Jeremiah understood Deut 24:1's "nakedness of a thing" to be applicable to cases of adultery. Second, Proverbs 6:32-35 says that adultery will destroy a man since the woman's husband will accept no ran-

---

2. Joe M. Sprinkle, "Old Testament Perspectives on Divorce and Remarriage," *JETS* 40.4 (1997): 531. Similarly, A. Phillips, *Ancient Israel's Criminal Law* (Oxford: Blackwell, 1970), 112.

3. Phillips, *Ancient Israel's Criminal Law*, 112.

4. E. Otto, "False Weights in the Scales of Biblical Justice? Different Views of Women from Patriarchal Hierarchy to Religious Equality in the Book of Deuteronomy," in *Gender and Law in the Hebrew Bible and the Ancient Near East* (JSOTSup 262; ed. Victor Matthews, et. al.; Sheffield: Sheffield Academic Press, 1998), 138.

5. Bruce Wells, "Adultery, its Punishment, and the Nature of Old Testament Law" (paper presented at the annual meeting of the Evangelical Theological Society, Orlando, FL, Nov. 1998); idem, "Sex, Lies, and Virginal Rape: The Slandered Bride and False Accusation in Deuteronomy," *JBL* 124.1 (2005): 63-72.

som (kōper) nor gift (šōḥad). This implies that the husband might accept money in lieu of the execution of his wife's lover. In biblical law, the option of ransom in lieu of execution is sometimes explicit (Exod 21:29-30; 1 Kgs 20:39), and arguably it was an option unless explicitly disallowed (Num 35:31). If so, the paramour might ransom his life with money, while the woman might save herself by forfeiting her dowry. Third, cuneiform laws and Egyptian laws allowed husbands the choice of having both wife and paramour executed or else neither.[6] If acceptance of ransom in place of execution were possible in cases of adultery, biblical law would be consistent with its ancient Near Eastern milieu, as it often is. Fourth, the false witness law of Deut 19:15-19 ("you will do to him just as he intended to do to his brother," v. 19) suggests that the man who falsely accuses his wife of adultery (Deut 22:13-21) should be executed. Instead he is fined and prohibited from ever divorcing her. If a typical outcome of adultery were divorce with forfeiture of the woman's dowry, then this man's penalty would be comparable. These arguments suggest a woman's adultery was punishable either by execution or divorce with loss of dowry; hence adultery would be a major reason for divorce.

The reason why "something indecent" is not specified is that the law is not attempting to define conditions under which a person may divorce—though it assumes that such conditions exist. Instead the law is primarily concerned about prohibiting remarriage after a divorce if the woman subsequently remarries.

Why God prohibits remarriage in such a circumstance has puzzled commentators, and a number of suggestions—none fully convincing—have been proposed as to the rationale. Was the law meant to discourage both divorce and remarriage?[7] Perhaps it discouraged divorce since there was a good chance that one would not be able later to remarry a wife one divorced, and it discouraged remarriage since a woman who so remarries is "defiled" (Deut 24:4), a term used elsewhere of adultery (Lev 18:20). Hence it is claimed that the text teaches the same thing that the NT teaches: that marriage after divorce is equivalent to adultery. Against this view it is hard to see how this law would hinder an angry husband from divorcing his wife. A possible future remarriage would not be on his mind. Moreover, it is only after marriage to another man that she is "defiled," and that defilement is mentioned in conjunction with her remarrying the first husband and is not necessarily in relationship to other men.[8] If remarriage is adultery, why is it not a capital offense or, at least, why is there no condemnatory aside? This view appears forced.

---

6. Law of Hammurabi §129; Middle Assyrian Laws A §§14-16, 22-22; Hittite Laws §198; David Lorton, "The Treatment of Criminals in Ancient Egypt through the New Kingdom," *JESHO* 20.1 (1977): 3-64, esp. pp. 14-15, 38-39.

7. J. C. Laney, "No Divorce & No Remarriage" in *Divorce and Remarriage* (ed. H. W. House; Downers Grove: InterVarsity, 1990), 21-25.

8. T. R. Edgar, Response to Laney, in *Divorce and Remarriage,* 64.

According to R. Yaron[9] the purpose of this regulation is to support and stabilize the second marriage from a destabilizing "love triangle" involving the woman and the two husbands. Such a love triangle is "defiling" since it is a kind of incest. To protect against such a contingency, all possibility of remarriage is prohibited. Pressler[10] argues similarly that this A-B-A pattern of marriage to the first husband, then to the second, then back to the first is disruptive of the boundaries that define a family. Instone-Brewer[11] suggests a second husband might have felt morally obligated to divorce a wife if the first husband wished to have her back. He cites as backdrop Middle Assyrian Laws A §36 and §45 that allowed a man who leaves the country and abandons his wife for as long as five years, or a man taken captive by enemies for two years, the right to reclaim his wife even if she remarries in his absence (compare David's reclaiming of Michal from Paltiel whom she married in David's absence, 2 Sam 3:13-16). These Assyrian laws are not exact analogies to Deut 24:1-4, however, since in neither does the first husband initiate a divorce. Moreover, in Deut 24:1-4 the continued prohibition of remarriage, even if the husband dies (v. 3b) and thus eliminates the triangle, appears difficult to reconcile with the approach of Yaron, Pressler, and Instone-Brewer.

G. Wenham[12] argues that the prohibition of remarriage draws on the logic of the laws of incest in Leviticus 18 and 20. According to this logic a woman's marriage, divorce, and remarriage makes the two men into brothers via the one-flesh principle of Gen 2:24, the wife in the OT sometimes being described as in some sense a "sister" of her husband. This interpretation, however, is highly speculative and contrary to common sense which suggests that a wife could be considered a "sister" in only the most figurative of ways.

R. Westbrook[13] holds that the primary purpose of this passage is economic. Comparative analysis of ancient Near Eastern and later Jewish marriage contracts suggests that if a man divorces his wife on the basis of a well-recognized violation of the marriage covenant, he could send her away without relinquishing her dowry. On the other hand, in the case of a purely subjective divorce—divorce because the husband just does not like his wife anymore—the husband would be obliged to return the woman's dowry to her. Westbrook argues that in the first case in v. 1 the woman was sent away without dowry because of the "something indecent" found in her. With the second marriage, however, she was sent away

9. R. Yaron, "The Restoration of Marriage," *JJS* 17 (1966): 1-11.

10. C. Pressler, *The View of Women found in the Deuteronomic Family Laws* (BZAW 216; Berlin: W. de Gruyter, 1993), 60-62.

11. D. Instone-Brewer, *Divorce and Remarriage in the Bible* (Grand Rapids: Eerdmans, 2002), 31-32.

12. G. J. Wenham, "The Restoration of Marriage Reconsidered," *JJS* 30 (1979): 36-40.

13. R. Westbrook, "The Prohibition on Restoration of Marriage in Deuteronomy 24:1-4," in *Studies in Bible 1986* (ScrHier 31; ed. Sara Japhet; Jerusalem: Magnes, 1986), 387-405.

just because the second husband "disliked" (Heb. *śāne'*) her, and so she would have taken her dowry with her. Westbrook thinks the law is preventing the man from taking advantage of the woman, remarrying her for her dowry. The point is not that the woman is unclean but that the first husband has asserted that she is unclean and has profited from that claim by confiscating her dowry. Hence having profited from declaring her unclean, he now wants to claim her to be "clean" for marriage so as to again claim her assets, the dowry of the second marriage. But Westbrook reads so much between the lines that it is hard to accept his view either. If the dowry money were so important, why is there no explicit mention of it?

Thus all the views are problematic, and I personally consider the matter unresolved. There are, however, several deductions that can be made from the law of Deut 24:1-4 at this point:

- We may deduce that the law of God under certain circumstances tolerated divorce.
- The expression "some indecency" implies that one could not divorce a wife for any reason whatsoever but that some "unseemly" breech of wifely duty must be involved. This limitation increased the wife's status and dignity in Israelite society.[14]
- Divorce required an official declaration of divorce, in this case in the form of a written document.[15]
- Remarriage after divorce was legally permitted for women with a certificate of divorce.
- A marriage can be dissolved, shown in the fact that return to a first husband after an intervening marriage was not allowed since the old marriage was dead.

---

14. E. Neufeld, *Ancient Hebrew Marriage Laws* (London: Longmans, Green, and Co., 1944), 176. Neufeld describes the requirement to find "something indecent" before divorcing a woman to be "a great advance in the attitude of the law to women" as compared with the notion that one could divorce a woman for any reason whatsoever. The requirement to find something indecent would "increase the assurance of the wife's position" and "limited the husband's power over her and in these ways added to her domestic and social dignity." This provision, by restricting male titles of disposal over women, bestows to women an elevated legal status. Similarly, Otto, "False Weights in the Scales of Biblical Justice?" 138.

15. Deut 24:1 states that a written document was in this case given, but as J. C. Laney observes ("No Divorce & No Remarriage," 23) this verse does not demand that a written certificate of divorce must be given. Nevertheless, in order for the divorced woman who remarries not to be subject to execution as an adulteress, she would have to have some official proof of divorce. An oral declaration before witnesses or judges could serve as an alternative public declaration, but our text suggests a divorce certificate was a common, if not the usual or even universal, method of doing this.

The last point is particularly interesting since it explicitly goes against the counsel of some Christians who argue that marriage cannot be dissolved and that therefore divorce is never valid. They suppose that divorced persons should under every circumstance return to their original spouses since their initial marital unions were indissoluble. God, on the other hand, commanded the Israelites never to return to a first marriage if a second one occurred in between. Marriages can become irreconcilably dissolved. And from this passage it is tempting to say: What God has put asunder, let no man join together.

2. *Deuteronomy 22:13-19, 28-29.* Deuteronomy 22 gives two other cases that assume the right to divorce. Verses 13-19 discuss the case of a man who falsely accuses a girl of not being a virgin at the time of her marriage to him. If the accusation turns out to be true, the law goes on to stipulate that the girl could be executed. But if "proof of the girl's virginity"[16] can be presented showing that she was a virgin at marriage, then not only does he pay an extremely high one hundred shekels to the father as a penalty but also the girl continues to be the man's wife. In addition, he forfeits all right of divorce.[17]

The formulation of this law clearly assumes that were this penalty not imposed an Israelite could divorce his wife.

Similarly, Deut 22:28-29 describes a case of what appears to be rape[18] in which the maiden is subsequently given to the offender as wife (after a fifty

---

16. G. Wenham, "*Bĕtûlâh,* 'A Girl of Marriageable Age,'" *VT* 22 (1972): 331-332, rejects the traditional view that the proof of the girl's virginity is the bloody bed-cloth resulting from the virgin's hymen being ruptured by her first intercourse with her husband. Instead Wenham believes that the woman has missed her period and shows no evidence of virginity (*bĕtûlîm,* which Wenham would rather translate "evidence of menstruation"). The newlywed husband charges that his wife is pregnant through adultery with another man during the betrothal period before marriage. One of Wenham's objections to the traditional view includes the unreliable character of evidence from a bloody marriage bedcloth since not all virgins bleed at their first intercourse. Either view fits into our application to the divorce question.

17. For a detailed exegesis of this passage with alternative interpretations see Wells, "Sex, Lies, and Virginal Rape," 41-72. He concludes that the husband who slanders his bride by accusing her of premarital infidelity is punished according to his intentions: with relatively minor humiliation if he simply wants to annul the marriage, but with severe additional punishments (heavy fines and obligations to provide for the woman's permanent support) if he sought the full measure punishment of the bride—i.e, her execution with the alternative of her saving her life through a ransom paid to him.

18. The usual interpretation of "seize" (*tāpaś*) is that the text implies that the man seizes the woman by force and rapes her. G. P. Hugenberger (*Marriage as Covenant: A Study of Biblical Law and Ethics Governing Marriage Developed from the Perspective of Malachi* [VTSup 52; Leiden: Brill, 1994], 255-260), on the other hand, argues that Deut 22:28-29 is a case of seduction rather than rape. One argument in favor of the seduction view is the expression, "they are found," which suggests that both the man and the woman are involved, whereas in the case of rape one would expect it to say "he is found." Another argument is that it seems unfair to force the woman to marry her rapist, whom

shekel marriage gift/fine to the father). In such a case the man "cannot divorce her as long as she lives." Again, were it not for the original offense, it would be assumed that he could divorce her.

III. CASES WHERE DIVORCE IS COMMANDED BY GOD

There are even passages where God requires divorce.

1. *Exodus 21:10-11.* Exod 21:10-11 involves the case of a slave-wife. If her husband takes a second wife, he must not reduce his support of the slave-wife.[19] He must give her the appropriate choice food and fine clothes. Also involved is a term that perhaps refers either to cosmetics or conjugal rights.[20] If he is unwilling to do these things, then "she is to go free, without payment of money."

The expression "she is to go free" can mean no less than formal divorce. The point being made is if this woman, sold as a slave-wife, is no longer to be a wife, she cannot be kept as a slave on the pretext that she is his wife. Instead she is to be given her freedom. The purpose of this law, then, was humanitarian: to assure

---

she may well hate. Against Hugenberger, however, it seems hard to reconcile this being only a case of seduction with the extremely high brideprice of fifty shekels, in contrast with Exod 22:16-17 where no such high price is set, and no forfeiture of the right of divorce is mentioned.

19. W. Kaiser (*Toward Old Testament Ethics* [Grand Rapids: Zondervan, 1983], 185) and Hugenberger, *Marriage as Covenant*, 113, 320-22) argue that Exod 21:10-11 does not refer to polygamy ("If he marries two wives at the same time") but rather to broken betrothal ("If he marries another woman instead of her"). This view, however, seems more an apologetic against polygamy in the law than dispassionate exegesis. The essence of the case of breach of contract has already been covered in Exod 21:8: "If she is displeasing in the eyes of her master who has not designated her" (Ketiv) or "If she is displeasing in the eyes of her master who designated her for himself" (Qere). With either reading (which I take to be an intentional double entendre) the woman purchased for marriage is rejected before the consummation of that marriage and must be redeemed which—given the binding and serious nature of ancient betrothals—is a kind of divorce. But v. 10 appears to have moved on to a case after the consummation of the marriage. In the case of a slave-wife purchased for purpose of marriage, one would not expect a long betrothal of the woman once "designated"—unless, of course, she has not reached puberty. This is one reason why I think v. 9 is more an adjuration that the slave-wife, despite her lack of dowry, be treated as a freeborn wife ("daughter[-in-law]," not "slave") after marriage rather than an adjuration to treat her as a daughter before marriage, though the language is applicable in both cases. If the traditional rendering of ʿōnātāh as "her conjugal rights" (v. 10) turns out to be correct (though it is admittedly uncertain), this would be fatal to this alternative view. More tellingly, the obligation of providing the woman with "food, clothes, and oil(?)" does not seem an appropriate stipulation for a breach of betrothal. Only complete release and freedom seems appropriate, as in v. 8.

20. The meaning of this last term, ʿōnātāh, is uncertain; cf. J. Sprinkle, *'The Book of the Covenant': A Literary Approach* (JSOTSup 174; Sheffield: Sheffield Academic Press, 1974), 53-54, for a discussion of the exegetical issues.

that a woman sold for the purpose of marriage would not be taken advantage of by being instead reduced to ordinary slavery.[21] Thus under these conditions and for the sake of the woman involved, God commanded the Israelite unwilling to give the woman full wifely privileges to divorce her without return of the original brideprice.

Ideally, of course, it would have been better for the man to fulfill his marital obligations and not divorce his wife. When Judah, portrayed as God's wife, gave God's food and clothes and sexual favors to idols (Ezek 16:16-18), God on analogy with Exod 21:10-11 (to which it alludes) had the same three grounds for divorcing Judah; but there he chose not to do so.[22] This law by no means condones the man's abandoning of his marital duties. But biblical laws are not utopian. In the real world, people often refuse to do the right thing. What this law does is indicate that where due to human sinfulness and stubbornness a man refuses to maintain his marriage, divorce can be prescribed as the lesser of evils.

2. *Deuteronomy 21:10-14.* Another law, Deut 21:10-14, also commands divorce. It describes a case where, after an Israelite victory over an enemy city, an Israelite man sees a beautiful foreign captive woman and is attracted to her. Rather than following the common practice among the nations in war—namely, killing the men and raping the women—this law states that an Israelite man can take this woman as a wife, but only after removing her beauty (she shaves her head and cuts her nails, making herself ugly) and providing a cooling-off period of one month in which the woman can mourn the loss of her family and the man can think over whether he really wants to marry this foreign woman with the stubbly hair. If he still wants her, he cannot simply violate her. He must marry her.

But if after marriage he is not pleased with her, the text says he cannot treat her as a slave and sell her to someone else. Instead, she has all the rights of a freeborn wife. If he no longer wants her as a wife, he must "let her go wherever she wishes" (*wĕšillaḥtāh lĕnapšāh*). The expression "let her go wherever she wishes" must imply "divorce her." The piel of *šlḥ* is commonly used for divorce (Deut 22:19, 29; 24:1, 3; Jer 3:1). So, if he is unwilling to treat her as a wife, God commands that he divorce her.

This command to divorce has a humanitarian purpose of preventing the sexual abuse of captive women. One who desires a beautiful captive woman cannot rape her and leave her. That man must marry her to have her. And if he no longer wants her as a wife, he cannot sell her as a slave, which morally would be tantamount to rape and abandonment. She must be treated with dignity as a full-fledged wife and be returned to freedom if not treated as a wife.

The text does not condone the man's choice of no longer accepting this woman as his wife. His reasons may well be morally unjustified. But if for what-

---

21. Sprinkle, '*The Book of the Covenant*', 72.
22. Instone-Brewer, *Divorce and Remarriage,* 47-48.

ever reasons he rejects her as wife, the text prescribes divorce and release as preferable to her continued subjugation.

3. *Genesis 21:8-14*. In Gen 21:8-14 God directs Abraham to divorce his slave-wife Hagar. The situation arises when after the birth of Isaac at the celebration of his weaning Sarah sees Ishmael "mocking" (v. 9).[23] Sarah then demands that Abraham drive away (*grš*) the slave-wife and her son (v. 10) lest her son inherit with Isaac. Abraham is grieved by the request. But God intervenes, telling Abraham: "Listen to [Sarah's] voice, for through Isaac your seed will be named" (v. 12). God goes on to promise divine blessing for Ishmael (v. 13). Abraham obeys: "he sent her away" (piel of *šlḥ*; v. 14).

The terms "to drive away" (piel of *grš*) and "to send away" (piel of *šlḥ*) can be used in a general sense, but the qal of *grš* is used of divorcées (Lev 21:7, 14; 22:13), and the piel of *šlḥ* often means "divorce" in the Hebrew Bible (as was noted above). Permanent divorce rather than temporary separation is clearly implied in this case.[24]

Sarah's motives were hardly entirely innocent. She was petty and selfishly jealous for her child's interests, a factor that partly explains why Abraham was so displeased with her request. But why then does God encourage Abraham to do what Sarah suggested? One reason is that the request corresponds with the broader purposes of God in the Abrahamic promises: "A family squabble becomes the occasion by which the sovereign purposes and programs of God are forwarded."[25]

But how could God ask Abraham to do evil if divorce is always a sin? The answer must be that divorce in this case either is not a sin or else is the lesser of two evils. When Hagar conceived, "her mistress was despised in her eyes" (16:4). This led to Sarah's treating her so harshly that Hagar fled into the desert (16:5-6). Read in the light of Exod 21:7-11 (treated above) and given both Sarah's and Hagar's attitudes, it would have been very difficult for Abraham to perform his husbandly responsibilities for both Sarah and Hagar at the same time. Since he could no longer treat Hagar as a wife, he would have been obligated by Exod 21:7-11 (had it been in effect) to let her go free. God's command in Genesis 21 is thus consistent with the later Mosaic law.

---

23. The LXX and some commentators (cf. RSV) take the piel of *ṣḥq* to mean innocent "playing," but something more sinister seems to be implied (cf. Gal 4:29 where Paul says Ishamel persecuted Isaac). There is also a word play, since the verb "mocking" (*mšḥq*) could be interpreted as a denominative, "acting the role of Isaac (*yṣḥq*)," the very thing Sarah feared.

24. G. Wenham, *Genesis 16-50* (WBC 2; Dallas: Word, 1994), 82, 84.

25. V. Hamilton, *The Book of Genesis: Chapters 18-50* (NICOT; Grand Rapids: Eerdmans, 1995), 81.

4. *Ezra 9-10.* Ezra 9-10 records how Ezra, the priest and scribe of God and an expert in the law, with help from Shecaniah, convinced many of the Jews of his day to divorce their foreign wives.

In Ezra 9:1-2 the leaders complain to Ezra that the people were violating the law against mixed marriages. These leaders had in mind such passages as Deut 23:3 where no Moabite or Ammonite was to enter the assembly of the LORD (this being, possibly, a leadership body) to the tenth generation and Deut 7:1-5 where Israel was commanded to have nothing to do with Canaanites. In 7:1-5 Hittites, Amorites, Canaanites, Perizzites, and Jebusites are not excluded from marriage but are devoted to destruction due to their abominations and the fact that they would lead Israel astray. Strictly speaking, the text in Ezra is careful not to iden-tify the "peoples of the land" (with whom Jewish men were marrying) with "Ca-naanites, Hittites, Perizzites, and Jebusites." In fact it is probable that these Ca-naanite groups condemned in the law no longer existed as separate entities by the time of Ezra.[26] In the view of these leaders, however, the abominations of the peoples of the land were like that of the Canaanites and would lead the Jewish people astray should intermarriage be allowed. Yet the Jews were marrying them in significant numbers.

Some interpreters question whether Ezra correctly understood and applied the law in this situation. After all, marriage with non-Canaanite foreigners was not prohibited. Ruth, a Moabitess, was accepted into Israel as a full wife and in-deed became an ancestress of David. Even the Canaanite Rahab was allowed to be assimilated into Israel (Josh 6:25; cf, Matt 1:5). Deuteronomy 21:10-14, as seen above, permits marriage to foreign, non-Canaanite wives taken in war. Al-though Moses married a Cushite wife (Num 12:1), God justified him, not his sis-ter and brother who opposed this marriage. Deuteronomy 23:7-8 explicitly states that one is not to despise an Egyptian and that in the third generation an Egyptian and an Edomite could become full citizens of Israel, which seems in conflict with Ezra 9:1's reference to Egyptians.

Only marriage with Canaanites was prohibited (Exod 34:11-16; Deut 7:1-5; 20:10-18). Even the patriarchs were aware of the danger of marriage with Ca-naanites (Genesis 24; 28:1-9). But if the "peoples of the land" are not, strictly speaking, Canaanites, then the prohibition, blurred by a thousand years of de-portations and assimilations that mingled various ethnic groups, had ceased to apply.

Were Ezra's actions racist in motive? The expression "holy seed" (9:2) sounds racist to some.

It could be argued that in the light of the NT Ezra's policy was un-biblical, contrary to both NT and OT morality. Compare 1 Cor 7:12-14 and 1 Pet 3:1-7 where Christians are exhorted to remain with unbelieving partners. Jesus teaches that those who divorce their wives to marry others "commit adultery" (Matt 19:3-

---

26. D. J. A. Clines, *Ezra, Nehemiah, Esther* (NCB; Grand Rapids: Eerdmans, 1984), 119; H. G. M. Williamson, *Ezra, Nehemiah* (WBC 16; Waco: Word, 1985), 130.

9). Moreover, Ezra's policy even seems to be contrary to the morality of the OT expressed in Mal 2:16, where the LORD shows disapproval of divorce.

In addition, it can be argued that forced divorces must have produced a terrible hardship on the women and children being in this way abandoned. It is also a violation of free will. They were unfairly bearing the punishment their husbands or fathers had deserved through arranging a wrongful marriage in the first place.

For these sorts of reasons, an interpreter might conclude that Ezra's actions are only partially justified. Our text describes what happens, one could say, but it does not prescribe what should have happened. In fact Ezra's actions were not altogether justified. Ezra and Shecaniah rightly saw that proliferation of mixed marriages would ultimately undermine the religious foundations of the Jewish community and eventually result in assimilation and the complete loss of Jewish identity. And yet Ezra's measures, while well-intended, were excessive. The racist attitudes that influenced the choice of action are regrettable. The application of the law of the Canaanite to "Egyptians" is an unjustified abuse of Scripture.[27]

In contrast, my view is that Ezra's actions were altogether justified.[28] Ezra was faced with a crisis situation. Though the actual number of mixed marriages was not extraordinarily large, the community was at a crossroads. If the trend towards mixed marriages continued to proliferate, it would have threatened the continued existence of the whole Jewish community. The only thing separating them from the world was their Jewish faith. Intermarriage would eventually destroy that distinction and hence the Jewish people as a distinct people of God. Under such pivotal conditions, severe measures were justified that would not be required had Israelite religion dominated society, nor does it apply in the later NT setting. It may have been an evil, but given the circumstances it was the lesser of evils.

Under these circumstances, the spirit of the law demanded an application broader than its original application. Hence Ezra was justified in applying a law limited to Canaanites to all pagan foreigners, even the Egyptians who were originally explicitly excluded.

Moreover, the divorce law of Deut 24:1-4 is applicable. At Ezra 10:3 Shecaniah appeals to acting "according to the law." He may have had Deut 24:1-4 in mind. If so, the openly pagan practices of the foreign wives seem to be that which constitutes the "unseemly thing" of Deut 24:1.

Many of these marriages may not have been innocent. The book of Malachi probably dates to around the mid-fifth century, near the time of Ezra. In Mal 2:16 God opposed certain divorces in which Jewish men divorced their Jewish wives without good cause in order to marry pagan ones. If this forms the backdrop of Ezra's actions, then what at first may seem to be innocent marriages to foreigners

---

27. This is the view of Williamson, *Ezra, Nehemiah*, 159-162.
28. Cf. W. Kaiser, *Hard Sayings of the OT* (Downers Grove: InterVarsity, 1988), 140-143, for a similar approach.

might not be so innocent after all since many of the men involved may have previously divorced their Jewish wives.[29]

As far as the hardships of divorce on the women and children are concerned, these should not be exaggerated. Divorced wives and children would be able to sustain themselves by returning to their extended families. They would presumably take with them their dowries as an economic base. Many could remarry. Indeed, Ezra does not command the assembly. He persuades them to adopt the covenant to put away wives. Their participation was not altogether involuntary. Only a handful opposed the community's decision.

It is reasonable to suppose that the investigations by Ezra's commission gave due process to those involved, which may have limited the number of divorces (only one hundred and thirteen are recorded). The commission to investigate matters could take into consideration whether the foreign wives were converts to Judaism. Where a wife was no threat to Judah's religious life, there would be no need of divorce. The matter may have been essentially religious, not racist.

What is the implication of this passage for the divorce question? It certainly underscores the spiritual harm of marriage to unbelievers—being "unequally yoked together," as Paul puts it (2 Cor 6:14). For very practical reasons such marriage is harmful. It sets a poor example for children. It limits what believers can do and may undermine their spiritual life. It puts strain on the marriage. Ezra's contemporary Nehemiah, though he does not explicitly demand divorce, asserted in the strongest terms—rebuking the men, calling curses down upon them, beating some and pulling out their hair, making them swear that they would do this no more—that entering into marriages with foreign women was wrong, as illustrated by the fact that such marriages had led Solomon into the sin of idolatry (Neh 13:23-27; cf. 1 Kings 11). Under the new covenant, although Paul encourages converts to remain with unbelieving spouses if they are already married in an attempt to convert them (1 Cor 7:10-14), for a believer deliberately to marry an unbeliever is at the very least a foolish thing to do.

But this part of Ezra implies something stronger. Ezra, commended by Scripture as an expert in the law of Moses (Ezra 7:6), expressing his understanding of the will of God from that law, adjures these Jews to divorce their wives. Now if Ezra was right, as I believe he was, then as tragic and painful as these divorces were, it was nonetheless God's will that they occurred. Might there not be similarly tragic circumstances where divorce is God's will today?

IV. CASES WHERE DIVORCE IS CONDEMNED BY GOD

We have already treated two cases in Deuteronomy 23 where divorce is prohibited: the case of a man who falsely accuses his wife of adultery and the case of a man who must marry the virgin he raped. There is, however, one other im-

---

29. J. G. McConville, *Ezra, Nehemiah, and Esther* (Philadelphia: Westminster, 1985), 70.

portant passage that condemns divorce: Mal 2:10-16. I will also treat another passage that is wrongly thought to condemn divorce: Lev 21:7, 14; 22:13.

1. *Malachi 2:10-16.* A text roughly contemporary with the fifth-century activities of Ezra and Nehemiah, Mal 2:10-16 condemns any Jew who divorces his Jewish wife and marries "the daughter of a foreign god" (v. 11)—that is, a foreign woman.[30] The fundamental offense is the violation of the marriage covenant: "you have broken faith with her . . . the wife of your marriage covenant" (v. 14).[31] There follows in the rendering of most translations the most comprehensive condemnation of divorce per se in the OT: "'I hate divorce,' says the LORD God of Israel" (v. 16; NIV; cf. NRSV, NASB).

But this rendering does not reflect the wording of the MT which lacks the first person pronoun. It could be justified on the basis of conjectural emendation, but there is no manuscript support for the first person pronoun.[32] It might also be justified on the basis of a paraphrased rendering of an awkward Hebrew expression. The verb *šānēʾ* ("hate") could be taken as a verbal adjective and rendered substantively: "'*He who hates* divorce,' says the LORD God of Israel." In that case God is obliquely referring to himself.[33] To smooth that out, one might paraphrase, "I hate divorce." But this still leaves an awkward syntax in the rest of the verse that makes this solution problematic.

The MT reads literally "*kî* [a particle with a wide variety of senses] he [third person, not first person] hated/hates (*šānēʾ*) sending away (*šallaḥ*), says the LORD." It is not grammatically impossible to render the verse as a command in favor of divorce. Hence some manuscripts of the LXX render, "If you hate your wife, put her away," which takes *šallaḥ* as an imperative rather than an infinitive. However, the LXX rendering hardly fits the context, where the divorcing of Jewish wives has already been condemned and where the second half of the verse again expresses a note of disapproval of these divorces.

If we keep the MT, I would like to render it something like "When he hates so as to divorce, says the LORD God of Israel, then he covers himself with lawlessness as with a garment."[34] The expression "he hates" may relate to the

---

30. Not a "goddess." Cf. Hugenberger, *Marriage as Covenant,* 34-36.

31. For a detailed defense that Malachi refers here to marriage as a covenant, see Hugenberger, *Marriage as Covenant,* 27-47.

32. C. J. Collins, "The (Intelligible) Masoretic Text of Malachi 2:16 or, How Does God feel about Divorce?" *Presb* 20.1 (1994): 36-40. The Qumran copy of this verse, though it varies from the MT, does not support the common emendation. Cf. R. Fuller, "Text Critical Problems in Malachi 2:10-16," *JBL* 110.1 (1991): 47-57. Fuller accepts the MT as the closest to the original.

33. Compare the HCSB margin, "The LORD God of Israel says that he hates divorce and the one who covers his garment with injustice."

34. Hugenberger (*Marriage as Covenant,* 72-76) independently comes to a very similar rendering: "If one hates and divorces." He takes *šallaḥ* to be the equivalent of a finite verb, perhaps as a bi-form of the infinitive absolute, whereas I take it to be a result clause.

divorce formula. In a fifth-century Jewish divorce certificate from Elephantine in Egypt, the divorce formula is "I hate my wife" or "I hate my husband" (see below). There is no need to emend Mal 2:16.

However one renders v. 16, what is condemned in context is not necessarily every divorce under every condition—as if the text is opposed to the actions of Ezra and Nehemiah[35]—but specifically the divorce of innocent Jewish wives simply because their husbands prefer foreign wives to their Jewish ones. There are thus two points of condemnation: (1) They are marrying pagan wives who will undermine Israel's religion and their covenant with God and (2) they are too cavalier in repudiating without cause the marriage covenant with their original Jewish wives.

We cannot conclude from this verse, however, that God opposes divorce in any and every circumstance. The context is a limited one. God is opposed to these particular divorces, not any and every divorce regardless of circumstance. Otherwise, one makes this text contradict the passages already considered above where divorce is prescribed.

2. *Leviticus 21:7,14; 22:13.* The Leviticus texts require that priests marry only virgins. They are prohibited from marrying prostitutes, divorced women, or even widows.

Does the prohibition of a priest marrying a divorcée constitute a stigmatization of divorced women as such?[36] Not unless by the same reasoning one is willing to stigmatize a widow.[37] The logic here probably pertains to matters of ceremonial uncleanness. In order to be qualified to perform their duties, priests had to be careful not to contract ceremonial uncleanness. Sexual intercourse produces ceremonial uncleanness (Leviticus 15). A woman previously married or sexually active would bring into a marriage with a priest an elevated degree of ceremonial uncleanness that could be transmitted to the priest by sexual contact, rendering him less fit for his duties. The fact that the divorcée is listed with the widow, who is in no way culpable for the death of her husband, proves that this prohibition does not necessarily stigmatize the divorcée as evil.

Nor is Scripture here condemning all second marriages. The widow Ruth marries Boaz as part of God's plan for her life (Ruth 4). A widow without child followed levirate marriage custom according to the law and remarried within the clan of her husband (Deut 25:5-10). In the NT Paul encourages younger widows to remarry and have children (1 Tim 4:14).

So even though OT priests were forbidden to marry widows, this prohibition related to their special calling that excluded them from many activities that were

---

35. Mentioned as an "unlikely" possibility by E. Good, annotations to Malachi 2:13-16, *New English Bible with the Apocrypha: Oxford Study Edition* (ed. S. Sandmel; New York: Oxford University, 1976), 1031. Hugenberger (*Marriage as Covenant,* 95-98) argues in detail against this view.

36. Laney, "No Divorce & No Remarriage," 25.

37. Edgar, Response to Heth, in *Divorce and Remarriage,* 64.

in no way immoral but which did convey ceremonial uncleanness. So, for example, in the same chapter where priests are prohibited from marrying prostitutes, divorced women, and widows, they were also forbidden from personally burying anyone other than members of their own immediate family because corpses convey ceremonial uncleanness (Lev 21:1-4). The high priest, moreover, could not even be in the same room as a corpse (Lev 21:11). Those prohibitions have nothing to do with morality—it is not morally wrong to bury the dead—but with avoiding ceremonial impurity that would make a priest unable to perform his priestly duties. Likewise the prohibition against priests marrying nonvirgins has to do with contracting ceremonial impurity, not morality.

. Interestingly this prohibition against priests marrying nonvirgins does not apply to prophets. Hosea was commanded by God to marry an immoral woman (Hos 1:1-9).[38] Would God command his prophet to sin? If not, then it must not have been inherently immoral to marry a woman who had previously been sexually active (whether divorced or widowed or promiscuous) even if such a marriage was not allowed to priests.

V. CASES WHERE GOD IS INVOLVED IN DIVORCE

In some places the language of divorce is used to describe the breach in God's covenant relationship with Israel.

1. *Isaiah 50:1.* "Thus says the LORD, 'Where is the certificate of divorce, by which I have sent your mother away? Or to whom of My creditors did I sell you? Behold, you were sold for your iniquities and for your transgressions your mother was sent away'" (Isa 50:1, NASB). The question here seems to be whether God gave Judah (whom he calls his audience's mother, the wife of Yahweh by covenant) a certificate of divorce so as to forsake her. As J. A. Motyer notes from Deut 24:1-4, divorce could set in train a series of events that would make reconciliation and reconstitution of a marriage (seemingly) impossible.[39] The implied answer to the question appears to be "No." It was true that Judah was to be punished, sold into slavery for her sins when she did not answer God's calling out to her through the prophets, and sent away into Babylonian exile. But she was given no certificate of divorce. God had not completely and finally dissolved the covenant relationship. And therefore there remained the possibility of redemption.

Here the language of the possibility of divorce is used, but no divorce between God and Judah actually takes place. The analogy does assume divorce as an established Israelite institution.

---

38. I accept the view, based on the syntax of Hos 1:2, that Gomer had been immoral before her relationship with Hosea and indeed had children by the immorality whom Hosea adopted when he married her. Cf. T. E. McComiskey, "Hosea" in *The Minor Prophets* (3 vol.; ed. T. E. McComiskey; Grand Rapids: Baker, 1992-1998), 1:15-16.

39. J. A. Motyer, *The Prophecy of Isaiah* (Downers Grove: InterVarsity, 1993), 397.

2. *Hosea 2:2.* "Plead with your mother, plead; for she is not my wife, and I am not her husband." It has been conjectured that this phrase, "She is not my wife and I am not her husband" is part of Israel's divorce formula (compare the formula in Sumerian divorce documents "You are not my wife"[40]). On the other hand, this is not the divorce formula of the Elephantine Papyri (see below). The consensus of exegesis is that Gomer (symbolizing Israel) is not in fact divorced at this point. But if the conjecture is correct, then by alluding to the divorce formula, God is threatening to make official what was *de facto* the case.[41]

3. *Jeremiah 3:1-8.* This text is the most interesting of those describing God using the language of divorce because it clearly portrays God as divorced. Verses 1-4 refer to the divorce law of Deuteronomy 24. Verses 6b-7 describe Israel's adultery. They assert that, although God thought she might return to him, she had not done so. She had gone up on every high hill and under every spreading tree and committed adultery there (with idols), and her "sister" Judah had seen her and was adversely influenced. Then comes v. 8: "I gave faithless Israel her certificate of divorce and sent her away because of her adulteries" (NIV). The text goes on to say that Judah had learned nothing from this experience and had not returned to God wholeheartedly.

In the first verse God's statement raises an issue of interpretation: Is it permissible for him to remarry Israel whom he has divorced, given the law in Deut 24:1-4? Israel is actually worse than the wife of Deuteronomy 24 who has merely married another man. Israel has lusted after many other gods. For this reason she has been "sent away" (the language of divorce)—that is, she has gone into exile and become joined to other gods. The analogy from divorce law suggests that Israel cannot come back to her husband (God). Yet despite the law, God calls upon Israel to return to him as her true husband (v. 14).

It is implied here that God is both divorced and polygamous—with sisters as wives, contrary to the incest laws. Now one can hardly blame God for the polygamy and the incest: God originally married only one woman (Israel), who subsequently split into two sisters (Israel and Judah).

But should we not blame God for the divorce? If we follow the policy in some circles, I suppose we would have to say that God is now disqualified for a leadership position in the Church by reason of his previous divorce with Israel. It makes no difference that God was entirely the innocent party in the divorce and that his justice demanded it. There is still an appearance of evil simply by virtue of being divorced.

But, you might say, it is absurd to suppose that God's divorce with Israel disqualifies him as leader in the Church. After all, he is God. And I agree. But does not this example show it to be equally absurd to adopt a rigid rule that per-

---

40. S.v. "Divorce," *EncJud* 123.
41. Similarly, Hugenberger, *Marriage as Covenant,* 233.

manently and unconditionally, regardless of all mitigating circumstances, excludes from church leadership everyone who has undergone a divorce?

I draw three conclusions from this analogy. (1) Divorce can be morally justified since it is not likely that God would portray himself doing a sinful act. Hence we may assume that initiating a divorce is not under all circumstances sinful. (2) Adultery could be grounds for divorce in Israel rather than always being a capital offense (as already discussed above). (3) Though I am admittedly pressing the analogy to its limits, this passage suggests that divorce does not automatically disqualify someone from leadership among God's people since to say that is to exclude God as leader of the Church.

VI. COVENANT AS RATIONALE FOR OT DIVORCE TEACHING

Some confusion on the indissolubility of marriages has come from a misunderstanding of the "one flesh" principle of Gen 2:24; 1 Cor 6:16. It is sometimes said that having sexual relations in and of itself constitutes marriage. But this is not true to the totality of biblical teaching of this topic. For example, Exod 22:16-17 is a case where a man seduces a virgin but marriage takes place if and only if the father consents to it. Otherwise, he pays a brideprice as a fine to the girl's family, but no marriage is considered to have occurred. In Gen 2:24 it is not "one-flesh" alone that defines the marriage relationship. Marriage also involves a man's leaving his father and mother and cleaving to his wife.[42] The leaving is not physical—culturally in Israel it was usually the wife who left her parents behind, not the husband—but psychological, consisting of transferring to his wife his first loyalty. And the cleaving refers to Israel's covenant with God, implying that a covenant relationship, not just sex, is involved.[43]

Marriage is explicitly called a covenant in the OT.[44] As we have seen above, Mal 2:14-15 refers to the "wife of your youth" as "your companion and your wife by covenant." This connection of marriage and covenant allows the prophets to push the analogy of God's relationship with Israel as resembling a marriage (cf. Hosea 1-3; Ezek 16:8). Likewise, an adulteress is said to be someone who has "left the partner of her youth and ignored the covenant she made before

---

42. Laney, "No Divorce & No Remarriage," 16-20.

43. William Heth ("Divorce but No Remarriage" in *Divorce and Remarriage,* 75) comments that *dābaq* ("cleave") is explicitly a covenant term when Israel is told to "cleave" to the LORD in affection and loyalty (Deut 10:20, 11:22, 13:4; 30:20, etc; cf. Hugenberger, *Marriage as Covenant,* 160).

44. Hugenberger (*Marriage as Covenant,* 4-8) notes that J. Milgrom (*Cult and Conscience: The Asham and the Priestly Doctrine of Repentance* [SJLA 18; Leiden: Brill, 1976], 134) denies that marriage in the OT was conceived as a covenant, in part because marriage lacked the "oath" used in covenants. However, Hugenberger (pp. 280-338) shows how various OT texts do portray marriage as a covenant. He also provides extrabiblical evidence that covenant treaties do not always include an oath and that some extrabiblical marriage contracts do include oaths (pp. 186-89).

God" (Prov 2:17). Given the parallelism, this covenant violation is probably in reference to the marriage covenant.[45]

The idea of marriage as a covenant is not unrelated to the marriage contract of that cultural setting. How early marriage contracts became the norm is not clear, but we have Jewish Aramaic marriage contracts and certificates of divorce from Elephantine, Egypt (fifth century B.C.).[46] Since nothing like this occurs in Egyptian documents, it is likely that these texts represent a uniquely Israelite practice.[47] There are also many extant marriage contracts known from Mesopotamia much earlier. Indeed, the Laws of Hammurabi declare that a marriage concluded without a formal contract is invalid (LH §128), though Middle Assyrian Laws consider a woman without a marriage contract to be married to a man if the two have lived together for two years (MAL A §36). Deuteronomy 24:1 speaks of a certificate of divorce, so legal documents pertaining to marriage were not unknown in OT times. It therefore seems probable that written marriage contracts were the norm among upper-class Israelites, though doubtlessly not as common among the poor.

One Elephantine marriage contract specifies the name of the wife-to-be, her father, and the groom; the brideprice (five shekels); and the groom's gifts to the bride (in this case, material goods worth more than 65 shekels). In addition, the contract specifies the inheritance rights of both partners in event of death without children (all goes to the surviving spouse) and the legal consequences of divorce. In this case if she divorces him (literally, "if she says, 'I hate my husband'"), he gets his brideprice back plus fifty percent interest and keeps his presents; but if he divorces her (literally, "If he says, 'I hate my wife'"), he forfeits the five-shekel brideprice. According to this contract, however, he gets his presents back; and she takes her personal belongings with her. The man also agrees to pay the first wife two hundred shekels as a penalty and to provide continued support should he take a second wife.

Elements of the marriage contract are mentioned in passing in the OT: the "brideprice" and the "dowry."[48] The ordinary custom was that the man acquiring a wife would pay a *mōhar* ("brideprice" or—if this sounds too much like the woman is being bought—"marriage gift") that would go to the father (Exod 22:16-17). The exact amount was subject to negotiation related to a family's standing in society.

This custom is assumed in OT laws. For instance, in the case of an unbetrothed woman who is given in marriage to a man who had first raped her, the

---

45. "Covenant of her God" might refer to the covenant at Sinai, but Hugenberger, *Marriage as Covenant,* 296-302, argues convincingly that marriage is in view.

46. *Aramaic Papyri of the Fifth Century B.C.* (ed. A. Cowley; Osnabrück: Zeller, 1967), 44-50, 54-56.

47. Hugenberger, *Marriage as Covenant,* 226, citing R. Yaron.

48. For a brief discussion of brideprice and dowry, see Sprinkle, `The Book of the Covenant', 156-59; for more detail, see R. Westbrook, "The Dowry" in *Property and the Family in Biblical Law* (JSOTSup 113; Sheffield: JSOT Press, 1991), 142-164.

brideprice is fifty shekels (Deut 22:28-29), the price of redeeming an adult male in his prime devoted to the sanctuary, which is probably the fair-market price of prime-male slaves (Lev 27:3).[49] Since wages for a day laborer was only between a half and one shekel per month in Old Babylonian times (and between three and twelve shekels per year by the fourth century B.C.),[50] the fifty-shekel brideprice appears extremely high—no doubt because it was also punishment for rape, as is the associated prohibition of divorcing the girl.

These are other examples: Abraham's servant gave costly gifts to Rebekah's brother Laban and his mother for the betrothal of Rebekah to Isaac (Gen 24:53b). Jacob, who lacked any money for a brideprice, worked for his uncle Laban for fourteen years in lieu of a brideprice for Leah and Rachel (Gen 29:18-20). David presented Saul with two hundred foreskins of Philistines as his marriage gift for Michal (1 Sam 18:24-27).

Once the brideprice was received, the woman was considered married, so that a virgin who is engaged who willingly had intercourse with another man could be executed as an adulteress (Deut 22:23-24); whereas, the penalty for the unbetrothed woman doing the same thing is possible marriage to her seducer, not death (Exod 22:16-17). Violation of the marriage covenant was considered a very serious matter.

In this cultural setting, if a man of modest social standing wanted to get married, he would have to save for quite a while before being able to afford a wife. The very poor would not be able to acquire a wife at all.

Having received the marriage gift, the father in turn would give some or all of that gift back to the woman as a "dowry" (šillûḥîm), literally "sending away [gifts]," a term mentioned only at 1 Kgs 9:16 and Mic 1:14. In 1 Kgs 9:16 the pharaoh at the time of Solomon conquered Gezer and presented it to Solomon as a dowry for his daughter who married Solomon. In Mic 1:14 the dowry given to the town of Moresheth Gath is metaphorical: Just as a bride receives a dowry before leaving her family for marriage, sometimes seeing them again, so her citizens were about to depart into exile, perhaps never to return. Though the word for "dowry" is not used, the concept is seen both in Gen 24:59, 61 where Rebekah's nurse and other female slaves who went with her were part of her dowry and also in Gen 29:24, 29 where Laban gave the slave girl Zilpah to Leah and the slave girl Bilhah to Rachel as dowries.

The dowry may be discussed indirectly in Gen 31:14-16. There Rachel and Leah complain that Laban their father "has sold us but he has used up what he paid for us" (NIV). This perhaps implies that Laban, in their view, gave them insufficient dowry but instead simply sold them off. The essence of their complaint

---

49. G. J. Wenham, "Leviticus 27:2-8 and the Price of Slaves," *ZAW* 90 (1978): 264-65.

50. For Old Babylonian wages, Wenham, *Genesis 16-50*, 235 (citing G. R. Driver and J. C. Miles, *The Babylonian Laws* [Oxford: Clarendon, 1952], 1:470-71); for neo-Babylonian wages cf. M. Dandamaev, *Slavery in Babylonia* (DeKalb: N. Illinois University Press, 1984), 115.

was that Laban had merely used the brideprice "money" (Jacob's fourteen years of service) without performing his paternal duty of returning most if not all of that value to the daughters as a dowry.[51] Laban, of course, would point to the gift of maidservants as their dowry. But the daughters perhaps felt that, in view of the benefit Laban had received from Jacob, they deserved more.[52]

The exact nature of the parting gift is clarified by reference to laws concerning brideprice and dowry in the Laws of Hammurabi and the Laws of Eshnunna (eigthteenth century)[53] and cuneiform marriage contracts at such places as Nuzi (thirteenth century).[54] From these sources, it is clear that the purpose of the dowry was to serve as security for the woman in case of a divorce. In other words, if the marriage were terminated, the woman would under ordinary circumstances take her dowry with her.[55] This would also serve to discourage divorce, since a considerable part of the family assets would be lost if one divorced his wife. Eventually, the dowry would become part of the family assets. At Nuzi this appears to be after the birth of the first child, though in Laws of Hammurabi §162 a husband cannot claim the wife's dowry after she dies since "it belongs to her children."

As a covenant or binding contract,[56] marriage gave certain responsibilities on the side of both parties. John Stott,[57] quoting Roger Beckwith, suggests that implicit in the marriage covenant would be the following: (1) marital love (including sexual privileges), (2) cohabitation as a single household (Gen 2:24), (3)

---

51. D. Garrett, *Rethinking Genesis* (Grand Rapids: Baker, 1991), 78; M. A. Morrison, "The Jacob and Laban Narrative in Light of Near Eastern Sources," *BA* (Sum. 1983): 160-61.

52. Wenham (*Genesis 16-50*, 273) thinks Rachel and Leah do not refer to dowries (since they both received handsome ones) but to the subsequent cheating of their husband by their father. I think they do refer to dowries, but their accusation has a fair degree of hyperbole.

53. R. Yaron, *The Laws of Eshunna* (Jerusalem: Magnes, 1969), 110-15.

54. K. Grosz, "Dowry and Brideprice at Nuzi," *Studies in the Civilization and Culture of Nuzi and the Hurrians* (ed. M. A. Morrison and D. I. Owen; Winona Lake: Eisenbrauns, 1981), 161-182.

55. LH §§138-40 states that the dowry must be returned to a woman before divorce. If she had no dowry, one mina (60 shekels) of silver was to be given as a divorce settlement (20 shekels for commoners). Laws of Ur-Nammu §11 indicates that if a woman committed adultery before the divorce, she forfeited the divorce settlement. Cf. also the MAL A §§37-38, where the father keeps the brideprice of the divorced woman, though Assyrian law seems to let the husband decide whether or not any of the dowry is returned.

56. Some modern Christian teachers say marriage is a covenant, not a contract. Although this language is a well-intended attempt to take a selfish *quid pro quo* attitude out of the marriage relationship, our discussion shows that the ancient Israelites would not have understood so sharp a distinction between contract and covenant as this slogan suggests. The same Heb. word is used for both: *běrît*. To them marriage was both.

57. J. Stott, *Divorce* (Downers Grove: InterVarsity, 1973), 9; idem, *Involvement: Social and Sexual Relationships in the Modern World* (Old Tappan, NJ: Revell, 1985), 178.

faithfulness to the marriage bed (Exod 20:14), (4) provision for the wife by the husband (Gen 30:30), and (5) obedience to the husband by the wife (Gen 3:16). The fact that the last of these seems strange to modern ears shows how profound the feminist revolution has been in western culture. And yet recalcitrance by either partner is surely a destructive character trait for marriage. To Beckwith's list of five responsibilities, I would add a sixth: Both partners, but especially the wife, must rear properly any children born to the union.

What happens if this analogy of marriage as a binding covenant is pressed? It is the nature of contracts or covenants that if one or the other party persistently fails to keep his or her end of the bargain, then the covenant can be declared null and void.

What about a marriage covenant? If any of the essential elements of a marriage covenant is persistently withheld or grossly violated, the party denied would have the moral and legal right to divorce. So, for instance, malicious cruelty (against the love obligation), flat refusal to grant sexual privileges (against the love and one-flesh principle), abandonment (against the one-household principle), adultery or even spiteful flirtatiousness (against the faithfulness principle), lack of support for the woman (against the obligation of husband to support her), and open and sustained defiance against the husband (recalcitrance) would all be legitimate grounds for divorce in OT times.

This concept of covenant and annulling of a covenant helps to explain the OT teaching on divorce. The "something indecent" of Deut 24:1-4 arguably fits into this matrix. The term then could be figurative for any wifely offense against the essence of the marriage covenant as defined above.[58] The cases of divorce marshaled above fits into this pattern: Yahweh divorced Israel for adultery (Jer 3:8); the slave-wife must be divorced because the husband was no longer willing to provide food and clothes and (possibly) "conjugal rights" (Exod 21:10-11); Abraham's divorce of Hagar is permissible for the same reason, to which might be added Hagar's (and Ishmael's) own unruliness (Gen 21:8-14); the woman captured in war must be divorced because the husband was no longer is willing to live together with her in sexual union (Deut 21:10-14); and wives in Ezra's day were divorced because of the improper rearing of children in the faith (Ezra 9-10).

Only two of these things (sexual immorality and abandonment) are (arguably) explicit grounds for divorce in the NT. If the covenant principle is behind these applications, however, we might be justified in concluding that the two examples in the NT are not intended to be exhaustive but that other grounds are likewise applicable under the new covenant.

If this analogy is valid, it would imply that women too would have the right to divorce on the basis of marriage-covenant violation. As was noted above, di-

---

58. Similarly Neufeld (*Marriage Laws,* 179) takes ʿ*erwat dābār* in Deut 24:1 to refer to "some gross indecency, some singular impropriety" which has nothing to do with her physical appearance, but refers to whatever the public or a popular law court would consider a shameful act for a wife.

vorces initiated by women were allowed for Jewish women at fifth-century Elephantine. Family laws are, after all, very incomplete in the OT. No systematic treatment on the topic of divorce is given in the OT, and references to the matter are only incidental. Hence, the lack of mention of a woman's right to divorce her husband may be accidental.

VII. THE NEW TESTAMENT PASSAGES

Can OT teaching about divorce be reconciled with the teaching of the NT?

I cannot improve on the conclusions of R. H. Stein,[59] who makes the following points: An analysis of Mark 10:2-12; Matt 5:31-32; 19:3-12; 1 Cor 7:10-11 indicates that Jesus in his statement about divorce had no exception clause, but said something like this: "Whoever divorces his wife and marries another commits adultery against her; and if she divorces her husband and marries another man, she commits adultery." His words, if taken literally, would disallow any and all divorce and remarriage. But Matthew provided inspired commentary on Jesus' words by adding the gloss "except for immorality (*porneia*)." Likewise Paul, in his application of Jesus' words, provides another exception in the case of desertion: "If the unbelieving partner leaves, let him leave; the brother or sister is not under bondage in such cases" (1 Cor 7:15). These modifications of Jesus' statement indicate that both Matthew and Paul understood Jesus' statement to be an instance of hyperbole, akin to Jesus' statement in Matt 5:29-30 (just before 5:31-32 about divorce) that one should pluck out his eye or cut off his hand if it causes him to sin—an obvious exaggeration. Hence Jesus' statement is not to be read as a legal maxim to cover every situation, but as a highly colorful condemnation of the extremely loose attitude to divorce among Jesus' opponents. This easygoing practice of divorce for any and every reason was in heart attitude the moral equivalent of adultery. One cannot simply trade in and barter spouses the way one can trade in an old automobile for a new or preowned car.[60] Even marrying an innocent divorced woman is like adultery (Luke 16:18b) in that it involves a man taking as wife a woman who ideally (had hardness of heart not produced violation of the original marriage covenant) should have remained with another man.

Note that Jesus does not deny the validity of OT teaching on marriage and divorce. Indeed, he denied that he came to "abolish the law" (Matt 5:17).[61] In-

---

59. R. H. Stein, "Is it Lawful for a Man to Divorce his Wife?" *JETS* 22.2 (1979): 115-121; idem, "Divorce," *DJG* 196-198.

60. D. E. Garland, "A Biblical View of Divorce," *RevExp* 84 (1987): 427.

61. D. Moo ("Law," *DJG,* 456) finds in the six antitheses between Jesus and the Law in Matthew 5 ("You have heard it said. . . . But I say unto you") only one "possible abrogation of the Law—that having to do with divorce and remarriage." The others give the true meaning of the commandments or deepen the commandments without contradicting them. But if our understanding is correct, he does not contradict this commandment either.

stead, he reinforces the OT's authority on this topic by pointing to Gen 2:24 as a corrective to his opponents' unbalanced understanding of Deut 24:1.

What about the contradiction between 1 Cor 7:12-15, where Paul directs believers not to divorce unbelievers, and Ezra 9-10, where Ezra encourages Jews to divorce pagans? Here the differences in circumstances are important, for Ezra was at a crisis point of salvation history so that more extreme measures were justified. Even so, the contradiction with 1 Corinthians 7 is not as blatant as it appears. Paul goes on to say, in v. 15, that if the unbelieving partner wishes to separate, then the believing partner is not "bound" in that case. In other words Paul, while discouraging divorce of one's unbelieving spouse, does not prohibit it if the unbeliever wishes to leave. Is his judgment, at least in part, an attempt to balance Jesus' teaching with that of Ezra?

Does the New Testament's injunction that the "elder" is to be the "husband of one wife" (1 Tim 3:2; Titus 1:6) not only condemn the practice of divorce and remarriage but also exclude all possibility of ministry by a divorced man? Taken literally, this verse would also exclude single people from ministry, which would exclude both Jesus and Paul—a dubious conclusion. But this expression, which reads literally, "of one woman a man," is listed among general character qualities such as "temperate, sensible, respectable, hospitable." In that context, "of one woman a man" could be understood as the character quality of being a "one-woman man"—that is, that he is a person who is faithful to his wife if married and, whether or not married, is not given to sexual impropriety towards women.[62] Taken this way, a divorced man and a single man alike could be a "one-woman man."

Although the above remarks are but a skeleton treatment of the NT texts on divorce, they are enough to show the plausibility of a line of interpretation which makes the NT teaching on divorce consistent with OT teaching. Since "all Scripture," including the OT, is both "inspired" as well as "profitable for teaching, for reproof, for correction, for training in righteousness; that the man of God may be adequate, equipped for every good work" (2 Tim 3:16-17 NASB), it is in principle preferable to accept a line of interpretation that affirms the continuing value of OT morality for teaching, reproof, correction, and training, as opposed to any view that sees the OT teaching as being completely supplanted by a higher, NT standard.[63]

---

62. Cf. R. L. Saucy, *The Church in God's Program* (Chicago: Moody, 1972), 146.

63. Contra Heth, "Divorce, but No Remarriage," 73-74. Heth finds three dispensations on this issue: creation/paradise in Genesis before the fall (no divorce), Mosaic (divorce and remarriage allowed as concession to sin and in contradiction with God's original intention for marriage), and NT (return to creation/paradise standard). But this interpretative grid which permeates all of Heth's analysis (cf. L. Richards' response in *Divorce and Remarriage*, 145-46) seems to me inconsistent with Paul's high view of the applicability of OT moral teaching in 2 Tim 3:16-17.

VIII. CONCLUSION

The OT view on divorce provides a realism to the discussion of divorce that is much needed in the Church where a neo-Marcionite approach to the OT has led many Christians to disregard its data. The OT shows that divorce, although always lamentable and ordinarily generating additional collateral sin and suffering, is tragically prudent under certain circumstances.

Without giving full weight to the OT teaching, readers of the NT's treatment of divorce are too quick to absolutize the words of Jesus, which in my view are no more to be taken literally than his command to pluck out your eye if it causes you to sin. Those, for example, who say divorce is absolutely forbidden and marriage is absolutely indissoluble in God's eyes must explain away the OT data where God's law clearly permits divorce (and implied possibility of remarriage) under some circumstances and even commands it in others.

Likewise, the OT data are a corrective to those who say that divorce is permissible in cases of adultery and abandonment only. I have heard of women who were hoping and praying that their husbands would commit adultery so that they would have biblical grounds for divorce. But in the OT divorce is allowed for "indecencies" (Deut 24:1), which appears to be a broad term for a whole variety of offenses against the marriage covenant including, but not limited to, adultery. When the notion of marriage as covenant is applied, it becomes clear that any behavior that violates the essence of the marriage covenant could serve as grounds for divorce: wife abuse, flat refusal of conjugal rights, lack of support of the wife financially, and so forth.

This approach derived from the OT is thus broader than idealized and absolutized interpretations of the NT passages divorced from their OT backdrop. It is an approach that is practical in the real, sin-cursed, fallen world in which we live where hardness of heart is often the rule rather than the exception. Indeed, laying more weight to this OT perspective would more often prevent the real moral evil of death and mayhem caused to some Christian women and their children who have continued to live with violent and abusive husbands because "the Bible" gave them no permission to divorce.

But despite the fact that the OT allowed divorce under certain conditions, it gives no license to irresponsible divorce. The OT assumes monogamous, lifelong marriage as the ideal in which marriage is a binding covenant relationship, just as Rom 7:3 says a married woman is bound to her husband as long as he lives. As in any case of breech of promise, violation of the marriage covenant involves sin. Thus, the OT gives no grounds for supposing that one could divorce his wife arbitrarily without any good reason and not incur guilt. There must be some "indecency" as a basis for justifying a divorce. Hence Malachi condemns as immoral the unprovoked divorce of innocent Jewish wives. As a general rule God opposes divorce since all divorce involves violation of covenant promises. The thrust of biblical teaching is that divorce should be sought only as a last resort, to be discouraged in all but the most aggravated of cases. Modern American culture, with its predilection for no-fault, easy divorce, has made a mistake akin to that of Jesus' opponents.

When scandalous and serious "indecencies" have occurred that destroy the essence of the marriage covenant, however, divorce (and the possibility of remarriage) is permitted. As in other covenants, if a marriage covenant is consistently violated by one partner, the covenant can be invalidated so that the other partner is no longer obligated morally or legally to keep his/her end of the bargain.

In fact, the OT indicates that under some circumstances divorce may be prescribed as the lesser of evils. It appears to have been God's will that Israelites at the time of Ezra divorce their foreign wives for their unlawful paganism. It was in accord with God's will for Abraham to divorce his slave wife Hagar. In Exod 21:10-11 and Deut 21:10-14 husbands who in their hardness of heart were unwilling to give their slave-wives full wifely privileges in accord with marriage-covenantal obligations were told to divorce them and let them go free, for that would be the lesser evil. And who are we to deny that God did the morally right thing in divorcing his adulterous and wayward wife Israel?

Finally, as far as leadership in the Church is concerned, Jeremiah 3 implies that undergoing divorce should not be considered an absolute and unconditional deterrent to leadership among God's people. For to argue otherwise would lead us to the absurd conclusion that God, who "divorced" Israel, must be disqualified from being head of the Church.

Chapter 10

THE LAW'S THEOLOGY OF SEX

Sexuality and sexual ethics form a very prominent theme in the Pentateuch. Its teachings show a frankness, a remarkable comprehensiveness, and an unprudish celebration of sex, balanced by reserve in language and acknowledgment of strict boundaries for sexual expression. Sex is considered by the Pentateuch to be a blessing from God to be enjoyed, and yet it has been marred by human sin and impurity. Thus the Pentateuch provides parameters guiding God's people how to enjoy the blessings of sex while avoiding practices that deviate from God's design and ultimately undermine the potential for blessing.

I. SEX AS DIVINE BLESSING

Procreation is viewed positively in the creation account as part of God's blessing to humankind: "God blessed them and said to them, 'Be fruitful and multiply'" (Gen 1:28). Thus the world, including sexuality, is pronounced "very good" (Gen 1:31). Only Eve (Heb. *hawwâ*; "producer of life"; Gen 3:20) through childbearing (Gen 3:16, 20) could "help" (Gen 2:18, 20) Adam fulfill the divine commission to "be fruitful and multiply" (Gen 1:28). Moreover, marriage is a cure for loneliness (Gen 2:18). Woman, coming from the man's rib/side (Gen 2:21), was made for man, of the same bone and flesh as man (Gen 2:23); she shares the divine image with man (Gen 1:27); and in marital union substantially restores the primordial "oneness" with him (Gen 2:24). Love between spouses and other family members is the expected norm (cf. Deut 28:54-56).

Sex is also central to the patriarchal narratives. God promised Abraham, Isaac, and Jacob countless "descendants (seed)" (Gen 13:16; 26:4; 28:14; 32:12); and Israel multiplied prolifically in Egypt (Exod 1:7; the censuses list over six hundred thousand adult males in the wilderness, Numbers 1-3, 26); thus God fulfilled his promise of making them numerous as the stars of heaven (Deut 1:10; cf. Gen 15:5; 22:17).

Childbearing, as opposed to barrenness and miscarriage, was considered God's blessing (Gen 1:28; Exod 23:26) and fulfillment of the patriarchal promise. Barrenness was thought a divine closing of the womb (Gen 16:2; 30:2) and was a social blemish and source of anguish for women (Gen 30:1). Every effort was made to conceive, including prayer (Gen 25:21) and the use of mandrakes, considered a fertility-herb (Gen 30:14-16). On the other hand, marriage remains a remedy for loneliness (as noted above) irrespective of whether children ensue, and the Song of Songs can celebrate erotic love without reference to the possibility of children. This suggests that in the OT love between the sexes can be a good thing in itself, not just as a means of bearing children.

Circumcision, the symbol of the Abrahamic covenant, was a reminder of the seed promise (Gen 17:7-14), and was associated with the covenant obligations to walk blamelessly before Yahweh (Gen 17:1), making the Israelite male sexual organ a symbol of dedication to God.

II. SEX AS SYMBOL OF UNCLEANNESS

The ideal sexuality of Eden changes with the fall. In place of openness comes shame; joy and love are marred by pain, lust, and domination (Gen 3:7, 16). This warping of sexuality is perhaps one reason why the Pentateuch makes sexual expressions a source of ceremonial uncleanness, whether by abnormal male discharges or even normal ejaculation during intercourse (Lev 15:1-18), or for women during their periods or any abnormal vaginal bleeding (Lev 15:19-30) and 40 or 80 days after the release of the bloody placenta in childbirth (Lev 12:1-8). These all, arguably, symbolize loss of potential life (blood) and vitality (the fatigue of men after ejaculation), and hence movement towards death in contrast with God who is associated with life.[1] The rule on childbirth additionally insured that the woman had time to heal before renewing sexual activity.

An Israelite had to refrain from sex before entering the presence of God, for sexual propriety was absolutely mandatory in worship (Exod 19:15; 20:26; 28:42-43). Thus, unlike certain ancient pagan cults in which sexual acts were performed, Israel totally separated sexuality from worship.

III. SEXUAL PRACTICES DEVIATING FROM GOD'S NORMS

Although sexuality is pronounced good at creation, not every sexual expression is considered good by God. Some expressions are inferior, and others are condemned as abominations. The following will catalog the various sub-standard sexual practices.

1. *Polygamy and slave wives.* Money in the form of a brideprice was paid both for a slave wife (Heb. *'āmâ*) and for a free wife, but only the free wife brought dowry into the marriage, giving her a higher social status. Mosaic law demands that slave wives be treated like freeborn daughters and given full wifely privileges (Exod 21:7-11).

Marriage to a slave wife was not necessarily a deviation from God's norms, but polygamy was. Typically, a man who had slave wives also had freeborn wives: Hagar was a slave wife to Abraham, who was also married to Sarah; and Zilpah and Bilhah were slave wives to Jacob, who also was married to Rachel and Leah (Gen 16; 30:3-8).

---

1. Jacob Milgrom, *Leviticus 1-16* (AB 3; New York: Doubleday, 1991), 766-768.

Although polygamy (but not polyandry) was allowed, Gen 2:24 ("For this reason a man will leave his father and mother and bond to his wife, and the two will become one flesh") assumes the ordinary pattern of marriage is that the "two" become one. Only the wealthy could afford to pay multiple brideprices, and even wealthy kings were adjured not to multiply wives to excess (Deut 17:17). Narratives describe, and laws regulate, the family strife polygamous marriages created (Sarah and Hagar [Gen 16:5; 21:10]; Rachel and Leah [Gen 29:30-33]; Hannah and Penniah [1 Samuel 1]; cf. Exod 21:10-11; Lev 18:18; Deut 21:15-16). That Lamech, the Bible's first polygamist, was also a murderer (Gen 4:23) of the linage of Cain hints at a negative evaluation of the practice.

Although polygamy seems alien to those in western cultures, the modern practice of serial marriages is, anthropologically speaking, akin to polygamy. Polygamy did serve a useful social function whenever the male population was decimated by war (cf. Isa 4:1).

2. *Divorce.* Divorce involves the abrogation of a marriage covenant and so can be considered a deviation from God's norms. See Chapter 9 of this book for a complete discussion of OT teachings about divorce and remarriage.

3. *Adultery.* The Decalogue unconditionally prohibits adultery (*nāʾap*) as a sin fundamentally incompatible with a covenant relationship with God (Exod 20:14; Deut 5:18). Mesopotamia also considered adultery a religious sin.[2] Adultery in the Pentateuch refers to intercourse with a woman who is married (Deut 22:22) or inchoately married (betrothed; Deut 22:23-27; similarly Laws of Ur-Nammu §6; Laws of Eshnunna §26). Adultery is condemned as a violation of the husband's prerogatives. The marital status of the woman is especially relevant, for a married man who had sex with a single woman would not be said to have committed *nāʾap* (but see below).

Both the adulterer and the adulteress were subject to capital punishment (Lev 20:10; Deut 22:24 [stoning]; contrast Laws of Ur-Nammu §7 that exonerates the man if the woman initiates the adultery). An exception is the case of an inchoately married slave girl (Lev 19:20-22) where the girl is not executed because she was not free to refuse and/or the betrothal was not fully established by money, but the man was required to offer a guilt/reparation offering to God (implying also restitution to the master) for his offense.

Execution for adultery depended upon several factors. The woman would escape culpability if she cried out indicating she was an unwilling participant (Deut 22:24; cf. Laws of Hammurabi §130, Middle Assyrian Laws A §12), and she is given the benefit of the doubt if she is violated where no one could hear her cries (Deut 22:25-27). The requirement of two or three witnesses for capital cases

---

2. S. Loewenstamm, "The Law of Adultery and the Law of Murder in Biblical and Cuneiform Law," *Comparative Studies in Biblical and Ancient Oriental Literatures* (AOAT 204; Kevelaer: Butzon & Bercker, 1980), 147-148.

(Deut 17:6-7) precluded most executions for sexual offenses. Even where adultery was provable in court, it is probable that a woman accused of adultery could avoid execution by forfeiting her dowry to her husband as a ransom for her life in conjunction with a divorce. A good case can be made that the usual outcome of adultery was, in fact, divorce rather than execution.[3]

Given the severity of the potential penalty, accusations of adultery were not to be made lightly. In Deut 22:13-21 a man at first intercourse defames his bride, claiming she was not a virgin. Contrary to the view of J. Tigay and C. Presler,[4] the accusation is not merely one of premarital sex since premarital sex was not a capital crime (see below). Rather she has committed adultery during the betrothal (inchoate marriage) period for which she could be stoned (Deut 22:20-21), though the real motive may be monetary: divorce with forfeiture of her dowry. A falsely accused bride could exonerate herself by producing "evidence of virginity" (bětûlîm), usually taken as the bloody bed cloth after the rupture of the woman's hymen during her first intercourse (Deut 22:14, 20), though G. Wenham,[5] noting that bleeding at first intercourse is an unreliable indicator of a woman's virginity and rejecting the view that bětûlîm denotes "virginity" per se, takes bětûlîm as a term of marriageability, contextually "evidence of nubility," that is, a menstrual cloth worn recently by the girl proving she was not pregnant before the consummation of the marriage. If the girl is exonerated, the man is flogged and pays an extremely large 100 shekel fine—the value of two prime adult male or three prime female slaves (Lev 27:3-4)—to the girl's father, twice the amount charged for rape (Deut 22:28-29). This "double" amount might be taken as a penalty for attempted theft of the woman's dowry.[6] Additionally, he is prohibited from ever divorcing her. If "evidence of virginity/nubility" is not found—presumably also collaborated with other evidence (cf. Deut 17:6; 19:15)—then punishment was death by stoning at the doorstep of her father's house (Deut 22:21) since she acted immorally while still under her father's jurisdiction. The purpose of this law was primarily to protect a woman against a husband's frivolous accusations of unfaithfulness (cf. Laws of Hammurabi §127 that prescribes flogging for defaming another's wife).

---

3. On divorce as an outcome for adultery, see Chapter 9 above.

4. Jeffrey Tigay, *Deuteronomy* (JPS Torah Commentary; Philadelphia: Jewish Publication Society, 1996), 477-478; Carolyn Pressler, "Sexual Violence and Deuteronomic Law," in *A Feminist Companion to Exodus to Deuteronomy* (ed. A. Brenner; FCB 6; Sheffield: Sheffield Academic Press, 1994), 105.

5. Gordon Wenham, "*Bětûlâh*, 'A Girl of Marriageable Age,'" *VT* 22 (1972): 326-348.

6. Concerning twofold restitution see my Chapter 6 on theft. According to Deut 19:19, the penalty for perjury is "you are to do to him as he meant to do to his brother." The thesis that the man's real goal in accusing his bride of infidelity is to obtain the woman's dowry explains why his false accusation is not a capital offense for the man on the principle of Deut 19:19 since he assumes she can ransom her life by forfeiting her dowry to him. This is discussed further in Chapter 9 on divorce.

The Pentateuch indicates adultery could also be punished by God through such things as plagues (Gen 12:17; 20:7). Numbers 5:11-31 gives a case where a husband, in a fit of jealousy, accuses his wife of adultery. To resolve the issue, the woman may undergo a self-curse ritual at the tabernacle with a priest. She drinks water mixed with tabernacle soil, the "waters of bitterness." The curse states that if she is innocent no harm will befall her, but if not, "let her thigh fall and her belly swell" (Num 5:20-22). The exact meaning of this curse is unclear, but thigh and belly probably refer to the woman's external and internal sexual organs, and so the curse may be sterility (Milgrom; cf. v. 28)[7] or the appearance of a false pregnancy (Brichto).[8] The result is that a guilty woman would live under the threat of divine curse, but an innocent woman would be exonerated by the oath-taking (similarly Laws of Hammurabi §131), and her husband precluded from further expressions of irrational jealousy.

4. *Seduction and rape.* Adulteresses and prostitutes seduce men (e.g., Tamar and Potiphar's wife; Gen 38:14-15; 39:7, 12), and Balaam apparently used Moabite/Midianite women's sexuality to seduce Israelites into idolatry and bring on them a curse (Num 31:15-18; cf. 25:1-2, 6-7). If a man seduced and deflowered an unbetrothed maiden—were she betrothed, it would be a adultery—then he was to pay the father the brideprice for maidens and marry her unless the father refused, in which case he still loses the brideprice (Exod 22:16-17 [MT 15-16]). Such a regulation served to discourage irresponsible premarital sexual behavior, for the man might suffer economic loss and still not get the girl he wanted, or he might end up with a wife he did not want. It also compensated the girl's family for economic loss since a deflowered maiden would command less brideprice.

This law may be compared with several ancient Near Eastern laws: The Sumerian Law Exercise Tablet §7'-8' perhaps prescribes "marriage" as penalty for deflowering a maiden, though if the identification of the culprit could not be proven, the suspect was still required to swear an oath. The Laws of Ur-Nammu §§6 and 8 state that deflowering a "virgin" wife was punishable by death, but deflowering a man's virgin slave resulted in a fine of five shekels. The Laws of Eshnunna §31 prescribes a fine of twenty shekels for a deflowering a slave girl.

Rape of an unbetrothed maiden carried a stronger penalty. In this case the guilty man had to pay a brideprice specified at fifty shekels, a very high price, that of a prime adult male slave (Lev 27:3)—a day laborer earned only about a shekel per month.[9] Furthermore, he is prohibited from ever divorcing her (Deut

---

7. Jacob Milgrom, *Numbers* (JPS Torah Commentary; Philadelphia: Jewish Publication Society, 1990), 41, 303.

8. H. C. Brichto, "The Case of the *sota* and a Reconsideration of Biblical Law," *HUCA* 46 (1975) 55-70.

9. For Old Babylonian period wages, see Gordon Wenham, *Genesis 16-50* (WBC; Dallas: Word, 1994), 235; for neo-Babylonian wages, cf. M. Dandamaev, *Slavery in Babylonia* (DeKalb: Northern Illinois University, 1984), 115.

22:28-29). That the father could veto the match is not stated, though may be assumed.

In the narratives, the rape (or possibly seduction) of Dinah (Gen 34:1-31) outrages her brothers. Shechem had "humiliated her" (Gen 34:2). The Hebrew *ʿānâ* ["humiliate, violate"] is used of enforced marriages, simple adultery, and rape (cf. Deut 21:14; 22:24, 29). He had also "treated her like a whore" (Gen 34:31) by indulging in sex without permission of her family. Nevertheless, Simeon and Levi's treacherous murder of Shechem's clan for a non-capital offense—profaning the sacred covenant rite of circumcision in the process—is even more reprehensible (cf. Gen 49:6-7 where Jacob curses this act of his sons).

Assyrian laws were harsh: Middle Assyrian Laws A §§55-56 says if someone rapes a man's unbetrothed maiden, the rapist's wife is to be raped, or else the rapist pays triple the value of the maiden (a triple brideprice) and is forced to marry her (cf. Deut 22:28-29), though as in Exod 22:16-17 [MT 15-16], the father can keep the money but refuse to give him the daughter. Middle Assyrian Laws A §9 states that if a man grabs a woman or kisses her, his finger could be cut off for the grab and his lip cut with blade of an ax for the kiss (cf. Deut 25:12 where a woman's hand could be amputated for grabbing a man's genitals).

5. *Incest*. The laws prohibit conjugal relations between close relatives, many of which were violated by the patriarchs who lived before these laws were given. Prohibitions include sex with a father's wife whether or not she is one's biological mother (Lev 18:7-8; 20:11; Deut 22:30 [MT 23:1]; 27:20; violated by Reuben who slept with Bilhah, Gen 35:22; 49:4; applied to Christians by Paul, 1 Cor 5:1), with sisters or stepsisters (Lev 18:9, 11; 20:17; Deut 27:22; violated by Abraham, Gen 20:12; cf. 2 Sam 13:7-14), with granddaughters (Lev 18:10), with paternal or maternal aunts (Lev 18:12-14; 20:19-20), with daughters- or sisters-in-law (Lev 18:15-16; 20:12, 21; violated by Judah with Tamar, Gen 38:11-19), with stepdaughters, step-granddaughters, and mothers-in-law (Lev 18:17; 20:14; Deut 27:23), and with two sisters at the same time (Lev 18:18; violated by Jacob, Gen 29:21-28). Exception is made for levirate marriage in which a man could (and is subject to shaming if he doe not) marry a childless, widowed sister-in-law to raise up an heir for the deceased (Deut 25:5-10; cf. Gen 38 and Ruth 3-4), a custom that served a social need to care for childless widows.

Strangely, there is no explicit statement about incest with one's daughter, though the narrative about Lot's daughters (Gen 19:31-38) clearly implies such Sodom-like behavior was reprehensible. Nor is there explicit prohibition of incest with a full sister. Leviticus 18 perhaps omits the most obvious cases to concentrate on those that are more doubtful. However, even the most obvious cases are covered in the general prohibition against sex with close relatives *(šĕʾēr bĕśārô*; Lev 18:6), an expression that is defined elsewhere (Lev 21:2) as including one's mother, sister, and daughter.[10]

---

10. Jacob Milgrom, *Leviticus 17-22* (AB 3A; New York: Doubleday, 2000), 1527.

Where incest was provable, it was a capital offense (Lev 20:11-12; 14); but other punishments are mentioned: being cursed (Deut 27:20-23), "bearing guilt" (Lev 20:19, perhaps explained by 20:20-21), dying childless (Lev 20:20-21), and being "cut off from one's people" (Lev 18:27-29; 20:17). This last expression probably denotes neither banishment nor human execution, but death and extir-pation of descendants by divine intervention or separation from the relatives in the afterlife. The afterlife view explains why some cases involved both execution and divine "cutting off" (Exod 31:14; Lev 20:2-3).[11] Threat of divine punishment in the case of incest was important since incest was, and is, a sin done in private and so is difficult to prosecute in court.

The Laws of Hammurabi (§154-158) condemn and prescribe punishment for incest with a daughter (banishment), a son's wife (water ordeal) or a son's be-trothed (thirty shekels to girl and marriage annulled), and one's mother (both burned). A son could be disinherited for being found in a deceased father's wife's lap. Hittite Laws §§189-198 allow marriage to a widowed stepmother and encourages marriage to the widow of one's deceased brother or son (levirate marriage). They allow marriage to the sister of a deceased wife. A man may sleep with two free sisters or a free daughter and her mother only if the women live in different geographic regions; if they are slaves it is allowed wherever. Brothers having sex with the same slave woman is allowed, as is brothers and/or their father sharing the same prostitute (contrast Amos 2:7b). But Hittite Laws prohibit a man having sex with his mother, daughter, son, stepdaughter, mother-in-law, or a sister-in-law while the brother is alive.

Inbreeding can produce genetic deformities in children, and this may be one reason for these prohibitions. However, such an explanation does not account for the prohibitions in the Bible against marrying biologically unrelated in-laws. Instead, the primary motivation appears to be to define and protect the integrity of the family, the basic building block of society, from socially destructive forces that promiscuousness within families would unleash, and to protect widows from the abuse of being reduced to concubinage for other male family members.

6. *Homosexual acts*.[12] Homosexual copulation was practiced with other sex-ual sins among the Canaanites (Lev 20:23). Mesopotamian laws leave homo-sexuality unregulated except Middle Assyrian Laws A §§19-20. These laws first condemn falsely accusing a man of being a "female" partner for homosexuals for which the penalty for the accuser included fifty blows with a rod, one month of servitude, and a fine. These laws go on to condemn sodomizing (raping?) another man, for which the penalty is to be sodomized, then castrated. Hittite Laws,

---

11. Milgrom *Leviticus 1-16*, 457-460 for a full discussion.

12. For a more detailed discussion of this topic, see R. A. J. Gagnon, *The Bible and Homosexual Practice: Texts and Hermeneutics* (Nashville: Abingdon, 2001). This chapter was written before I consulted this work, but Gagnon independently reaches conclusions very similar to my own.

while condemning bestiality, did not consider homosexual acts to be sins[13] except when it involved incest with one's own son (Hittite Laws §189). In contrast, Leviticus 18:22 unequivocally prohibits sex between men and Leviticus 20:13 states that it was punishable by death. That Canaanites practiced it does not sufficiently explain the prohibition. Rather, at issue in context (Lev 18:6-23) is the integrity of the family.

This regulation presupposes that in creating mankind as "male and female" and decreeing that sex is to occur "according to its kind" (Genesis 1), God established a design for sexuality, disruption of which is both a revolt against the divine word and a disruption of the social life.

Although the OT generally speaks of acts and had no vocabulary for sexual-orientation, this reasoning suggests biblical authors would consider homosexual orientation a form of sexuality gone awry. Sexuality's purpose from creation was to drive humans to heterosexual union, which in turn produces the blessing of procreation (Gen 1:27-28) in contrast with homosexual sterility. The prohibition against women wearing men's clothing and visa versa (Deut 22:5) supports this thesis. This law, akin to other rules of forbidden mixtures (Deut 22:9-11), prohibits the blurring of sexual identities.[14] Transvestite behavior confuses the God-intended differences between male and female (cf. Lev 18:22).

No mention is made in the OT of lesbian homoerotic behavior perhaps because it was less common. J. Milgrom[15] argues that the silence concerning lesbianism in the Holiness Code implies that it was not prohibited. He reasons that lesbianism was permitted because it involved no spilling of seed. However, this kind of argument from silence is by nature weak. Such logic might lead one to conclude that incest between a man and his own daughter was permitted because it is not explicitly prohibited, though that view is highly dubious (as argued above). Biblical law is by no means exhaustive in detail. The condemnation of female transvestite behavior in Deut 22:5a ("A woman is not to wear a man's garment") provides a better point of reference. It suggests that lesbian behavior would be categorized as an "unlawful mixture" that wrongly blurs the distinctive roles of male and female assigned to humanity at creation. In any case, the NT does directly condemn lesbian behavior (see Rom 1:26).

The Sodom and Gomorrah narrative (Genesis 19; cf. English word "sodomy") tells how the men of Sodom demanded homosexual relations with the two men (actually angels) who had come to visit Lot (Gen 19:5), but he dissuaded them and offered the mob his virgin daughters instead (Gen 19:8; contrast Lev 19:29's prohibition against prostituting one's daughter). Read in the light of the

---

13. Harry A. Hoffner, "Incest, Sodomy, and Bestiality in the Ancient Near East," *AOAT* 22 (1973): 81-90.

14. P. J. Harland, "Menswear and Womenswear: A Study of Deuteronomy 22:5," *ExpTim* 110.3 (Dec 1998): 73-75.

15. Jacob Milgrom. *Leviticus: A Book of Ritual and Ethics* (CC; Minneapolis: Fortress, 2004), 196-197.

Pentateuch's sex laws, the men of Sodom's request was doubly offensive: not only a homosexual act but also gang rape.

J. Boswell's influential work, *Christianity, Social Tolerance, and Homosexuality*,[16] argues that the Sodom narrative has been fundamentally misunderstood and that the essential sin at Sodom was a lack of hospitality (a virtue valued more then than now), not homosexuality. Lot violated custom at Sodom by entertaining foreign guests without permission of the city elders, and so they came, not wanting to "know" (Heb. *yāda*ʿ) the guests sexually, but to "know" who they were (similarly, Calvin's commentary). Elsewhere the sins of Sodom are listed as injustice, adultery, pride, indifference to the poor, and general wickedness (Isa 1:10; 3:9; Jer 23:14; Ezek 16:46-48), not homosexuality. Boswell claims that Jesus, who mentions Sodom in conjunction with the failure of cities to receive his disciples (Matt 10:14-15; Luke 10:10-12), also interpreted this narrative as a lack of hospitality and that this story is at most tangentially related to sexuality. It follows that those who show lack of hospitality towards homosexuals are the real sodomites.

Such a reconstruction is hardly sufficient, however. What the men of Sodom wanted to do to the angels was, to be sure, an act of inhospitality; but the homosexual element cannot easily be eliminated. That to "know, experience" someone (Heb. *yāda*ʿ) can be used as a euphemism for copulation is well-established elsewhere in the Bible (see Gen 4:1; 19:8; Num 31:17) and also in the immediate context where Lot offers to the men his two daughters "who have not known a man" (Gen 19:8). Lot's offering the men sexual gratification with his daughters as a substitute clearly indicates that the men wanted to "know" Lot's guests in the sexual sense. In Judges 19:22-26, a narrative clearly modeled after Genesis 19, the Benjaminites of Gibeah who want to "know" a Levite guest accepted as substitute his concubine whom they proceeded to rape and abuse all night. Boswell's reading of Genesis 19 involves wrenching it from its canonical context, ignoring that the Sodom narrative is woven into a literary work, the Pentateuch, which includes laws. In such a context, narratives were meant to be read by a person informed by these laws, and the laws condemn all homosexual intercourse.

As for the other passages, the sins of Sodom were not limited to homosexual acts. Genesis 18:20 and 19:13 speak of the "outcry" (*zaʿăqâ/ṣaʿăqâ*) of Sodom and Gomorrah, a term that can refer to the outcry of those who are oppressed; and this justifies the prophetic usage of Sodom as symbol against Judah, whose sins were not primarily homosexual. Nevertheless, scriptural repugnancy towards homosexual acts—that such an act was, as it were, the last straw before Sodom's destruction—contributed to Sodom's becoming proverbial for wickedness. According to Ezekiel 16:47-50, the richness of Sodom ("like a garden of the LORD," Gen 13:10) led to pride and callousness in committing "abominations"

---

16. John Boswell, *Christianity, Social Tolerance, and Homosexuality* (Chicago: U. of Chicago, 1980), 91-117.

and to injustice to the poor. The reference to "abominations" (Heb. *tô'ēbâ*) is probably an allusion to the "abomination" of homosexual sex in Lev 18:22 and 20:13. There was no need, contrary to biblical preference for euphemism in sexual matters, to spell out the homosexual element of Sodom's sins in subsequent texts: the name Sodom itself sufficed. Moreover, contrary to Boswell's thesis, no prophetic text that mentions Sodom specifies its sin as lack of hospitality to strangers. In Matthew 10:14-15 and Luke 10:10-12, associating Sodom with lack of hospitality is a possible inference, but an alternative is that failure to receive God's (angelic or apostolic) messengers brings judgment.[17] On the other hand, Jude 7 does refer to certain angels who similarly to Sodom and Gomorrah "likewise" acted immorally and "went after strange flesh" (*sarkos heteras*); thus, Jude compares pejoratively what is probably the angel-to-women unions of Genesis 6:1-4 with the male-to-male lusts at Sodom.

In terms of Christian ethics, it has been argued that the law of Leviticus 18:22, like the nearby prohibition against sex with a menstruating woman (Lev 18:19; see below), is ceremonial rather than moral and so is no longer binding on Christians under the new covenant.[18] Sometimes it is claimed that *tô'ēbâ* ("abomination") is specific to ceremonial matters. Jewish scholar J. Milgrom[19] also tries to severely limit the applicability of this commandment: only for Israel not the nations, only in the Holy Land not the rest of the world, and only for males not lesbians. Milgrom also passes on the suggestion of his former student, David Stewart, that the prohibition against homosexual acts may apply only to incestuous homosexual relationships.

Attempts to limit the scope of this command seem problematic, however, for several reasons. If the prohibition against homosexual sexual intercourse is written off as merely ceremonial, then the applicability of the incest and bestiality laws of Leviticus 18 can also be questioned on the same grounds. But those laws are more obviously moral in nature. Moreover, the OT ceremonial laws were binding on Israel but not the nations, who instead were only held responsible for more purely moral obligations (cf. Isaiah 13-23; Amos 1-2). And yet Leviticus 18:27 and 20:23 indicate that the failure to keep these laws of incest and homosexuality was the reason why God would drive the Canaanite nations from the land. This suggests that these laws were not merely ceremonial laws and not limited solely to Israel, but were moral obligations that applied to other peoples as well. J. Milgrom's attempt to limit the moral obligation of the homosexual command solely to the Holy Land and/or only to incestuous homoeroticism seems to be strained apologetics by someone intent on finding a legal loophole to

---

17. D. A. Carson, "Matthew," *The Expositor's Bible Commentary* (vol. 8; ed. Frank E. Gaebelein; Grand Rapids: Zondervan, 1984), 246.

18. Thomas M. Thurston, "Leviticus 18:22 & the Prohibition of Homosexual Acts," *Homophobia and the Judaeo-Christian Tradition* (ed. M. L. Stemmeler and J. M. Clark; Dallas: Monument, 1990), 13.

19. J. Milgrom, *Leviticus: A Book of Ritual and Ethics*, 196-197; *idem, Leviticus 17-22*, 1786-1790.

justify current homosexual practice. The prohibitions against homosexual intercourse are too broadly worded to support the incest interpretation, and limiting the applicability to the Holy Land seems inappropriate for the neighboring incest laws.

The LXX of Leviticus 20:13 provides a link to the NT that indicates that this a moral law still applicable for Christians and not a temporary ceremonial law. The LXX of Leviticus 20:13 states, "Whoever sleeps with a male in the manner of bedding (intercourse with) a woman [*meta arsenos koitēn gynaikos*], they have both committed an abomination." The second of Paul's words for homosexuals in 1 Corinthians 6:9, *arsenokoitai*, combines elements of the word "male" (*arsēn*) and the word "bed/intercourse" (*koitē*). This compound word, not found in any extant Greek text earlier than 1 Corinthians, is probably derived directly from the LXX of Leviticus 20:13. Thus, Paul's use of the term presupposes and reaffirms Leviticus' condemnation of homosexual acts for the Christian.[20]

Homosexual prostitutes (Heb. *qādēš, keleb*; Deut 23:17-18 [MT 18-19]) will be discussed below under prostitution.

7. Bestiality. A man or a woman who copulated with an animal was subject to execution along with the animal (Exod 22:19 [MT 18]; Lev 18:23; 20:15-16; Deut 27:21). This prohibition is based on the perception that such acts violated the divinely prescribed hierarchy and division between humankind in the image of God and the beasts and the rule that mating be "according to their kind" (Gen 1:24-31). Bestiality is an unlawful "confusion/mixture/perversion" (Heb. *tebel*, from *bālal* "to mix, tangle up") between the species (Lev 18:23). That no animal was a suitable "helper" for Adam implies a rejection of bestiality (Gen 2:18-22). Transgression of this rule results in punishment not only of the person, but also of the beast (similarly, a human-goring ox is "executed," Exod 21:28-30). For Israel such acts brought defilement that could, ultimately, expel the whole nation from the land (Lev 18:23-25).

Ancient Near Eastern secular law collections did not regulate bestiality, and ancient Near Eastern gods sometimes engaged in bestial acts: Innana in a Sumerian hymn copulates with horses; Babylonian Ishtar copulates with a bird, a lion, and a stallion in the Gilgamesh Epic (lines 48-56); Ugaritic Baal copulates with a heifer.[21] Whether these gods took the form of animals during these acts is unclear. The Hittites, like Israel, viewed both incest and bestiality as sins of impurity (Hittite Laws §§187-188, 199) that could provoke the gods to wrath, were punishable by death, and required sacrificial cleansing rituals,[22] though bestiality with horses and mules was only mildly punished: the offender could not approach the king or become a priest (Hittite Laws §200a).

---

20. Richard B. Hays, *The Moral Vision of the New Testament* (San Francisco: HarperSanFransisco, 1996), 382-383.

21. B. L. Eichler, "Bestiality," *IDBSup* 96-97.

22. Hoffner, "Incest, Sodomy, and Bestiality in the Ancient Near East," 85-86.

8. *Prostitution, harlotry*. The Hebrew verb *zānâ* and its related cogates (*zônâ* "harlot"; *zĕnûnîm, zĕnût* "harlotry") refer to all forms of illicit sex between a man and a woman, whether that be professional prostitution (Tamar; Gen 38:15), freely offered sex outside of marriage (Moabite women; Num 25:1), or marital unfaithfulness as in the metaphorical usage of Israel "whoring after" other gods though betrothed to Yahweh (Exod 34:15-16; Lev 20:5-6; Deut 31:16).

Harlotry is a term of contempt in the Pentateuch. Fathers are admonished not to give their daughters into prostitution since that fosters further debauchery in the land (Lev 19:29), but no penalty is stated for violation. Israelites were not to be either female or male prostitutes, and money acquired through prostitution could not be given to the sanctuary (Deut 23:17-18 [MT 18-19]). When Dinah was violated by Shechem, her brothers were outraged because their sister was "treated like a harlot" (Gen 34:31). Tamar was in threat of execution for becoming pregnant through harlotry (Gen 38:24), though not because she gave sex in exchange for money—only the daughters of priests were subject to legal sanction for simple harlotry (Lev 21:9; see below)—but because being in effect betrothed to Shelah, her illicit sex amounted to adultery.[23]

Does the Pentateuch refer to "sacred prostitution," that is, ritualized sexual intercourse at a temple? There was in Corinth the famous brothel of Aphrodite. At Babylon (and similarly at Cyprus) according to Herodotus (*Hist.* 1.199), though not confirmed by cuneiform sources, every woman was obligated to prostitute herself once at the temple of a goddess (Ishtar?). These practices have often been associated with Deut 23:17-18 [MT 18-19] that prohibits any female from being a *qĕdēšâ* ("holy one [fem.]"), seemingly defined in the next verse as a "prostitute" (*zônâ*), and any male from being a *qādēš* ("holy one [masc.]"), seemingly defined as the "dog" of the next verse, and prohibits their wages from being given to the sanctuary.

The exact meaning of "dog" (*keleb*) in this passage is uncertain. Though literal dogs are mentioned in association with prostitutes (1 Kgs 22:38) and halakhic exegesis took the verse as referring to money obtained by selling a literal dog (*m. Tem.* 6:3), it is probably a term for male prostitutes, not canines.[24] The reason for this metaphor is conjectural: Did he take the stance of a dog during sex? Is this some sort of title for a "faithful" cult official (a fourth-century B.C. inscription at Kition lists "dog" as a minor cult official[25])? Is it pejorative slang for male prostitutes? Did he service only men, or possibly women also? Moreover did the *qĕdēšâ* and the *qādēš* engage in sex with each other in a form of sympathetic magic to induce the gods to give fertility to the land? The present state of knowledge allows no certain answers to such questions.

---

23. Wenham, *Genesis 16-50*, 369.
24. Against the view of Elaine A. Goodfriend, "Could *Keleb* in Deuteronomy 23:19 Actually Refer to a Canine?" *Pomegranates & Golden Bells* (ed. David Wright, et al.; Winona Lake: Eisenbrauns, 1995), 381-397.
25. Elaine A. Goodfriend, "Prostitution (OT)," *ABD* 5:507.

That "sacred prostitution" was part of a rite to give fertility to the land has been widely speculated, but no solid evidence supports it. Recent scholarship radically questions whether the OT refers to sacred prostitution at all.[26] Tamar becomes a *qĕdēšâ* (Gen 38:21-22), but she seems to be an ordinary harlot, not a cult prostitute. The basic idea of "holiness" (root *qdš*) has to do with "separation," and could refer to the *qĕdēšâ*-harlot in the sense that prostitutes are separated or alienated from the larger community.[27] Hosea 4:14 speaks of men offering sacrifice with the *qĕdēšâ* (parallel with *zônâ*), which could be a part of sacred prostitution, but the offense could be that of bringing the ceremonially unclean (secular) prostitute into the sanctuary. On the other hand, in Kings the masculine *qādēš* is regularly mentioned in conjunction with cultic offenses (1 Kgs 14:23-24; 15:12; 2 Kgs 23:6-16), and so the idea of cultic prostitution cannot be altogether ruled out.

9. *Indecency*. In Genesis 9:20-27 Noah, having become drunk, lay down in his tent naked. Ham, his son, came in and "saw the nakedness" of his father; but his brothers Shem and Japheth instead took a garment on their shoulders and, walking "backwards," covered their father's nakedness. When Noah awoke to learn what had happened, he cursed Canaan, Ham's son, for the act. The brothers' exaggerated modesty indicates, at the very least, they considered Ham's behavior indecent and disrespectful to their father. Modesty, especially in worship, was important in the Pentateuch (cf. Exod 20:26). However, that the act resulted in a curse has suggested to many commentators that something more serious had occurred, perhaps homosexual incest. Leviticus 20:17 condemns siblings "looking on the nakedness" of each other in the context of incest.

10. *Intercourse with a menstruant*. Menstruation (the "way" of a woman, Gen 18:11) rendered a woman ceremonially unclean for seven days (Lev 15:19-20). If her husband touched her bed, he was unclean till evening, though if he "lay with her" he too is unclean seven days (Lev 15:21-24). Accordingly, couples were not to engage in sex during menstruation (Lev 18:19). Leviticus 20:18 adds that whoever "uncovers the nakedness" and "lays bare the flow" of a woman was subject to being "cut off from their people." The discrepancy between these rules is sometimes explained by source-critical scholarship as conflicting viewpoints between P and the harsher H, though it is preferable to say "lying with" in Leviticus 15:24 is either literal (not a euphemism for sex) or refers to inappropriate sex, the man not realizing the woman's period had begun, whereas Leviticus 20:18 describes a flagrant, deliberate act. In both cases the quality of penalty is similar: danger of sudden death from God for defiling the sanctuary (Lev 15:31) versus being "cut off" (Lev 20:18), probably another case of divine punishment.

---

26. Tigay, *Deuteronomy*, 480-481; K. van der Toorn, "Prostitution (Cultic)," *ABD* 5:510-512.

27. Goodfriend, "Could *Keleb* in Deuteronomy 23:19 Actually Refer to a Canine?" 385.

Menstruation was much less frequent before the twentieth century because women were more often pregnant, breast-fed longer (children through age three), and had a poorer diet that delayed onset of their first menses to age fourteen and brought on menopause around thirty-five to forty, as compared with ages twelve to fifty today.[28] Thus these rules were less a practical problem then than they would be today.

The rationale for these rules is probably unrelated to the fact that conception is less likely during menstruation (contra S. Melcher);[29] for if that where the reasoning, one would also expect laws prohibiting sex with a pregnant or a post-menopausal woman, but no such prohibitions are given.[30] Furthermore, we have the example of Abraham and Sarah portrayed positively by the narrator as engaging in sex in their old age. Nor does it relate primarily to a woman's discomfort with sex during her periods, though prohibiting sex during a woman's menstrual "infirmity" may imply a broader prohibition of unwanted advances during times of "weakness."[31] Primarily, however, this regulation has to do with the sacredness and symbolism of blood within priestly theology.[32] Menstrual bleeding represents movement towards death, an uninhabitable womb undergoing self destruction, whereas intercourse and its life-giving semen represents potential for life, and the mixture of these contradictory symbols is incongruous. Additionally, these rules teach that sexual self-control is a virtue and that men do not have absolute ownership of their wife's sexuality.

11. *Special restrictions for priests.* Priests were more restricted than the general population in marriage. They were not to marry widows, divorced women, or any who had been sexually immoral (Lev 21:7, 13-15). Such women, because of previous sexual activity, brought elevated levels of ceremonial impurity that would contaminate the priest, who in turn would profane the sanctuary and threaten the community with divine wrath (Lev 15:31). Similarly, a sexually loose daughter of a priest was subject to being "burned with fire" because her uncleanness defiled her father (Lev 21:9). "Burned with fire" may refer to cremation after execution (cf. Gen 38:24; Judg 15:6), though branding is another possible interpretation.[33]

12. *Other sexual matters.* After the death of Er, his brother Onan was expected to act as *levir* (cf. Deut 25:5-10) to Tamar, but Onan "corrupted [the seed]

---

28. Milgrom, *Leviticus 1-16*, 953.

29. Sarah J. Melcher, "The Holiness Code and Human Sexuality," *Biblical Ethics & Homosexuality* (ed. Robert L. Brawley; Louisville: Westminster John Knox, 1996), 99.

30. Milgrom, *Leviticus 17-22*, 1790.

31. Milgrom, *Leviticus 17-22*, 1755.

32. Milgrom, *Leviticus 1-16*, 941, *passim.*

33. David Lorton, "The Treatment of Criminals in Ancient Egypt through the New Kingdom," *JESHO* 20.1 (1977): 15, takes a similar "burning" in Egyptian law as "branding."

to the ground not giving seed/posterity to his brother." This displeased God, who caused him to die (Gen 38:9-10). The exact nature of Onan's sin is debated: Was the sexual act masturbation (cf. English "onanism") or *coitus interruptus* (withdrawal before ejaculation)? In either case, was it the sexual act that was sinful, or the breech of duty as *levir* to his sister-in-law? Does this text condemn birth control generally as a wasting of seed? Or was the spilling of seed a pagan fertility rite, giving semen to some deity (P. Grelot)?[34] The questions are more easily raised than answered.

Giving one's "seed" to the Ammonite god Molech (Lev 18:21; 20:2-4) is usually understood as human sacrifice (cf. 2 Kgs 23:10; Jer 32:35 where "sons and daughters" pass through "fire" to Molech), and yet in Leviticus 18 the expression is in a context of illicit copulations—incest and adultery before, homosexuality and bestiality after—where "seed" (*zera*ʿ) means "semen" (Lev 18:20), not "children." It has been taken as reference to mixed marriages with pagans, as sacred prostitution, or as dedication (rather than sacrifice) of children to a pagan deity.[35] But if *zera*ʿ means "semen," it could refer to some sort of ritual involving semen dedicated to this pagan god (compare Grelot's view of Onan above).

Deut 23:1-2 [MT 2-3] states that men with crushed testicles or severed penis, as well as the *mamzēr*, were ineligible to enter the "assembly of Yahweh." This assembly is perhaps a governing body,[36] certainly not the whole national throng. If so, ineligibility to serve in this assembly that represented the rule of God to the people politically is similar to the ineligibility of priests with genital or other defects to conduct services representing the people to God religiously (Lev 21:18-20). Both groups required elevated levels of holiness symbolized by being "without blemish." The term *mamzēr*, whose descendants are excluded to the tenth generation, is unclear in meaning. "Bastard" (KJV, modern Hebrew), "child of a prostitute" (LXX), "offspring of incest" (Talmud; cf. Deut 22:30 [23:1]), "half-breed" (*HALOT*) are guesses.

A woman who seized the genitals of a man fighting with her husband was subject to having her hand amputated (Deut 25:12). She could probably avoid the actual amputation of her hand by paying a ransom,[37] but the described penalty underscores the seriousness of this offense: It was not only a breech of modesty and an unfair "blow below the belt" but it was also an act that threatened the man's ability to father children.

IV. CONCLUSION

The Pentateuch sees sexuality as a good thing when lawfully expressed, but destructive if uncontrolled. Sexual gratification is not its highest value. Its theol-

---

34. P. Grelot, "La péché de 'Onan (Gn., XXXVIII,9)," *VT* 49 (1999): 143-155.

35. John Hartley, *Leviticus* (WBC 4; Dallas: Word, 1992), 333-337.

36. Tigay, *Deuteronomy*, 210.

37. See Chapter 5 above on the role of ransoming in biblical law.

ogy of sex is incompatible with certain modern theologies that see sexual activity as one's birthright. When homosexual sex is approved because it is a "right" to act according to one's desires, the default morality of sexual conduct becomes "whatever consenting adults decide to do together." The Pentateuch, in contrast, bases its view of sex on the creation ordinances and divine instruction. The Creator provides instructions by which Israelites would be set apart from the nations (Lev 18:1-5; 20:22-26) and would know how to express their sexuality within their covenant relationship with God. Failure to control one's sexual expression according to those standards was detrimental to that relationship, to the integrity of the family, to social identity and societal order, and to the individual's felicity.

Christians seeking moral guidance in sexual matters from the Pentateuch must make certain adjustments. There are culturally bound elements: slavery, arranged marriages, brideprice, ransoms, and polygamy to name a few. Some of the rules are specific to priests or to the OT ceremonial setting. Some applied to Israel as a nation that do not apply directly to the Church, such as the specific punishments for sexual offenses which were so severe, in part, because of the special holiness required of a people having God's tabernacle in their midst. Interpreters may differ as to which elements are culture-bound and which are universally applicable. Nonetheless, the several cases where the NT uses and applies these regulations—adultery (Rom 13:9; James 2:11), incest (1 Cor 5:1), and homosexual acts (1 Cor 6:9)—suggest that many abiding moral principles on sexual matters can and should be deduced by Christians from them, even from those regulations that are not clearly repeated in the NT.

Chapter 11

"JUST WAR" IN DEUTERONOMY 20 AND 2 KINGS 3

I. INTRODUCTION

Second Kings 3 contains many problems of interpretation.[1] Among these, I will deal here with two problems: the problem of Elisha's predictions and the problem of the "great wrath" that came upon Israel. Are Elisha's predictions intended by the narrator to be an instance of failed prophecy in that Elisha's prediction of unconditional victory did not come true? Secondly, what is the meaning of the "great wrath" that came upon Israel (v. 27)? Could the wrath be that of the god Chemosh, the national god of Moab? Some readers claim that this narrative affirms the existence and the power of a pagan god, even to the extent of his being able to thwart the power of Yahweh. In contrast, we will argue that the best reading of the text finds in it neither failed prophecy nor the genuine existence of a pagan god. Instead, the mystery of the wrath of 2 Kgs 3:27 is explained on the basis of the "just war" instructions in Deut 20:10-20 that Israel violated and for which Yahweh punished Israel.

II. VIEWS ON THE GREAT WRATH (2 KINGS 3:27)

The identification of the great "wrath" (*qeṣep*) that came upon Israel after Mesha's sacrifice of his son as a burnt offering (2 Kgs 3:27) has long been a crux of interpretation. Is the wrath human or divine? If human, which humans: Israel and/or their allies (Judah and Edom) or Moab? If divine, which divinity: Yahweh or Chemosh? Several views exist as to how to understand this verse.

1. *The view that qeṣep means "regret" on the part of the invaders.* One view is that the "wrath" is human on the part of the Israelites in the sense of some combination of "horror, dismay, apprehension, consternation, regret."[2] For

---

1. For a discussion of questions concerning the historicity of this narrative in comparison with the Mesha Inscription, see Joe M. Sprinkle, "2 Kings 3: History or Historical Fiction," *BBR* 9 (1999): 247-270.

2. J. A. Montgomery, *Kings* (ICC; Edinburgh: T. & T. Clark, 1951), 364, "The Israelites lost all heart in sight of the gruesome act." D. J. Wiseman, *1 & 2 Kings* (TDOT; Downers Grove: InterVarsity, 1993), 202, "Israel's horror and dismay made them withdraw." E. Merrill, *A Kingdom of Priests* (Grand Rapids: Baker, 1987), 351, "Appalled by the horror of this human sacrifice, Israel and Judah retreated, leaving Moab untaken."

example, the REB renders 3:27b, "There was such great consternation among the Israelites that they struck camp and returned to their own land." Josephus (*Ant.* 9.3.2) took a similar view: "And, when the [invading] kings saw [the son sacrificed], they felt pity for him in his necessity, and, being moved by a feeling of humanity and compassion, they raised the siege and returned, each to his home."[3]

The premise of this view is that the invaders or their leaders were so appalled, horrified, indignant, and/or saddened by the sight of a human sacrifice, they refused to engage the Moabites in battle any further. Based on examples from Ugarit[4] and Carthage, Margalit even argued that this psychological reaction was the primary purpose of the sacrifice, a kind of psychological warfare: "The word denotes the psychological breakdown or trauma that affected the Israelite forces when they beheld the sign of human sacrifice atop the walls of Kir-Hareseth . . . [resulting in] mass hysteria."[5]

G. R. Driver[6] makes the philological case that "great wrath" (*qeṣep gādôl*) of 3:27 should be rendered "great remorse" or similar. Driver observed that the Syriac cognates *qĕṣipa* and *qĕṣapa* mean "sad" and "sadness" respectively, and the cognate *qĕṣûpâ* means "sorrow" in Mishanic Hebrew. The translators of the LXX took a similar view, translating *qeṣep* with *metamelos* "repentance, regret." All this suggests that *qeṣep* here could mean "regret" rather than "wrath."

The philological basis for Driver's rendering, however, is not very substantial for Biblical Hebrew. The Mishnaic form *qĕṣûpâ* appears in the expression, "house of *qĕṣûpâ*" in parallel with "house of mourning," but may mean not "house of *sadness*" but "house of *death* [understood as a visitation of divine anger]."[7] The Syriac *qĕṣapa* also can mean "grudging" or "meanness"[8] more in accord with the usual sense of the Hebrew root. The sense "sadness, regret" is not otherwise attested in biblical Hebrew for *qeṣep*.

It is also psychologically a doubtful view. Since the Israelites had already numbed their consciences in the process of killing many Moabites while devastating their towns and fields in operations leading up to the besiegement of Kir Hareseth, it hardly seems probable that one more act of senseless killing would change their heart, especially when total victory lay within their grasp. Mesha's

F. W. Farrar, *The Second Book of Kings* (London: Hodder & Stroughton, 1903), 39, limits the wrath to Judah and Edom: "The armies of Judah and Edom were roused to anger by the unpitying spirit which Israel had displayed."

3. Flavius Josephus, *Jewish Antiquites Books IX-XI* (LCL; Cambridge, Mass.: Harvard U. Press, 1937), 25.

4. A. Herdner, "Nouveaux Textes Alphabetique de Ras Shamra," *Ugaritica* 7 (1978): 31-38.

5. B. Margalit "Why King Mesha of Moab Sacrificed his oldest Son," *BAR* 12, no. 6 (Nov./Dec. 1986): 62-63.

6. G. R. Driver, *JTS* 36 (1935) 293. Cited by *HALOT* 3:1124.

7. M. Jastrow, *A Dictionary of the Targumim, the Talmud Babli and Yerushalmi, and the Midrashic Literature* (Brooklyn: P. Shalom, 1967), 1404.

8. *Qĕṣapa* is defined as "jealousy, grudging, meanness; sadness, anxiety" in R. Payne Smith, *A Compendious Syriac Dictionary* (Oxford: Clarendon, 1903), 516.

act of human sacrifice would more likely bring joy to these hardened soldiers, joy that their enemies in desperation were killing each other so that victory must surely be near, just as the Moabites had rejoiced when they thought the confederate armies had fought with one another (2 Kgs 3:23).

Margalit's claim of an "age-old Canaanite tradition of sacral warfare" that used human sacrifice for its psychological effect[9] is not proven by the texts to which he points. Burns[10] observes that other scholars question whether the Ugaritic text cited by Margalit really refers to human sacrifice at all and that, even if it does, it and Carthaginian holocausts of noble children cited by Margalit are inadequate parallels since neither give evidence that the sacrifices took place in the view of the invading army. Burns goes on to observe that where Egyptian reliefs show what some scholars consider to be examples of child sacrifice on the walls, no "mass hysteria" broke out; but Pharaoh pressed his assault to successful completion.

Hence, this view that *qeṣep* means "regret" is questionable both philologically and psychologically.

2. *The view that qeṣep refers to the wrath of Moab against Israel.* A second view is that the wrath is that of the Moabites against the Israelites.[11] The idea is that upon seeing Mesha's sacrifice of his son, the Moabites were so angry that they fought harder against Israel and were able to force the invaders to withdraw.

An advantage of this view is that *qeṣep* can retain its ordinary meaning "anger, wrath." Against it, however, is that in its twenty-seven other occurrences in the Hebrew Bible, the noun *qeṣep* is used twenty-five times for divine wrath, but only twice for human wrath (Esther 1:18; Eccl 5:16).[12] This evidence suggests that in an ambiguous case, such as 2 Kgs 3:27, the probability is that the wrath is divine rather than human. This argument also applies to the first view, above.

Another disadvantage of this view is contextual. Verse 26 suggests that Mesha had exhausted his military options before the sacrifice of his son: "When the king of Moab saw that the battle was too strong for him [to withstand], he took seven hundred swordsmen to break through to the king of Edom, but they were unable to do so." In addition, taking the wrath as that of the Moabites fails to explain the apparent discrepancy between Elisha's positive sounding prophecy and the failure of the campaign against Kir Hareseth. With this reading, the story concludes with an awkward and unresolved tension that Elisha predicted military victories, but the story ends in a military defeat. A reading that does not require this internal inconsistency would be a more satisfying one.

---

9. Margalit, "Why King Mesha Sacrificed," 63.

10. J. B. Burns, "Why did the Besieging Army Withdraw? (II Reg 3,27)," *ZAW* 102.2 (1990): 188-190.

11. Mentioned as a possibility by D. J. Wiseman, though Wiseman wrongly attributes the view to Josephus (*1 & 2 Kings*, 202).

12. *HALOT* 3:1125; G. Sauer, "*qṣp*," *TLOT* 3:1156-1158. The verb is also usually, if less overwhelmingly, of deity rather than humans: twenty-two times to eleven times.

3. *The view that qeṣep refers to the wrath of Chemosh.* A third view holds
that the "wrath" of 2 Kgs 3:27 refers to that of the god of Moab, Chemosh.[13] In
other words, Chemosh, in response to the supreme sacrifice by Mesha of his own
son, acted on Moab's behalf to drive off the Israelites. G. H. Jones, for example,
states:

> On balance, it seems that the implication here is that the wrath of Chemosh
> drove out the Israelites. It was Chemosh that had control over the land of Moab,
> and the supposition behind the extreme act of sacrifice was that he could be
> roused to action. Although it is not explicitly stated, v. 27b contains the imme-
> diate result of the action taken in 27a; in other words, Chemosh caused a panic
> among the Israelites, cf. the *Mesha Inscription*, 'he . . . let me see my desire
> upon my adversaries' (1.4).[14]

Likewise, Cyrus Gordon writes:

> Mesha sacrificed to the national god Chemosh his crown prince on the town
> wall, where everyone could see it. The Israelites and their allies chose this mo-
> ment to withdraw to their homeland lest the rage of Chemosh should destroy
> them in his own territory. His pity, aroused by the extreme sacrifice of King
> Mesha, had brought "his great rage against Israel" (2 Kings 3:27). The incident
> shows that Israel still shared with her neighbors the national concept of divinity.
> Just as Yahwe had His land and people; Chemosh had his land and people."[15]

However, such an interpretation is contrary to the ideological framework
found generally throughout biblical narratives. Kaufmann correctly notes that in
biblical narratives,

> No god other than YHWH ever appears at work in Israel's early history or in the
> battles between Israel and its neighbors. YHWH fights against Israel's enemies,
> but no god ever appears as his living antagonist; when the Bible tells us of
> YHWH's battles with foreign gods, it is always idols that are meant.[16]

Typical of the Deuteronomistic History's attitude is the humiliation of the
god Dagon in 1 Samuel 5. There the idol first falls prostrate in the position of
worship before Yahweh (v. 3), and then falls with its head and hands broken off,
showing the idol to be lifeless and powerless. Accordingly, Brichto is right to
label as "absurd" any interpretation of a biblical narrative that would imply even

---

13. E.g., Burns, "Why did the Besieging Army Withdraw?" 187-94.

14. G. H. Jones, *1 & 2 Kings* (Vol. 2; NCB; Grand Rapids: Eerdmans, 1984), 400.

15. Cyrus H. Gordon, *The World of the Old Testament* (Garden City: Doubleday,
1958), 205.

16 Yehezkel Kaufmann, *The Religion of Israel* (tr. M. Greenberg; New York:
Schocken, 1972), 11.

an indirect "praise to the power of Moab's god Chemosh,"[17] for such an interpretation makes this text contradict the consistent ideology of biblical narratives.

In all the other cases where *qeṣep* refers to divine wrath, it is the wrath of Yahweh, not the wrath of another god. Indeed, P. Stern, quoting Y. Kaufmann, observes that the Hebrew Bible does not know of an alien god who expresses any emotion, much less wrath.[18] The biblical attitude is that foreign deities are inept if not non-existent. It follows that if the wrath here is divine, it is probably the wrath of Yahweh, not Chemosh.

4. *The view that qeṣep refers to the wrath of Yahweh.* The considerations above leads us to agree with those commentators who affirm that the wrath of 2 Kgs 3:27 is that of Yahweh.[19] But if it be the wrath of Yahweh, why did Yahweh's wrath break out against Israel? As Cogan/Tadmor observe, "A proper biblical explanation would have been to point to some wrongdoing on the part of Israel which then brought the divine wrath."[20] Does the text imply some sort of wrongdoing?

III. JUST WAR THEORY IN DEUTERONOMY 20

The key to understanding 1 Kings 3:27 is found in the laws of war in Deut 20:1-20.[21] That passage gives the most detailed rules of war of all the Pentateuch. It begins by adjuring the Israelites not to be afraid in battle, "for it is the YHWH your God who goes with you, to fight for you against your enemies, to give you victories" (v.4). In vv. 5-7 it gives exemptions from the army to those who had just built a new house but not dedicated it, who had just planted a vineyard but had not yet enjoyed its fruit, and to those who had become engaged for marriage but who had not yet consummated that marriage. This law thereby avoided the tragedy of persons losing their lives in war before enjoying these milestones of life. It thereby also excluded persons whose worldly distractions might hinder their wholehearted participation in battles. In addition, this regulation excluded

---

17. H. C. Brichto, *Toward a Grammar of Biblical Poetics* (New York: Oxford, 1992), 207.

18. P. Stern, "Of Kings and Moabites: History and Theology in 2 Kings 3 and the Mesha Inscription," *HUCA* 64 (1994): 11, quoting Y. Kaufmann, *From the Furnace of Biblical Invention* (Dvir; Tel Aviv, 1966/67), 206 [Hebrew].

19. C. F. Keil, *The Books of Kings* (Biblical Commentary; by C. F. Keil and F. Delitzsch; Grand Rapids: Eerdmans, 1978), 307; M. Cogan and H. Tadmor, *II Kings* (AB 11; ed. D. N. Freedman; New York: Doubleday, 1988), 51 and D. N. Freedman (editor's remark) cited on p. 52 n. 8; Brichto, *Biblical Poetics*, 201-209; Stern, "Of Kings and Moabites," 11-14.

20. Cogan and Tadmor, *II Kings*, 51-52.

21. Brichto recognizes the importance of Deuteronomy 20 for 2 Kings 3, but fails to draw out as fully as our discussion the extent of that connection (*Poetics*, 207-208).

cowards (v. 8) whose faintheartedness might become infectious to the other troops.

Deuteronomy 20:10-20 goes on to distinguish between two kinds of war: war against the Canaanite tribes within the promised land where "anything that breathes" was to be utterly destroyed (vv. 16-18) and war "very far from you, which are not of these nations nearby" (v. 15); that is, war outside of the promised land where the destruction was to be strictly limited (vv. 10-14).[22]

The rules of war in Canaan that operated at Jericho and the Israelite conquest according to the book of Joshua have received a great deal of attention. Insufficient attention, however, has been focused on the other rules for war, the rules that governed war outside the land of promise and that were meant to govern all war once Israel occupied the land. These rules have been called a primitive form of "just war theory."[23] We will argue that this is correct.

There are three main elements to the rules of war outside of the land, plus an exception:

1. *Offer terms of peace (Deut 20:10-11).* Deuteronomy 20:10-11 reads: "If you approach a city to fight against it, you are to offer her [terms of] peace. If she accepts your [terms of] peace and opens to you, all the people found in it may become your forced labor and serve you." A city about to be besieged by the Israelites was to be offered terms of peace before Israel was permitted to make war on it. If terms of peace were accepted, the population would become subservient to Israel, but all killing would be avoided.

Gottwald[24] finds it strange that the Deuteronomistic Historian in 1 Kgs 20:42 portrays an unnamed prophet as rebuking Ahab for sending away the Syrian king Ben-Hadad rather than executing him since, according to Deut 20:10-12, Ben-Hadad as a surrendering non-Canaanite ought to have been spared. There are at

---

22. M. Fishbane *Biblical Interpretation in Ancient Israel* (London: Oxford University Press, 1985), 199-200, and Alexander Rofé, "The Laws of Warfare in the Book of Deuteronomy," *JSOT* 32 (1985): 23-45, are among those that suppose a harsher law demanding complete annihilation of the Canaanites (vv. 16-18) has here been placed over an earlier, softer law that allowed those who surrendered to live (vv. 10-14), the two being joined together by a harmonizing deuteronomic link (v. 15). This supposedly limits the earlier, softer law to those outside the land. As it stands, however, the contrast between vv. 10-14 and 15-18 serves as a rhetorical device to express complexity. Nadette Stahl (*Law and Liminality in the Bible* [JSOTSup 202; Sheffield: Sheffield Academic Press, 1995], 15, 33, 41, 52, etc.) has shown that this rhetorical device is fairly common in legal and legal-like materials in the Bible, an observation that raises doubts about the propriety of positing sources where such contrasts occur. However such source critical speculations need not detain us since our interest here is in the final form of the text.

23. Susan Niditch, *War in the Hebrew Bible* (New York: Oxford University Press, 1993), 26; Roland H. Bainton, *Christian Attitudes towards War and Peace* (Nashville: Abingdon, 1960), 43.

24. Norman K. Gottwald, "'Holy War' in Deuteronomy: Analysis and Critique," *RevExp* 61 (1964): 299.

least two ways to resolve the tension between these two passages. One solution is to say that this is a special prophetic judgment against the Syrian king as an individual, just as Samuel gave Saul a special prophetic judgment against the Amalekites to put them under the ban (Heb. *ḥērem*), that is, to dedicate them to God for complete destruction. Though the Amalekites were non-Canaanites, they came to be placed under the ban on account of Amalek's attacking of Israel at the time of the exodus (1 Sam 15:2-3).

Another solution is offered by H. C. Brichto.[25] He argues that the essence of Ahab's offense, according to this unnamed prophet, was this: Ahab had willingly and rightly consulted prophetic oracles before the battle, but he did not consult God's oracle in the matter of disposing the enemy king. Thus he failed to acknowledge properly that the victory was owed to Yahweh. Instead Ahab sent Ben-Hadad away, a man whom Yahweh calls "my *ḥērem*." To be God's *ḥērem* means to be dedicated to God, typically for destruction but not always. For example *ḥērem* can refer to a person dedicated to the sanctuary as a slave (Lev 27:28-29).[26] The term here, according to Brichto, does not imply that Yahweh was a blood-thirsty deity demanding Ben-Hadad's death. It merely means that Ben-Hadad was "a man owed to me" (Brichto's translation). The point is that Ahab, by claiming Ben-Hadad as his own captive and claiming that the victory was his own rather than Yahweh's—not to mention his other sins—had brought himself under divine retribution. Taken this way, 1 Kgs 20:42 does not contradict Deut 20:10-11.

2. Limit killing to the fighting men, not the women, the children, or animals (Deut 20:12-14). In the event that no terms of peace can be agreed upon, Israel is allowed to kill men—there is no other option if war is to be permitted at all—but not the women, the children, or animals who are explicitly excluded. Note the stark contrast with the rules for war within Canaan. Not even all the men needed to be killed. Translators have arguably mistranslated v. 13. This verse is usually rendered something like, "you *shall/must* strike all the men with the edge of the sword," the imperatival use of the imperfect, whereas it is better understood as permissive use of the imperfect.[27] I translate this law in Deut 20:12-14 as follows to bring out this permissive use of the imperfect:

> (12) Now if it [the city] is unwilling to make peace with you, but instead makes war with you, then you are *permitted* to besiege it. (13) Now when YHWH your God gives it into your hand, then you *may* kill any of its men with the edge of the sword; (14) however, in the case of the women and the children, the live-

---

25. Brichto, *Poetics,* 174.

26. Cf. N. Lohfink, "*ḥērem,*" *TDOT* 5:199.

27. R. J. Williams, *Hebrew Syntax* (2nd ed.; Toronto: U. of Toronto Press, 1976), 31, §170, illustrates the category from Gen 2:16 ("from any tree of the garden you certainly *may eat*") and Gen 42:37 ("You *may kill* my two sons if I do not return him to you").

stock, and everything else that is in the city (all of its spoil), you are instead[28] to take these for yourself as booty, for you are *allowed* to enjoy [literally, "eat"] the spoil of your enemies whom YHWH your God will give to you.

Taken this way, the verse not only states that the Israelites must limit the killing to the men, which means the fighting men as Rofé[29] observed, but does not even require that all the fighting men be killed. The text simply allows the killing of men. In contrast, they are ordinarily not allowed to kill the women and the children who are non-combatants.

The general rule of exempting the women from the slaughter could be forfeited under specific conditions. For example, in Num 31:9-18 non-Canaanite, Midianite women who at the bidding of Balaam had seduced the Israelites into idolatry and immorality (an allusion to Numbers 25) were executed. By their actions they had ceased to be innocent non-combatants. Accordingly, Moses had the non-virgin women killed along with the men. More stringent rules of war were applied as retributive justice against those Midianite women responsible for the seduction of Israelites into sin that in turn had led Yahweh to send a plague against Israel.

Further protection for the women captured in war is given in Deut 21:10-14. Here, in contrast to the standard operating procedure in wars throughout history where the victors typically slaughter the men and rape the women at will, an Israelite man is prohibited from sexual contact with a captive woman unless he marries her. Even if he chooses to marry her, the woman must be allowed a month of mourning and adjustment before the marriage; and once married, given all the rights and privileges of a wife, including her full freedom in case the marriage fails rather than servitude as a slave. By ancient standards, this represents quite humane treatment of captive women

3. *Avoid unnecessary destruction (Deut 20:19-20).* Deuteronomy 20:19-20 states: "You are not to destroy its trees by swinging an ax against them . . . only the non-fruit trees you may destroy and cut down to construct siege-works." This is arguably an example of synecdoche, one example of a category of things to illustrate the whole category. Compare Rabbinic exegesis that took this rule as a broad principle of avoiding purposeless destruction of all sorts.[30] Why would one deliberately cut down the fruit trees in a land during war, especially trees such as

---

28. "Instead" represents Heb. *raq*, a particle that typically qualifies or restricts a previous statement. The first clause indicates what can be done to the "men/males" (v. 13), but the *raq* clause qualifies and clarifies that such a rule does not apply to women, children and spoil. Cf. B. Waltke and M. O'Connor, *IBHS*, 669-670, §39.3.5c.

29. Rofé, "Laws of Warfare," 29.

30. J. H. Tigay, *Deuteronomy* (JPS Torah Commentary; Philadelphia: Jewish Publication Society, 1996), 190, 380 n. 37. Citing Maimonides, Tigay states, "Rabbinic exegesis expanded this rule into a broad prohibition, not limited to wartime, of destroying anything useful, such as vessels, clothing, buildings, springs, or food."

olives that require many years before they produce fruit? It would in many cases simply be a malicious act intended to deprive the enemy of any future benefits that those trees might render. Thus the case of the "fruit trees" illustrates an underlying principle that condemns all cases of militarily unnecessary, malicious acts of destruction. [31]

It is sometimes supposed on the basis of Israel's rules of war against the Canaanites that those who composed the Hebrew Bible lacked the kind of sensitivity to the moral aspects of war that modern people have. However, Robert Good[32] has shown from narrative and prophetic texts that war was often interpreted as the expression of the legal verdict of Yahweh as judge, a metaphor that in turn assumes standards of fairness that necessarily govern the exercise of legal authority. The above discussion has attempted to show how Deuteronomy 20 and 21 specifically define such standards of fairness. The rules there advocate measures reminiscent of the Geneva Convention. As C. Wright[33] correctly observes, these laws provide for humane exemptions from combat; require negotiations and give preference to nonviolence; limit killing to combatants; put restraints on the treatment of captives, especially captive women; and reduce the ecological damage associated with war. Such elements have been part of just war moral theory in the West since the Middle Ages,[34] but they were anticipated by the rules for war in Deuteronomy.

4. *The Canaanite exception (Deut 20:15-18; 7:1-5).* The morally more difficult question is why these more humane rules were not applied to the Canaanites where instead total destruction of *ḥērem* was prescribed. The biblical answer—as unpalatable as it may seem—is essentially that the Canaanites deserved it. According to the Hebrew Bible, by virtue of the extreme sinfulness of Canaan that expressed itself in human sacrifice among other abominations (Lev 18:6-30) and the pervasive, negative influence they would have upon Israel if allowed to remain (Deut 20:18), God, having waited patiently for four hundred years for the sins of the Canaanites to reach critical mass so as to justify their eradication (Gen 15:16), commanded Joshua as an act of divine judgment to destroy them completely.

---

31. An example in modern times of a violation of this principle is when Saddam Hussein of Iraq set many of Kuwait's oil wells on fire as his army was being driven out of that country at the end of the Gulf War of 1990. This was arguably an act of pure maliciousness, his way of saying "If I cannot have Kuwait's oil, you cannot have it either."

32. R. Good, "Just War in Ancient Israel," *JBL* 104.3 (1985): 385-400.

33. Christopher J. H. Wright, *Deuteronomy* (NIBCOT; Peabody: Hendrickson, 1996), 230.

34. R. Bainton, *War and Peace*, 89-93. shows how Christian just war theory has its roots in St. Ambrose and St. Augustine in the fourth and fifth centuries A.D. Ambrose drew on Stoic philosophy, the OT, and the Roman pagan writer Cicero.

Even so, according to the book of Joshua, some exceptions were allowed: Rahab the harlot (Josh 7:22-25), the Gibeonites (Josh 9), and possibly the city of Shechem (Josh 8:30-35). Joshua 8:30-35 narrates a covenant renewal ceremony at Shechem despite the fact that Shechem was a major power during the Late Bronze Age as the fourteenth century B.C. El Amarna tablets from Egypt indicate. This suggested to J. Bright that Shechem was absorbed into Israel rather than being conquered, and so the covenant renewal ceremony was on the occasion of additional people being added to the covenant.[35]

Further exceptions are implied in the language used to describe the anticipated conquest. Israel was to "drive out" the Canaanites (Exod 23:28; 33:2; 34:11, 24; Num 33:52, 55; Deut 4:38; 7:22; 11:23; Josh 13:13, etc.). If Israel had continued to conduct war strictly and successfully according to the rules of *ḥerem*, including the total destruction of populations that those rules demanded, the natural reaction of the native Canaanite population would have been to flee for their lives. Thus the goal of *ḥerem* was not genocide, but ethnic cleansing in which most Canaanites would have survived as refugees outside the promise land.

The rules of *ḥerem* do not seem to be applied uniformly even in the book of Joshua. Sometimes *ḥerem* applied to everything that breathes, as well as goods (Joshua 6, Jericho). Sometimes it applied only to the people, but not the livestock and goods (Joshua 8, Ai; Joshua 11, Hazor; cf. Deut 2:34-35 and 3:6-7, Sihon and Og).[36] Such exceptions suggested to S. Kang that

> the Dtr theologians were more interested in the theological meaning of *ḥerem* than its actual practice. For them this utter destruction symbolizes a radical break or discontinuity with the old Canaanite society and the new covenant society of Israel.[37]

The same thing is true for Deuteronomy. By the time of the canonization of the Pentateuch in its final form, there was no longer any question of applying literally the rules of *ḥerem* to the Canaanites, for the Canaanites by the time of the late monarchy had been by and large assimilated into Israel. By that time the abiding value of the *ḥerem* regulations was solely ideological: It was a repudiation of the Canaanite lifestyle. Their actual implementation had ceased to be applicable.

N. Lohfink suggests that even within Deut 20:10-20 application of *ḥerem* had more exceptions than are usually recognized. He asserts that the requirement to offer terms of peace (Deut 20:10-11) "holds not only for the cities that are 'very far' (v. 15), but also for the cities that Yahweh has designated for Israel's inheritance (v. 16)" and that within the land complete destruction follows only

---

35. J. Bright, *A History of Israel* (2nd ed; Philadelphia: Westminster, 1972), 132.

36. Niditch, *War in the Hebrew Bible*, 34-35.

37. Sa-Moon Kang, *Divine War in the Old Testament and the Ancient Near East* (BZAW 177; Berlin: Walter de Gruyter, 1989), 143.

upon rejection of the terms of peace.[38] Taken this way, the rules for war in Deut 20:10-20 outline as follows:

1. Offer terms of Peace—all war, whether or not in Canaan (vv. 10-11)
2. If peace is rejected—
   - In the case of war with cities "far from you" limit the killing to men, not women, children, or livestock. (vv. 12-15)
   - In the case of war with the Canaanites tribes utterly destroy everything that breaths (vv. 16-18)
3. Do not cut down fruit trees—all war, in or out of Canaan (vv. 19-20)

According to this reading, ideally war was to be avoided even with the Canaanites so long as they were willing to accept Israel's terms of peace.

Lohfink's outline has in its favor that it makes logical sense out of what is otherwise a jumbled series of laws. Moreover, Josh 11:19-20 may lend support.[39]

> There was not a town that made peace with the Israelites, except the Hivites, the inhabitants of Gibeon; all were taken in battle. For it was the LORD's doing to harden their hearts so that they would come against Israel in battle, in order that they might be utterly destroyed, and might receive no mercy, but be exterminated, just as the LORD commanded Moses. (NRSV)

This text is often taken to mean that God hardened the hearts of the Canaanites in order to make sure that Israel obeyed the command utterly to destroy them rather than yielding to the temptation to show them mercy in violation of God's decree. However, it could be understood to mean that "mercy" in the sense of offering them terms of peace was in theory possible even to Canaanites had their hardness of heart—expressed by their ill-advised attacks on Israel—not rendered that impossible. Taken in this latter way, Joshua 11:19-20 supports Lohfink's view that Deut 20:10-11 applied to both Canaanites and non-Canaanites.

Lohfink's thesis is not without difficulty, however. As Fishbane[40] observes, it appears to be on the basis of this regulation (and deception) that the Gibeonites—who falsely claimed to be from a distant land (Josh 9:6)—were able to make a peace treaty with Israel and avoid the harsher measures of the war against the Canaanites. Although God tells Joshua to honor the treaty with the Gibeonites, the narratives make clear it was not the choice God intended. Deuteronomy 7:2 prohibits making a treaty with the Canaanites, but it is not obvious under Lohfink's view what distinction there is between offering terms of peace (Deut 20:10), which is permitted and offering a treaty which is not. Could

---

38. N. Lohfink, "ḥērem," TDOT 5:197.

39. Cf. E. Noort, "Das Kapitualationsangebot in Kriegsgestz DTN 20,10ff. und in den Kriegserzählungen," Studies in Deuteronomy (ed. F. G. Martínez, et al.; Leiden: Brill, 1994), 200.

40. Fishbane, Biblical Interpretation, 206.

it be that "terms of peace" involved repudiation of the Canaanite lifestyle
whereas "making a treaty" did not?

Whatever one makes of Lohfink's interesting proposal, it remains incorrect
to say that Deuteronomy looked upon the indiscriminate destruction of all enemies with moral indifference.

IV. 2 KINGS 3 IN THE LIGHT OF DEUTERONOMY 20

With these rules in mind, we now turn back to 2 Kings 3. Since Noth first
coined the term, the books of Joshua through Kings are often labeled by scholars
the Deuteronomistic History, a label that recognizes that this history is written in
the light of teachings found in Deuteronomy. 2 Kings 3 has no doubt drawn from
various sources. The statements about Jehoram's reign and the date of Mesha's
rebellion (2 Kgs 1:1; 3:1, 4) may go back to Israelite and Judean royal chronicles,
and the narrator has drawn on traditions about the prophets Elijah and Elisha as
well. But whatever his other sources, a good case can be made that the narrator
has put the story in its final form in the light not only of Deuteronomy generally
but also of the rules for war in Deuteronomy 20 in particular.

Since Moab is outside the land of Canaan, the rules in Deuteronomy 20 for
war outside the land rather than the rules of complete destruction for Canaanites
apply. Indeed, Deuteronomy specifically states, "Do not harass Moab, nor provoke them to war, for I will not give you any of their land as a possession" (Deut
2:9). Yet it appears that the Israelites violated every element of Deuteronomy
20's rules for war outside the land in the narrative of 2 Kings 3.

They certainly violated the rule concerning the cutting down of fruit trees
(2 Kgs 3:25; lit. "good trees"). Hobbs claims that Deuteronomy's prohibition of
cutting down the fruit trees did not apply in this case because Deut 20:19-20 "is
designed to ensure that the army's food supply would not be cut off."[41] Even if
Hobbs were right about the meaning of Deuteronomy 20, why would this prudent
advice not still apply? But if our analysis above is correct, Deut 20:19-20 is concerned with morality rather than practical prudence. Not only did Israel violate
the letter of the law in cutting down the fruit trees, they also violated the spirit of
that law in various maliciously vindictive measures: marring the fields with
stones so the Moabites would have more difficulty in engaging in agriculture in
the future and stopping up the springs/wells of water to make the Moabites dig
them again before they could once again live there.

They arguably violated the first two rules as well. The rules for war demand
the offering of terms of peace and limiting of the killing to the fighting men, but
2 Kgs 3:24 states, "Israel arose and struck Moab so that they fled before them,
wayyabbû bāh so as to smite Moab." The Heb. *wayyabbû bāh* (Qere
wayyakkû bāh "they struck her") is problematic and should probably be corrected
on the basis of the LXX's *eisēlthon eisporeuomenoi* to read *wayyābo'û bô'* (vav-

---

41. T. R. Hobbs, *2 Kings* (WBC 13; Waco: Word, 1985), 37.

consecutive plus infinitive absolute), "they kept on coming [so as to smite Moab]." In other words, there was no stopping of their slaughter of the Moabites. As they took each fortified city (v. 19), they did to its population what Mesha, according to his own inscription, had done in slaughtering all the inhabitants of Gad at Ataroth, and what Mesha did to the population of Nebo where he "slew all that was in it, seven thousand men and women, both natives and aliens and female slaves" (Mesha Inscription, lines 10-12, 14-17). There was no mercy for any Moabite regardless of age or gender nor any offer of terms of peace.

The lack of any offer of terms of peace is evident in the desperation of Mesha at Kir Hareseth. If reasonable terms of peace were offered, Mesha would certainly have accepted them. Instead Mesha appears to have been surrounded by a militarily superior enemy who gave him no terms of surrender and who had vindictively and maliciously destroyed his land, cut down his civilian population, and seemed bent on the utter destruction of both Mesha and all who were in his city. Supposing that he had nothing to lose, Mesha, as a last ditch attempt to provoke his god to pity, offered up to his god Chemosh the most valuable offering he could: He offered his firstborn son (2 Kgs 3:27; cf. Micah 6:7).

And Mesha's appeal was heard, our text implies, not by Chemosh whom biblical writers dismiss as powerless to hinder invading Israelites (Num 21:29) or even to prevent his own exile (Jer 48:7). Rather, it was heard by Yahweh whose wrath came upon Jehoram of Israel, a king whose wickedness in general was explicitly stated by the narrator in the introduction to this episode (2 Kgs 3:2, though less than Ahab's) and was underscored in the narrative by Elisha's dismissive remarks in vv. 13-14 ("What do we have to do with each other? Go to the prophets of your father and the prophets of your mother. . . . were it not that I respect King Jehoshaphat of Judah, I would not look at you or notice you"). Jehoram was a member of the house of Omri, a dynasty in whose evil the biblical narrator has taken special interest. Accordingly, the narrator was happy to show "that God would not permit an Omride to have undiluted victory."[42]

Jehoshaphat is not innocent in this matter either. To his credit, Jehoshaphat seeks a prophet of Yahweh (2 Kgs 3:11), just as he had in the parallel story of 1 Kgs 22:5-7, and the prophet Elisha acknowledges respect for Jehoshaphat (2 Kgs 3:14). The lack of explicit condemnation of Jehoshaphat elsewhere in the narrative indicates to Stern that in this narrative "Jehoshaphat the Good" as a character "shines."[43] But upon closer examination this is not true.

Later biblical traditions condemn Jehoshaphat. The Chronicler records the prophet Jehu's rebuke of the king: "You help the wicked and love those who hate YHWH and so bring wrath [qeṣep] upon yourself from YHWH" (2 Chr 19:2). The reference there is to Jehoshaphat's helping the wicked Ahab king of Israel in battle against the Arameans (2 Chronicles 18; cf. 1 Kings 22). A similar condemnation is implied here. After Jehoram's request for his assistance,

---

42. D. N. Freedman quoted by Cogan and Tadmor, *II Kings*, 52 n. 8.
43. Stern, "Of Kings and Moabites," 8, especially n. 23.

Jehoshaphat said, in language reminiscent of the words he used in the story of 2 Kings 22, "I will go up: me and you alike, my and your peoples alike, my and your horses alike" (2 Kgs 3:7; cf. 1 Kgs 22:4). Why does Jehoshaphat so readily cooperate with wicked Israelite kings? Moreover, if he were so good, why in 2 Kings 3 had Jehoshaphat not consulted with a prophet of Yahweh earlier, before he agreed to work with the king of the wicked northern kingdom? Rather than shining as a faultless character, Jehoshaphat receives poetic justice as a sinner: Jehoshaphat and his people went up with Jehoram "alike," and, accordingly, Jehoshaphat, his people, and Jehoram receive divine wrath "alike."

On this reasoning the divine "wrath" of 2 Kgs 3:27 affected Jehoshaphat (as part of "Israel") because of Jehoshaphat's excessive cooperation with wicked Israelite kings and his failure despite his piety to adhere strictly to Deuteronomic law. Moreover, the Jehoshaphat narratives initiates a theme in the books of Kings of Judah's failure to fulfill her vocation as true Israel. Judah instead identified herself with the northern kingdom in character and purpose, and that in turn leads to an identity of destiny, namely exile.[44]

In sum, Yahweh's wrath fell upon Israel in general because of Jehoram's own wickedness and that of the house of Omri and specifically because of Jehoram's (and Jehoshaphat's) violation of Deuteronomy 20's guidelines for a just war—allowing massacres and militarily unnecessary destruction.

V. ELISHA AND THE QUESTION OF FAILED PROPHECY

If the wrath that came upon Israel is to be interpreted as Yahweh's for violation of the rules of war in Deuteronomy 20, how does Elisha's prophecy fit in to the narrator's purposes? Did Elisha's prophecy fail?

De Vries holds that Elisha's prophecies are portrayed as fulfilled, but De Vries despaired of integrating that view with the conclusion of 2 Kgs 3:25b-27 and, therefore, hastily dismisses those verses as a secondary addition.[45] K. Koch, on the other hand, uses the same verses to argue that "the prophetic word did not always prevail"; for in this case, says Koch, Elisha's prophecy failed by being thwarted by a foreign god whose power was superior to that of Yahweh's on his own land.[46] But to suppose there to be a reference to the "wrath of Chemosh" by the biblical narrator is, as we have seen, absurd. In addition, the notion that the narrator's heroic figure of Elisha would be portrayed as giving false prophecy is similarly absurd. According to Deut 18:22, a prophet whose prophecies fail to come true would be considered a false prophet. But our narrator's Elisha is no false prophet.

---

44. J. G. McConville, "Narrative and Meaning in the Book of Kings," *Bib* 70 (1989): 40.

45. S. J. De Vries, *Prophet Against Prophet* (Grand Rapids: Eerdmans, 1978), 88 n. 48.

46. K. Koch, *The Prophets. Volume One: The Assyrian Period* (Philadelphia: Fortress, 1983), 29.

Indeed the narrator does portray Elisha's prophecies as coming true: The trenches dug by the Israelites did fill with water apart from rain (2 Kgs 3:17, 22). What is described is a ground-swell of subterranean waters that reached the Israelite side before it reached the Moabite side and thus filled the trenches from below.[47] Moreover, Israel did strike and destroy cities, cut down fruit trees, stop up wells, and ruin fields with stones just as Elisha predicted (3:19, 25). What Elisha did not say, however, was that after Israel fulfilled these prophecies, Yahweh would punish them for doing what Elisha predicted they would do.

Being judged for doing what the prophet predicted, however, seems unfair. Was not the prophet's prediction *de facto* a granting of permission for the kings to do the things predicted? Not necessarily. In 2 Kgs 8:12 Elisha predicted how Hazael would devastate Israel and weeps over the prospect. There prediction was no permission.

In addition 2 Kgs 8:10 is instructive in terms of prophetic ambiguity. Hazael had been sent to Elisha by the ill king Ben-Hadad of Aram to inquire of the prophet whether or not Ben-Hadad would recover. Elisha responds, "Go and say to him, 'You will indeed live (*lô ḥāyōh tiḥyê*)' but YHWH has revealed to me that he will die." There is a lack of clarity here in the Hebrew, reflected by the Qere that reads the homonym *loʾ* ("not, no") instead of *lô* ("to him"). Spoken verbally the same words could mean, "say *to him,* 'You will live'" (Ketiv), or "say: 'You will *not* live'" (Qere), or even "say: '*No.* You will live'" (Qere). The ambiguity here seems to be intentional.

Likewise the predictions of 2 Kgs 3:19 are grammatically ambiguous. The verbs are all either imperfects or "converted" perfects whose meaning could be either simple indicative (what "will" happen) or be imperatival (what "is to" happen) or permissive (what the authority is "granting permission" to allow to happen). Jehoram assumed that these verbs implied both prediction and license to do what was predicted. But Elisha meant only simple prediction.

The fact that Jehoram assumes the prophecy gave him license to do what was predicted indicates his lack of moral sensitivity. Were Jehoram interested in following Deuteronomic law, he would have immediately seen the conflict between what Elisha predicted and what the law allows.

Nor was Jehoshaphat innocent. As a godly king, he especially should have known at the time of the prophecy that the kind of war Jehoram was about to practice was contrary to Deuteronomy's laws and made some kind of protest. Deut 13:1-5 indicates that any prophet who explicitly encourages behavior contrary to God's commandments was to be condemned, so the fact that a prophet prophesies the wicked behavior was no excuse. But ironically it is not the godly Jehoshaphat, but the wicked Jehoram who recognized in the unfolding events the impending judgment of Yahweh: "Alas, for Yahweh has called these three kings to give them into the hand of Moab" (2 Kgs 3:10). Jehoshaphat's failure to ques-

---

47. Brichto, *Biblical Poetics*, 206.

tion Elisha concerning the atrocities he predicted resulted in Jehoshaphat too experiencing God's "wrath" along with Jehoram.

But what about the failure to take Kir Hareseth? Is that not a failure of prophecy? Related to the answer to this question is determining the nature of the "wrath" that came upon Israel. It is not stated how this wrath specifically manifested itself, but there is good reason to suppose the narrator has a plague in mind. In Num 16:46 (MT 17:11) in conjunction with Korah's rebellion, God's wrath (*qeṣep*) took the form of a plague against his people. In 2 Samuel 24, though the Hebrew root *qsp* is not used, God's anger against David's census manifests itself as a plague. In the close quarters and unsanitary conditions of a besiegement, outbreak of rapidly spreading disease would surely have been rather common in ancient times. That was probably the act of God what forced Sennacherib to break his besiegement of Hezekiah's Jerusalem in 701 B.C. Isaiah 37:36 (= 2 Kgs 19:35) describes the devastation of one hundred eighty-five thousand of Sennacherib's army as an act of God, but earlier Isa 10:18 describes this same event in terms of a sick man wasting away. This suggests that this act of God in fact worked though the mechanism of a plague. Moreover, in biblical times any outbreak of disease might well be attributed to deity.[48] The outbreak of plague—described as "wrath [from deity]"—is what leads to the conclusion of our story, namely Israel's abandoning of the military operation despite having the upper hand. A reader trying to do gap-filling might read between the lines and speculate that the plague led first to introspection and then to a sense of guilt and ultimately to a sense of dread as soldiers drew the conclusion that this plague must be a judgment from God for the atrocities they had recently committed.[49]

If the "wrath" of 2 Kgs 3:27 is understood as a plague, then there would be no failure of prophecy. The Israelites were successful in all battles against Moab as predicted but then were thwarted not by man but by an act of God.[50]

---

48. J. Liver, "The Wars of Mesha, King of Moab," *PEQ* 99 [1967]: 30, defends the "plague" interpretation of the wrath of 2 Kgs 3:27. He observes the extra-biblical example of a plague sent by deity against a besieging army in Homer's *Iliad.* There the god Apollo became angry with the Greeks who were besieging Troy and so afflicted them with a plague.

49. Compare Joseph's brothers in prison who concluded that their misfortune was God's providential judgment for what they had done twenty years earlier to their brother (Gen 42:22-23).

50. Biblical narratives also suggest a second, less likely, interpretation: that God's wrath expressed itself via military defeat. Josh 22:20 refers to God's wrath (*qeṣep*) on the congregation of Israel as a result of Achan's sin, a wrath that manifested itself through military defeat at Ai (Josh 7:1-12). Similarly in 2 Chr 29:8-9 God's wrath against Judah results in men falling victim to the sword and their wives being taken into captivity. Cf. the Mesha Inscription where Mesha believed Israel oppressed Moab because "Chemosh was angry (*y'np*) with his land" (line 5). Against taking Yahweh's wrath as expressed through a military defeat is the explicit failure of Mesha to break through Israel's lines militarily (v. 26), suggesting that Mesha had exhausted his military options. But even if the "wrath" were understood as a military reversal, there would not be a contradiction

Elisha did not spell out the consequences of Israel doing what Elisha predicted for the very reason that it was God's will that these kings be judged: Jehoram for his family trait of wickedness and Jehoshaphat for having too close an association with a wicked Israelite king and his deeds. Elisha was the son of Shaphat (2 Kgs 3:11), that is, son of "[God] judges"; and fittingly he was a "son of judgment," an instrument of judgment through whom the judgment of God was meted out to these kings for the way in which they conducted war. The prophet Micaiah served the same role in the parallel narrative in 1 Kings 22 where Jehoshaphat joined Ahab, Jehoram's father, in war.

VI. CONCLUSION

The "great wrath" (*qeṣep gādôl*) that came upon Israel (2 Kgs 3:27) was not that of any human being, nor any pagan deity, but of Yahweh whose anger probably manifested itself as a plague. The reason for Yahweh's anger was Israel's violation of the rules for just war as found in Deut 20:10-15, 19-20. This violation consisted of engaging in unnecessary massacres and vindictive destruction while offering the enemy no terms of peace. When Elisha was pressed to prophesy concerning the anticipated military engagement, he knew that it was God's will to judge both the wicked Jehoram of Israel and the godly but compromising Jehoshaphat of Judah. He therefore gave a prophecy predicting that these kings would commit certain atrocities, but gave no explicit warnings or moral indictments of these acts, and used verbal forms that were ambiguous as to whether this was the permissive will of Yahweh. The fact that Jehoram and even the relatively godly Jehoshaphat were both silent about this predicted violation of Deuteronomy's laws of war, and indeed seem to have taken the prophecy as Yahweh's permission to carry this violation of Deuteronomy's laws, confirms in the narrator's mind God's justice in sending his wrath upon them.

---

with prophecy in the mind of the narrator. In that case, the battles up until Kir Hareseth fulfilled Elisha's prediction, but the military reversal would be the unstated thing that followed the fulfillment of what Elisha predicted as a sign of Yahweh's displeasure. Jeremiah 18:9-10 states that Yahweh can reverse any good prophesied for a nation by his prophets if that nation disobeys God's voice. In 2 Kings 3 Israel disobeyed the laws of Deuteronomy 20. Taken as a military reversal, Jehoram's words would ironically turn out to have been correct: Yahweh had "gathered these three kings to give them into the hands of Moab" (2 Kgs 3:10).

Chapter 12

LAW AND JUSTICE IN THE HISTORICAL BOOKS

Law plays a very prominent role in the Pentateuch, but it also plays an important if less prominent role in the OT historical books. This chapter will discuss the two major terms for "law" in the historical books, the influence of Mosaic law on the historical books, and the administration of law from the time of Joshua to the end of the OT period.

I. TERMS FOR LAW IN THE HISTORICAL BOOKS

There are many terms for law in the historical books, including *hôq/huqqâ* "statute," *mišpaṭ* "judgment, decision," and *miṣwâ* "commandment." But only the two terms *tôrâ* and *dāt* will be treated here.

1. *Torah in the Historical Books.* The term *torah* (*tôrâ*) meaning "law, instruction" is the most important term for law in the OT. It also occurs frequently in the historical books of the OT. Of special interest related to the term *torah* is the identity of various "books of the law" mentioned in the historical books and the judicial reforms of Jehoshaphat.

In the Deuteronomistic History (Joshua through 2 Kings), God exhorts Joshua to adhere to the law (*torah*) that Moses commanded and to meditate on the book of the law day and night (Josh 1:7-8), an exhortation Joshua passes along to the Transjordan tribes of Reuben, Gad, and half of Manasseh (Josh 22:5), and to all Israel (Josh 23:6). There is reference also to building an altar at Mount Ebal of unhewn stones in accord with instructions in the Mosaic law (Josh 8:30-31), archaeological remains of which may have been found though the interpretation is disputed.[1] On the stones of that altar was inscribed a copy of "the law of Moses," and Joshua read the blessing and the curse written in the law of Moses and indeed every word of that law to the people (Josh 8:32-34).

Precisely to what this "book of the law" refers is not immediately obvious. In canonical context, where Joshua appears to be a continuation of the story of the Pentateuch, the book of the law might be thought to refer to all the laws of the Pentateuch, including the book of the covenant written at Sinai (Exod 24:7), or perhaps even the Pentateuch itself that later Jewish tradition labeled the *Torah*. The usual interpretation of critical scholarship, on the other hand, is that it refers

---

1. A. Zertal, "Mount Ebal," *ABD* 2:255-258.

to an earlier version of Deuteronomy. In the Pentateuch, "the book of the law" is used only for the teachings in Deuteronomy (Deut 28:61; 29:21; 30:10; 31:26). Passages in Joshua that mention the book of the law of Moses also strongly allude to matters found in Deuteronomy: the death of Moses (Josh 1:1-2; Deut 34:1-8), a promise of conquest that closely echoes Deuteronomy (Josh 1:3-5a; Deut 11:24-25a), and God's exhortation for Joshua to have courage repeating the exhortation Moses gave Joshua in Deuteronomy at his commissioning (Josh 1:5b-6, 9; Deut 31:7-8, 23). Also drawing from Deuteronomy is the warning not to turn to the right or the left in following the law (Josh 1:7b; 23:6; Deut 5:32; 28:14), the admonition to obey with all one's heart and soul (Josh 22:5; Deut 6:5), and Moses' command to build an altar of stones on Mount Ebal and inscribe on it "all the words of this law" (Josh 8:30-35; Deut 27:1-8), including the blessing and the curse (Josh 8:34; Deut 27:9-28:68). In Deut 27:8 "all the words of *this* law" that Moses commanded to be put on the stones of the altar at Mount Ebal presumably refers in context to the various laws of Deuteronomy. These many allusions to Deuteronomy fit well with the hypothesis that Joshua is part of the Deuteronomistic History, a history highly influenced by Deuteronomy. Martin Noth thought that Josh 8:30-35 was directly composed by the Deuteronomist [Dtr].[2]

Reference to the *torah* of Moses is absent from 1-2 Samuel, but 2 Samuel does refer to a "*torah* of mankind" (2 Sam 7:19) in David's prayer after receiving God's promise of an eternal dynasty. This expression is variously interpreted: "instruction for mankind/people" (ESV, NRSV); "manner/custom of man " [as opposed to the manner/custom of God] (NASB; BDB); "[This (promise) is] a charter for mankind";[3] or as a question "[Is this your] usual way of dealing with man?" (NIV). Since the meanings "manner, custom" and "charter" are not well attested for *torah*, and the usual meaning "law, instruction" does not seem apt, some scholars prefer to emend the text after the parallel in 1 Chr 17:17 that reads *tôr* (meaning uncertain; perhaps "rank" or "group" or "turn") rather than *tôrat* (cf. RSV where "future generations" assumes an emended text, either "the turn [*tôr*] of mankind" or "the generations [*dôrōt*] of mankind").

Jehu of Israel (2 Kgs 10:31) specifically, and Israel and Judah generally (2 Kgs 17:13, 34, 37) are rebuked for not following God's *torah*. Although God would have allowed the people to remain in the land had they followed the *torah*, Manasseh led them astray (2 Kgs 21:8-9; 2 Chr 33:8-9). King Amaziah of Judah, on the other hand, is commended for following Deut 24:16 ("children are not to be put to death because of their fathers"), for he did not execute the sons of assassins along with the perpetrators themselves (2 Kgs 14:6; 2 Chr 25:4).

During Josiah's reign, Hilkiah the priest discovered in the house of Yahweh the lost "book of the *torah*" also called "the book of the covenant" (2 Kgs 22:8;

---

2. M. Noth, *The Deuteronomistic History* (JSOTSup 15; Sheffield: JSOT Press, 1991), 63.

3. Walter Kaiser, "The Blessing on David: A Charter for Humanity," *The Law and the Prophets* (ed. J. Skilton; Philadelphia: Presbyterian and Reformed, 1974), 311-315.

23:2). When Josiah heard the words of this book he tore his garments in a gesture of grief (2 Kgs 22:11) and proceeded to carry out that law by removing mediums and idols from the land (2 Kgs 23:24). Indeed, Josiah is said to have followed the *torah* of Moses with all his heart and soul more than any other Israelite king (2 Kgs 23:25). Part of his activity involved putting down idolatry and destroying the high places of Judah and Samaria that Manasseh had allowed, thereby restricting the place of sacrifice to Jerusalem (2 Kgs 21:3; 23:5-9, 15, 19-20).

Julius Wellhausen and his school generally accept the thesis of W. M. L. de Wette's 1805 dissertation (published in 1807) that Josiah's "book of the law" was a version of Deuteronomy and was in fact a pious fraud prepared by Hilkiah or other priests in Jerusalem for political gain.[4] The purpose of Deuteronomy, according to de Wette, was to get the king to exalt the Jerusalem priesthood at the expense of the high places by making Jerusalem "the place that Yahweh your God chooses" of which Deuteronomy speaks (Deut 12:5).

Josiah's "book of the law" probably does refer to a version of Deuteronomy, as does the same expression in the Pentateuch and the book of Joshua (see above). It is not so clear, however, that Deuteronomy commanded an immediate end to all altars outside the central sanctuary as the Wellhausen school believes, nor does it specify the place that God will choose as Jerusalem. In fact, the version of Deuteronomy that now exists in fact directed Israel to build an altar of stone at Mount Ebal upon entering the land (Deut 27:1-8) and foresaw that Israel would build other legitimate altars in the land besides the place God would choose (Deut 16:21).[5] What Deuteronomy 12 does do, however, is predict a time in the future in which God would centralize sacrificial worship (but not profane slaughter) to the one place that God chooses.

The Deuteronomistic History reflects a similar tension. It clearly portrays various biblical characters after the time of Moses as constructing or using legitimate altars outside the central sanctuary. These characters include Joshua (Josh 8:30-35, fulfilling Deut 27:1-8), Gideon (Judg 6:24), Manoah (Judg 13:19-20), Samuel (1 Sam 7:17), Saul (1 Sam 14:35), David (2 Sam 24:18-20), and Elijah (1 Kgs 18:30). And it mentions various other altars of Yahweh wrongly torn down by the people (1 Kgs 19:10). On the other hand, this history foresees a day when all such altars would be supplanted. In the context of Solomon's using the altar at Gibeon, the text comments, "The people, however, were still sacrificing at the high places, because a temple had not yet been built for the name of Yahweh" (1 Kgs 3:2). This text assumes that other altars were permissible at least until the temple was built; but at some point after the construction of the temple, they would become obsolete. Josiah (c. 621 B.C.) then comes along to

---

4. Ronald E. Clements, *One Hundred Years of Old Testament Interpretation* (Philadelphia: Westminster, 1976), 7-8, 18.

5. J. G. McConville, *Law and Theology in Deuteronomy* (JSOTSup 33; Sheffield: JSOT Press, 1984), 29-33.

fulfill the centralization of the cult[6] predicted by Deuteronomy 12 and anticipated by the narrator in 1 Kgs 3:2.

The Chronicler also shows interest in *torah*, though for him the term is clearly broader than Deuteronomy and includes priestly regulations. He condemns Rehoboam who "forsook the *torah* of Yahweh" (2 Chr 12:1). God speaking to Asa though the prophet Azariah remarks that Israel had long been "without teaching priest and without *torah*" (2 Chr 15:3), probably a hendiadys meaning "without priest giving authoritative instruction" as Weingreen suggests.[7] The Chronicler also repeats the book of Kings' evaluations of Amaziah and Manasseh (2 Chr 25:4; 33:8-9; see above).

The Chronicler commends others for following the law. In portraying positively David's interest in the cult, the Chronicler notes that David had the Zadokite priests offer the regular burnt offerings in accord with "the *torah* of Yahweh" (1 Chr 16:40), i.e., the priestly regulations of the Pentateuch (e.g., Exod 29:38-42; Num 28:3-4). The Chronicler quotes David as admonishing his son Solomon to "keep the *torah* of Yahweh" (1 Chr 22:12), and Asa directed Judah to "observe the *torah* and the commandments" (2 Chr 14:4). In Solomon's prayer of dedication for the temple, the Chronicler modifies 1 Kgs 8:25 where the king must "walk before me" with the clarifying paraphrase that the king is to "walk in my *torah*" (2 Chr 6:16). Jehoiada, who after Athaliah's idolatrous reign of terror ran the government until Joash came of age, returned control of the temple to the Levitical priests "as is written in the *torah* of Moses" and "the order of David" (2 Chr 23:18). Hezekiah is commended for seeking God "in *torah* and commandments" (2 Chr 31:21). Hezekiah's religious reforms included having the festivals celebrated "as is written in the *torah* of Yahweh" (2 Chr 31:3) and having the Levites take their stations "according to the *torah* of Moses" and receive financial support of tithes so they could devote themselves to "the *torah* of Yahweh" (2 Chr 30:16; 31:4). Josiah's piety "as written in the *torah* of Yahweh" is also commended (2 Chr 35:26).

The Chronicler repeats the account drawn from Kings of the discovery of the Deuteronomic "book of the *torah*" (2 Chr 34:14-19; cf. 2 Kings 22 above). One variation of wording about the book of the *torah* is worth mentioning: In Kings Shaphan "read it" (*wyqr'hw*; 2 Kgs 22:8); whereas, Chronicles says Shaphan "read in it" (*wyqr' bw*; 2 Chr 34:18). It is possible that the Chronicler rewords Kings' account because the Chronicler intends his audience to apply this language to a broader "book of the law" (i.e., the Pentateuch), not merely the (part of) Deuteronomy to which the Kings account refers.[8] On the other hand, Dillard

---

6. Though in popular usage "cult" can be used for unorthodox and/or excessively authoritarian religious sects, in the study of religion the term "cult" often refers to any system of religious beliefs and rituals. In that sense ancient Israel's organized worship centered around the temple was its cult.

7. Cited by H. G. M. Williamson, *1 and 2 Chronicles* (NCB; Grand Rapids: Eerdmans, 1982), 267.

8. Williamson, *1 and 2 Chronicles*, 402.

rightly observes that grammatically the meaning of the two phrases could be equivalent and so the two wordings may infer no difference in meaning.[9]

Jehoshaphat is said to have appointed priests and Levites to teach the cities of Judah from "the book of the law of Yahweh" (2 Chr 17:8-9), and he reorganized the judiciary, appointing judges from the priests, Levites, and heads of families to decide cases involving "bloodshed, *torah* and commandment, statues and rules" (2 Chr 19:10). Although some consider Jehoshaphat's "book of the law" to consist of royal edicts, evidence is lacking to confirm this hypothesis.[10]

Noting that this whole matter is missing from the parallel in Kings and defending his post-exilic dating of the P source, J. Wellhausen took the Chronicler's account of Jehoshapat's judicial reforms as a retrojection of what happened after the exile into the earlier history of Israel, a retrojection that builds on an aetiology[11] built off Jehoshapat's name that means "Yahweh judges."[12] G. Knoppers[13] argues that the Chronicler's account of Jehoshaphat's judicial reforms is based on Deut 17:8-13, Exod 18:13-27, and Deut 1:9-18 rather than reliable sources. Other scholars, while acknowledging that the Chronicler uses language influenced by texts in the Pentateuch, are more willing to give the Chronicler the benefit of the doubt,[14] suggesting that the Chronicler probably did not simply invent his account but is consulting a source that describes a pre-Deuteronomic reform of Israelite legal traditions. W. F. Albright[15] defended the historicity of Jehoshapat's judicial reforms as similar to those of Haremhab in 14th century Egypt, a reform that also involved priests serving as judges.[16]

---

9. Raymond Dillard, *2 Chronicles* (WBC 15; Waco: Word, 1987), 281.

10. Keith Whitelam, *The Just King: Monarchial Judicial Authority in Ancient Israel* (JSOTSup 12; Sheffield: JSOT Press, 1979), 212.

11. An aetiology tries to find the origins or causes of things. In biblical studies this term is often used of supposed legendary explanations for the meaning of proper names. For example, it is alleged that the stories of Joshua's conquest of Ai are derived from a speculative aetiology on the meaning of that city's name that means "heap, ruin." The aetiology theory in Ai's case supposes that the stories of Joshua's conquest of Ai are based not on historical record but on speculations as to why this site was given a name that means "heap," which in turn led people to associate that site with the developing legends of Joshua's conquests. If the account of Jehoshapat's judicial reforms are aetological, it means they are legends built upon speculations as to why Jehoshapat should be given a name that in Hebrew means "YHWH judges."

12. Julius Wellhausen, *Prolegomena to the History of Israel With a Reprint of the Article 'Israel' from the Encyclopedia Britannica* (Gloucester, Mass.: Peter Smith, 1983), 191.

13. Gary N. Knoppers, "Jehoshaphat's Judiciary and the 'Scroll of Yahweh's Torah,'" *JBL* 113.1 (1994): 59-80.

14. E.g., Dillard, *2 Chronicles*, 148; Williamson, *1 and 2 Chronicles*, 287-88; Whitelam, *The Just King*, 185-206.

15. W. F. Albright, "The Judicial Reforms of Jehoshaphat," *Alexander Marx Jubilee Volume* (New York: Jewish Publication Society, 1950), 61-82.

16. Roland de Vaux, *Ancient Israel* (2 vol.; New York: McGraw-Hill, 1965), 154.

The book of Ezra-Nehemiah[17] also refers to *torah*. After the exile Zerubbabel built an altar on which Jeshua and the priests sacrificed burnt offerings "as is written in the *torah* of Moses" (Ezra 3:2). The narrator remarks that Ezra was "a scribe skilled in the *torah* of Moses" (also called the *"torah* of Yahweh" and *"torah* of God") which he studied and taught (Ezra 7:6, 10). Ezra is portrayed as bringing the "book of the *torah*" (Neh 8:1, 3, 5, 8, 18) before an assembly of men and women of Judah at the Western Gate during the days of Nehemiah.[18] The people listened to his book of the law from early morning to midday, and assistants explained the *torah* and gave the sense (Neh 8:7-8).

Ezra's prayer (Ezra 9:6-15) where Ezra confesses his people's disregard of God's commands influenced Shecaniah to propose that Jews divorce their foreign wives "in accord with the *torah*" (Ezra 10:2-3; cf. Deut 7:1-5). This particular claim is problematic since there is no law requiring a divorce from non-Canaanite foreign spouses. There are also contrary examples in the OT: Ruth the Moabitess, ancestress of David, is very positively portrayed in the book of Ruth. Deut 21:10-14 allows marriage to foreign captive women. And God sided with Moses rather than his bother Aaron and sister Miriam regarding his marriage to a Cushite woman (Num 12:1-9). Some of these wives seem explicitly non-Canaanite (Moabites and Egyptians are mentioned in Ezra 9:1). Moreover, it is doubtful that "the peoples of the land" are actually Canaanites. Their abominations are said to be "like" those "of the Canaanites" (NIV) and other groups, but they are not actually identified as Canaanites. Canaanites as such may have ceased to exist by this point in history. Some conclude therefore that Shecaniah and Ezra misapplied the law out of racist zeal to preserve the "holy seed" (Ezra 9:2).[19]

On the other hand, the biblical narrator gives no hint of disapproval. Given the narrator's previous portrayal of Ezra as an expert in the *torah*, he probably agrees with the actions taken. A more positive reading is possible: The demand to divorce foreign wives "according to the law" was probably understood in terms of principles rather than explicit command. Because the sins of these foreigners were "like" those of the Canaanites, so the command not to marry Canaanites could be applied by analogy to intermarriage with such foreigners. Moreover, Shecaniah may also have had Deut 24:1 in mind where the openly pagan practices of the foreign wives constituted the "unseemly thing/indecency" that justified divorce.

The nature of the *torah* in which Ezra was expert and which he taught the people in Nehemiah 8 is subject to speculation. Scholarly opinions as to the contents of Ezra's *torah* have included the following: a collection of legal materials (R. Kittel, G. von Rad, M. Noth, C. Houtman), the Priestly Code P (A. Kuenen,

---

17. Ezra-Nehemiah is considered a single book in the Hebrew Bible.

18. Contra the view of H. G. M. Williamson, *Ezra, Nehemiah* (WBC 16; Waco: Word, 1985), 409 n. 9a, who takes "Nehemiah" here as a secondary insertion and dates this event to c. 458 B.C.

19. Williamson, *Ezra, Nehemiah*, 159-162

W. O. E. Oesterly, H.-J Kraus), the Deuteronomic laws (L. Browne, R. Bowman, M. F. Scott, U. Kellermann), and the Pentateuch (J. Wellhausen, E. Sellin, O. Eissfeldt, W. Ruldoph, K. Galling, S. Mowinckel, W. F. Albright, F. Cross).[20] There seems little basis at this late date to limit *torah* to Deuteronomy. Ezra 3:2 uses *torah* in the sense of cultic law. If (as some scholars believe) the Chronicler also edited Ezra-Nehemiah, then the Chronicler's broader usage that includes cultic law would be expected. Ezra is repeatedly called a priest as well as a teacher of law (Ezra 7:11-12, 21; 10:10, 16; Neh 8:2, 9; 12:26); so he would have had a natural interest in cultic matters. C. Houtman argues that the law book pre-supposed in Ezra-Nehemiah does not refer to P, nor to Deuteronomy, nor to our current Pentateuch in whole or part, but to some other law book, now lost, analogous to the *Temple Scroll* found at Qumran whose laws overlapped with those in the Pentateuch, but which contained some laws that were unique to it.[21] But against this view, it seems doubtful that a book associated with Moses in the post-exilic community would have been entirely lost, and the alleged discrepancies that Houtman sees between statements about the law in Ezra-Nehemiah and the laws of the Pentateuch can be otherwise explained.[22] Wellhausen[23] took this "book" as essentially the Pentateuch as we now have it, and indeed suggests Ezra was its final and principal editor, adding P to the earlier JED document. It is also possible that Ezra brought with him a version of the Pentateuch from Babylonia.[24] Either way, it is probable that the Ezra's law book is in fact related to our current Pentateuch.

   2. *Dāt in the Esther and Ezra.*   In Hebrew and Aramaic portions of Esther and Ezra, the Persian loan word *dāt* occurs in the sense of "law." Of special importance here is the question of what precisely Ezra was authorized to do with *dāt* by the Persian monarch Artaxerxes.

   The term *dāt* is often used in reference to Persian law. The noun *dāt* in the singular can be a collective for Persian jurisprudence generally (Esther 1:13; 4:16) or refer to individual decrees of Persian kings whose edicts constitute law (Ezra 8:36; Esther 1:19; 2:8; 3:14-15; 4:3, 8; 8:14; 9:1, 13, 14). Even Ahasuerus' pronouncement that everyone drink freely is considered a *dāt* (Esther 1:8). The plural of *dāt* can refer to the total body of royal edicts and laws in Persia (Esther 1:19; 3:8b) or a specific group of royal directives such as those Artaxerxes sent to sanction Ezra's mission (Ezra 8:36).

   The story of Esther revolves around the *dāt* issued by Ahasuerus to annihilate the Jews of his empire (3:9, 14). According to the Bible, a Medo-Persian *dāt* cannot be repealed (Esther 1:19). This has been taken to mean no more than that

   20. Edwin Yamauchi, *Persia and the Bible* (Grand Rapids: Baker, 1990), 256-257.
   21. Cornelis Houtman, "Ezra and the Law: Observations on the Supposed Relation between Ezra and the Pentateuch," *OTS* 21 (1981) 91-115.
   22. Williamson, *Ezra, Nehemiah*, xxxviii-xxxix, 288.
   23. Wellhausen, *Prolegomena to the History of Israel*, 408-9, 497.
   24. Yamauchi, *Persia and the Bible*, 258.

Persian decrees must be quickly carried out,[25] but the story of Daniel takes it to mean that a king cannot invalidate his own decrees (Dan 6:8, 12, 15). In Esther Ahasuerus evidently cannot simply reverse his own decree to annihilate the Jews, but instead must issue a new one allowing the Jews to defend themselves (Esther 8:8, 13). Possible extra-biblical evidence of this quirk in Persian law comes from Diodorus 17.30.6 where Darius III, despite his royal powers, is unable to undo the death sentence he had pronounced on a man whose words had offended him. That text is not clear, however, whether the king's regrets came before or after the man had actually been executed.

Dāt is also used as a synonym for the Heb. term *tôrâ*. Artaxerxes' letter to Ezra in Aramaic authorizes Ezra's mission. There Ezra is called a "scribe of the *dāt* of the God of heaven" (Ezra 7:12, 21). This "God of heaven" is described as "your [Ezra's] God" (Ezra 7:25-26), but it may also have been a title of the Persian celestial god Ahuramazda who was portrayed as winged figure and is known to have been worshiped by Darius and Xerxes.[26] Artaxerxes may have identified Yahweh with Ahuramazda. In the Hebrew portion of the book, Ezra is similarly called a scribe skilled in the *torah* of Moses and the *torah* of Yahweh (Ezra 7:6, 10). It thus seems that in this Aramaic letter, *dat* is a synonym for Hebrew *tôrâ*.

The scope of what Ezra was being authorized to do by Artaxerxes has been subject to debate. The key verses are Ezra 7:25-26 where Ezra is authorized to appoint magistrates and judges who "know the laws [pl. of *dat*] of your God," to teach the law, and to punish those who disobey the law. This has been understood in several ways:[27] Persia authorized a version of the Pentateuch as the law of Judah (Peter Frei). Persia merely authorized Ezra to appoint judges to carry out Persian law with limited influence from Jewish legal traditions (Lisbeth Fried). Persia authorized the Pentateuch in a token way as the "official" law of Judah, though with little actual attention to that law's form or content (James Watts). Persian authorization of Jewish law is fictional rather than historical (Lester Grabbe).

One complication in this discussion regarding Ezra's making Jewish law the law of the state has to do with whether Ezra's book of law is in fact the Pentateuch (discussed above). Another complication is that not all the norms of the Pentateuch are "laws" in the sense of norms ever meant to be enforced by the state. A norm such as the Decalogue's "do not covet" (Exod 20:17; Deut 5:21) is purely a moral precept not easily enforceable by the state. The formulation of certain injunctions lack penalty clauses for non-compliance (e.g. the slave laws of Exod 21:2-11). To make these into "laws" rather than moral admonitions requires the addition of penalty clauses that goes beyond the Pentateuch. Some

---

25. David J. A. Clines, *Ezra, Nehemiah, Esther* (NCB; Grand Rapids: Eerdmans, 1984), 282

26. Yamauchi, *Persia and the Bible*, 430-433.

27. James W. Watts, ed., *Persia and Torah: The Theory of Imperial Authorization of the Pentateuch* (Atlanta: Society of Biblical Literature, 2001), 1-4 and subsequent essays.

regulations specify God as enforcer not the state (e.g., the admonition to treat sojourners, widows, and orphans decently; Exod 22:21-24). For this very reason, even if Ezra had made the Pentateuch in some sense the law of the Judah, Nehemiah as governor would still have had to cajole rather than demand that his fellow wealthy Jews not charge interest to those sacrificing to work on Nehemiah's wall, as he does in Neh 5:6-13. Nehemiah as governor had no legal authority under Mosaic law to stop his fellow aristocrats from taking interest because the regulations against taking interest from the poor are ones enforced by God rather than the state (Exod 22:25-27; Lev 25:35-38; Deut 23:19-20). More generally, since biblical law covers only a limited number of legal topics, the Pentateuch is not adequate by itself to serve as a complete law code. It could serve at most as one element of the legal standards of Ezra's day.

II. INFLUENCE OF MOSAIC LAW ON THE HISTORICAL NARRATIVES

In addition to statements about law associated with the vocabulary of law given above, there are from time to time allusions in the historical books to concepts found in Pentateuchal laws even where the term "law" is not used. A sampling follows.

The historical books refer to holy days found in the law including sabbaths (though not till the divided monarchy, 2 Kgs 4:23 + 22x), the feast of Passover/Unleavened Bread (28x), the feast of weeks (2 Chr 8:13), and the feast of tabernacles (Judg 21:19[?]; 1 Kgs 8:2; 2 Chr 8:13; Ezra 3:4; Neh 8:14-17). The changing of the date of tabernacles from the seventh to the eighth month—along with appointing non-Levitical priests—is part of the sin of Jeroboam (1 Kgs 12:32-33; cf. Lev 23:34) that is condemned repeatedly in the book of Kings.

Joshua in accord with the law circumcised every male (Josh 5:2-9; cf. Gen 17:10-14), removed hung corpses of his enemies before sundown (Josh 10:26-27; cf. Deut 21:22-23), and set up Levitical cities of refuge (Josh 20:2-9; cf. Num 35:9-15; Deut 4:41-43; 19:1-13). Achan's taking of things "under the ban" brought punishment on Israel as threatened by the law (Josh 7:12, 20-25; cf. Deut 13:17). Samson's parents are warned that he must not drink wine, shave his head, or eat anything ceremonially unclean in accord with the rules for Nazirites (Judg 13:4-14; cf. Num 6:1-8), though Judges makes no mention of the prohibition against corpse contamination that Samson clearly violates. In Ruth 3-4, the customs surrounding the right of a near relative to redeem and marry Ruth resembles (with some variation) the law of levirate marriage (Deut 25:5-10). Hannah's vow that were she to have a child, no razor would come on his head (1 Sam 1:11) is explained by the law as an application of the Nazirite vow (Num 6:5).

The sons of Samuel by taking bribes perverted justice contrary to the law (1 Sam 8:3; cf. Exod 23:6, 8; Deut 16:19). When David failed to come to eat with Saul's family the fellowship/peace offering associated with the new moon, Saul supposed that David must have been ceremonially unclean (1 Sam 20:26;

cf. Num 10:10; Lev 7:20). Saul applied for a time the laws against sorcery and divination (1 Sam 28:9; cf. Exod 22:18; Deut 18:10-14). David was prepared to apply the law requiring fourfold restitution for theft of a sheep (2 Sam 12:6; cf. Exod 22:1). Joab sought asylum at the sanctuary, an option allowed in the law for murderers (1 Kgs 2:28-29; cf. Exod 21:13) and perhaps here expanded to include political offenses.[28]

Solomon violates the laws against kings multiplying wives, intermarriage with pagans, and idolatry (1 Kgs 11:1-8; cf. Deut 17:17; Exod 20:3; 34:12-17; Deut 7:1-5). Arguably "great wrath" came against Israel in 2 Kgs 3:27 because Israel had violated the rules of war outside the land (Deut 20:10-20).[29] Naboth was falsely accused of violating the law concerning unspecified offenses against God and the ruler (1 Kgs 21:10; cf. Exod 22:28). Amaziah obeyed Deut 24:16 (see above). Nehemiah urged his fellow aristocrats to follow the laws against usury (Neh 5:10; cf. Exod 22:25; Lev 25:36-37; Deut 23:19).

Whitelam[30] argued that in many of these cases later royal edicts came to be retrojected back into Mosaic law. However, it could just as well be true that royal practice was directly or indirectly influenced by earlier Mosaic law. In principle the king was not so much to promulgate law but to administer the law of Yahweh.[31] Yet in practice, given the limited scope of the corpus of biblical laws, the creation of additional, new laws by kings was both inevitable and legitimate so long as any new laws were compatible with those received from God through Moses by revelation.

III. ADMINISTRATION OF LAW IN THE HISTORICAL BOOKS

Administration of justice was diverse in the historical narratives, but there does seem to be development over time as to how the law was administered.

While in Genesis it appears that the head of household (the *paterfamilias*) had primary authority,[32] by the time of Joshua-Judges this authority was shifting to elders, leaders, and judges (Josh 23:2; 24:1). Although only one "major" judge is described as sitting at court (ironically the female Deborah; Judg 4:5), the "minor" judges of the book of Judges may have served this function. Elders at the city gate served as both witnesses and judges (Ruth 4:1, 11; cf. Deut 21:19-20).

In Deuteronomy priests were to serve as judges, especially for hard cases (Deut 17:8-11; 19:17-18), sometimes administering an oath or self-curse to help

---

28. P. Barmash, "The Narrative Quandary: Cases of Law in Literature," *VT* 54.1 (2004): 15.

29. J. M. Sprinkle, "Deuteronomic 'Just War' (Deut 20:10-20) and 2 Kings 3:27," *ZABR* 5 (2000): 285-301, and Chapter 11 above.

30. Whitelam, *The Just King*, 218.

31. de Vaux, *Ancient Israel*, 150.

32. Hans Jochen Boecker, *Law and the Administration of Justice in the Old Testament and the Ancient East* (Minneapolis: Augsburg, 1980), 30.

divine the truth (Num 5:19; Exod 22:11). In the historical books, Samuel serves as both priest, who blesses and conducts sacrifices, and judge (1 Sam 7:15-17; 9:13; 10:8; Ps 99:6). Jehoshaphat's judicial reforms involved appointment of Levites and priests, along with heads of families, to administer justice (2 Chr 19:8-10). Jeremiah towards the end of the monarchy mentions that the job of the priest was closely related to *torah* (Jer 18:18), and Ezra the scribe of the law of God was also a priest (see above).

After the establishment of the monarchy, kings are portrayed as rendering judicial decisions.[33] In times of war kings like Saul naturally oversaw martial law over soldiers and civilians (1 Sam 22:6-19). This authority eventually passed to kings in other conditions. Kings thus took the role once belonging to the judges (1 Sam 8:1, 5). Solomon built the Hall of Justice for the purpose of conducting court (1 Kgs 7:7). In principle administering law so justice occurred for his people (2 Sam 8:15; 2 Chr 9:8; Ps 45:4; 72:1-2), a king might be called upon to decide an especially difficult case, such as the dispute without witnesses over possession of a child (1 Kgs 3:16-28 [Solomon]). Sometimes the king evidently served as a court of appeals, as in the (fictional) case of the wise widow of Tekoa who asked the king to save her son from her "family" or clan who intended to execute him for killing his brother (2 Sam 14:4-8).[34] In other cases the king may have had primary jurisdiction from the beginning (2 Kgs 6:26-29, a special case during besiegement; possibly also the case of a woman seeking to repossess her house and field in 2 Kgs 8:3, and the fictitious case of theft recounted by Nathan to David, 2 Sam 12:1-6).[35] It would be impossible for a king to hear all cases and appeals, a fact exploited by Absalom to incite discontent (2 Sam 15:1-6). The innovation of kingship naturally shifted the jurisdiction of some cases from the other judges to kings and so made the king the highest judicial authority in the land, though how and why some cases went to the king while other cases remained in the sphere of lower courts is not clear.

In theory even kings were subordinated to the *torah* of Yahweh (Deut 17:18-20); hence kings were admonished to obey God's commandments (2 Sam 12:14-15; 1 Kgs 2:3-4). This is what Solomon expresses desire to do (1 Kgs 8:58). And yet David seems not to have been subject to human punishment after committing adultery with Bathsheba and having Uriah her husband murdered (2 Samuel 12). Ahab king of Israel (unlike his wife Jezebel) thought that even he as king was subject to the law of property rights (1 Kgs 21:4).[36] Josiah is portrayed positively as renewing his commitment to obey God's commandments (2 Kgs 23:3; 2 Chr 34:31). Saul, on the other hand, is said to have lost his kingship because he failed to keep Yahweh's command (1 Sam 13:14; 15:23), and Solomon's successor lost control of the northern kingdom because Solomon did not follow God's

---

33. See Boecker, *Law and the Administration of Justice*, 40-49; de Vaux, *Ancient Israel*, 150-152; Whitelam, *The Just King*, *passim.*

34. Cf. Barmash, "Cases of Law in Literature," 11-14.

35. Whitelam, *The Just King*, 124.

36. Barmash, "Cases of Law in Literature," 14.

commandments (1 Kgs 11:10-11). Moreover, if Solomon's dynasty failed to keep God's commands, it too might prove temporary (1 Chr 28:7).

After the exile, it was the law of the Persian king that authorized Ezra to administer the law of God (Ezra 7:26), thus showing the preeminence of Persian law for that state.

IV. FINAL OBSERVATIONS

This chapter has surveyed law and the administration of justice in the historical books. It is interesting to note the development of law over time. Mosaic law gives only a few guidelines as to how it was to be administered. This non-specificity was a good thing since it allowed Israel flexibility in applying God's law as its society changed from being an agrarian, tribal society to being more of an urban society ruled by kings. In that process, because the Mosaic law was non-specific, Israel was free to make adjustments to its administration of law by granting more power to kings in one period and more to administrators such as Ezra in other periods. When certain laws, such as the law against intermarriage with Canaanites, became obsolete so far as literal application is concerned, its application could be properly adjusted though application by analogy (Ezra 10). All this is within the parameters allowed by the law.

What Israel was not free to do, which it in fact did do, was to alter the fundamental principles of the law. Jeroboam had no license to change the date of the feast of tabernacles or to appoint non-Levitical priests (1 Kings 12). Israel was not free to practice idolatry or divination or violate the other various laws. Prophets like Amos condemn Israel for its social injustice in violation of the law, and Hosea and Zephaniah condemn Israel and Judah respectively for their idolatry.

It is noteworthy that the Sabbath Year and Year of Jubilee laws (Leviticus 25), in which slaves were freed and the land was to return to its original owners, appear never to have been fully instituted during the period covered by the historical books. Jeremiah 34 indicates that compliance with the demand to release slaves periodically (the slave law of Exod 21:1-6 and the Year of Jubilee regulation) was nil. There is no evidence of even recognizing the date of the Year of Jubilee until after the Babylonian exile at which point there are references to the Sabbath Year in Maccabees and Josephus (see 1 Macc 6:49, 53; Josephus *Ant.* 12.378 [163/162 B.C. during Maccabean Revolt]; 13.234 [135/134 B.C., John Hyrcanus]; 14:202-206, 475 [37/36 B.C.,]),[37] though Nehemiah earlier made an

---

37. An attempt to find allusions to the Year of Jubilee in the preexilic period is made by Lisbeth Fried and David N. Freedman, "Was the Jubilee Year Observed in Preexilic Judah," in *Leviticus 23-27* (by J. Milgrom; AB 3b; New York: Doubleday, 2000), 2257-2270, but I find their arguments unconvincing. See Shmuel Safrai, "Sabbath Year and Year of Jubilee: Jubilee in the Second Temple Period," n.p., *EncJud CD-Rom Edition.* Version 1997. He states, "there is no evidence throughout the whole Temple period of the actual observance of the Jubilee."

attempt to reinstitute the Sabbath Year (Neh 10:31). This lack of institution is understandable since there would be many practical difficulties in instituting these laws, and doing so would be expected to generate considerable opposition from landowners. The Year of Jubilee was difficult to institute initially since it assumes the full conquest and division of the land, but the land was not fully taken until centuries after Joshua at the time of David (2 Samuel 8, 10). By that time identifying the "original owners" of various lands was difficult to impossible. Nonetheless, completely ignoring this law was but one more example of the failure of Israel to comply with its covenant with Yahweh.

It is also worth noting that many of the key institutions associated with the law in later periods are completely absent from the historical books of the OT. For example, although by NT times they were central institutions of Judaism, in OT times there is no evidence of synagogues or rabbis. The oldest archaeological remains of a synagogue building come from Egypt and date to the second century B.C.[38] Exactly when and where the synagogue as a formal institution develops is uncertain. The synagogue institution seems to have developed because of lack of access to the temple due to the Babylonian exile. They may have developed informally out of prayer and Bible study groups meeting in homes. Eventually formal, lay (non-Levitical) teachers called rabbis come to have prominence, and specialized buildings come to be built. The origins of the rabbinic approach to the law might be seen in Ezra the scribe. Rabbinic tradition looked back to Ezra and his reading the law and having his representatives give the sense (Nehemiah 8) as justifying the use of oral law (rabbinic interpretation) and translation (Aramaic targums) alongside the written law.

Thus the role of law in the OT historical books is primitive as compared with later Judaism where the oral tradition came to seek application of the laws to every conceivable situation—see the Mishnah and Talmud for a compiling of these once oral traditions. On the other hand, the historical books lack the excesses found in later Judaism: legalism (seeking to merit salvation by law-keeping), letterism (obsessive devotion to details of legal obedience), and putting a fence around the law (making up oppressively numerous, non-biblical rules to keep one from breaking the biblical statues themselves).

---

38. Eric M. Meyers, "Synagogue," *ABD* 6:253.

Chapter 13

CONCLUSION: IS THE LAW RELEVANT FOR TODAY?

This book raises the question of whether biblical law is relevant for today, and if so, how.

New Testament statements about Mosaic law indicate that the law does have lessons for Christians under the new covenant and that in some sense Christians are to establish the law. I have tried to construct an adequate methodology consistent with New Testament teachings about the law by which a New Testament Christian can derive legitimate moral and religious lessons from the laws despite the changes in historical and redemptive settings between Old Testament times and New Testament times. This methodology has been shown to be exhibited in the New Testament uses of the law. It has been found that the basis of the giving of the law was God's grace, that the law as originally given was neither a system of legalism (earning salvation by law-keeping) nor oppressively letteristic, and that the law expresses a worldview and ideology superior to that found in the law collections of Israel's ancient Near Eastern neighbors (though the latter can be illuminating in understanding Israel's laws). It has also been shown how the law portrays the character of God, illustrating this in detail from Exodus 19-24, and how the law was meant to foster a closer relationship between God and Israel (with implications for our relationship with God as well). It has also been observed why it is essential to grasp the teachings in the law in order to understand correctly biblical narratives (and visa versa), giving many examples, but illustrating this in greatest detail in the case of 2 Kings 3. I have also described how the law came to be applied in Old Testament history, contrasting that application with the application of the law by the rabbis in NT times.

The abiding relevance of the Mosaic law concerning many ethical issues has been affirmed in these chapters. I argue that the *lex talionis* was meant to be a just, legal principle of allowing punishments to correspond to the crime, not a justification of personal revenge. I have found principles in the law that show the full humanity of subservient persons such as slaves and that make it unlikely that biblical writers would have approved of elective abortions of fetuses. Biblical laws of theft help us to reflect on many religious and ethical issues: divine blessings, property rights, maintenance of peace and harmony in society, the role of repentance in the spiritual life, the need for proper attitudes towards the possessions of others, and the need to treat the poor decently. The laws of purity sear into our consciences the profound holiness of God and sinfulness of us humans, the need to reflect God's holiness in our worship, and the call for believers to be a separated and holy people themselves.

One area of ethics where Old Testament laws are very helpful is in the realm of sexual ethics. I argue vigorously that the Old Testament's perspective on divorce and remarriage is essential for establishing a correct biblical ethic on divorce, and that failure to have done this has led to misguided practices among Christians. The relevance of the other laws about sexuality has also been affirmed: how moral principles (though not necessarily the legal sanctions) of the incest laws, the adultery laws, and the laws about homosexual acts are still valid under the new covenant (and not to be explained away), and how the laws about sexuality fit into the matrix of a larger biblical theology of creation and blessing.

Finally, the Bible's ethics of war have been defended against critics who say they are unjust. The laws of war have been shown instead to constitute an early form of just war theory that was quite humane and whose principles we should continue to follow today.

The Mosaic laws are not always easy to understand, and I do not pretend to have unraveled correctly every interpretative mystery. Nonetheless, it is my hope that this book has led some readers to a deeper understanding and appreciation of the relevance of this often neglected portion of the Bible and of the Lawgiver who inspired this material. If that should prove to be true, I will be most gratified.

Bibliography

Albright, W. F. "The Judicial Reforms of Jehoshaphat." Pages 61-82 in *Alexander Marx Jubilee Volume*. New York: Jewish Publication Society, 1950.

Alexander, Patrick H., et al., eds. *The SBL Handbook of Style*. Peabody, Mass.: Hendrickson, 1999.

Alexander, T. D. "The Composition of the Sinai Narrative in Exodus XIX 1-XXIV 11." *VT* 49.1 (1999): 2-20.

Averbeck, Richard. "Clean and Unclean." Pages 4:477-486 in *NIDOTTE*.

Bahsen, Greg. *Theonomy and Christian Ethics*. Nutley, NJ: Craig Press, 1979.

Bainton, Roland H. *Christian Attitudes towards War and Peace*. Nashville: Abingdon, 1960.

Barker, W. and W. R. Godfrey, eds. *Theonomy: A Reformed Critique*. Grand Rapids: Zondervan, 1990.

Barkhulzen, J. H. "A Short Note on John 1:17 in Patristic Exegesis." *Acta Patristica et Byzantina* 8 (1997): 18-25.

Barmash, P. "The Narrative Quandary: Cases of Law in Literature." *VT* 54 (2004): 1-16.

Barrett, C. K. *The Gospel According to St. John*. 2nd ed. Philadelphia: Westminster, 1978.

Beasley-Murray, G. R. *John*. WBC 36. Waco, Texas: Word, 1986.

Beentjes, P. C. *The Book of Ben Sira in Hebrew*. VTSup 68. Leiden: Brill, 1997.

Berlin, Adele. "On the Meaning of *PLL* in the Bible." *RB* 96 (1989): 345-351.

———. *Poetics and Interpretation of Biblical Narratives*. Bible and Literature 9. Sheffield: Almond Press, 1983.

Boecker, Hans J. *Law and the Administration of Justice in the Old Testament and the Ancient East*. Minneapolis: Augsburg, 1980.

Bonar, A. A. *A Commentary on Leviticus*. 1852. Repr., London: Banner of Truth, 1966.

Book of Concord: Confessions of the Evangelical Lutheran Church. Trans. Theodore Tappert. Philadelphia: Fortress, 1959.

Bornkamm, Heinrich. *Luther and the Old Testament*. Trans. E. W. and R. Gritsch. Ed. V. Gruhn. Philadephia: Fortress, 1969.

Boswell, J. *Christianity, Social Tolerence, and Homosexuality*. Chicago: University of Chicago Press, 1980.

Brawley, R. L., ed. *Biblical Ethics and Homosexuality*. Lousiville: John Knox, 1996.

Brenner, Athalya. *Color Terms in the Old Testament*. JSOTSup 21. Sheffield: JSOT Press, 1982.

---, ed. *A Feminist Companion to Exodus-Deuteronomy*. FCB 6. Sheffield: Sheffield Academic Press, 1994.

Brichto, H. C. "The Case of the *śoṭâ* and a Reconsideration of Biblical Law," *HUCA* 46 (1975) 55-70.

———. *Toward a Grammar of Biblical Poetics*. New York: Oxford, 1992.

Bright, John. *A History of Israel*. 2nd ed. Philadelphia: Westminster, 1972.

Brown, Raymond E. *The Gospel according to John*. AB 29-29a. Garden City, N.J.: Doubleday, 1966-1970.

Bruce, F. F. *The Gospel of John*. Grand Rapids: Eerdmans, 1983.

Brueggemann, Walter. "The Book of Exodus." In *The New Interpreter's Bible*. Vol. 1. Nashville: Abingdon, 1994.

Bultmann, R. *The Gospel of John*. Trans. G. R. Beasley-Murray. Philadelphia: Westminster, 1971.

Burns, J. B. "Why did the Besieging Army Withdraw? (II Reg 3,27)." *ZAW* 102.2 (1990): 187-194.

Carmichael, Calum M. *The Origins of Biblical Law: The Decalogues and the Book of the Covenant*. Ithaca, New York: Cornell University Press, 1992.

Carson, D. A. *The Gospel According to John*. Grand Rapids: Eerdmans, 1991.

————. "Matthew." Pages 1-599 in *The Expositor's Bible Commentary*. Vol. 8. Ed. Frank Gaebelein. Grand Rapids: Zondervan, 1984.

Casselli, Stephen J. "Jesus as Eschatological Torah." *TJ* 18.1 (1997): 15-41.

Cassuto, U. *Commentary on Exodus*. Trans. I. Abrahams. Jerusalem: Magnes, 1951.

Cazelles, H. *Études sur le code de l'alliance*. Paris: Letouzey et Ané, 1946.

Chirichigno, G. C. "The Narrative Structure of Exodus 19-24." *Bib* 68 (1987): 457-479.

Clark, G. R. *The Word Ḥesed in the Hebrew Bible*. JSOTSup 157. Sheffield: Sheffield Academic Press, 1993.

Clements, Ronald E. *One Hundred Years of Old Testament Interpretation*. Philadelphia: Westminster, 1976.

Clines, D. J. A. *Ezra, Nehemiah, Esther*. NCB. Grand Rapids: Eerdmans, 1984.

Cogan, M. and H. Tadmor. *II Kings*. AB 11. Ed. D. N. Freedman. New York: Doubleday, 1988.

Collins, C. John. "The (Intellibible) Masoretic Text of Malachi 2:16, or, How Does God Feel about Divorce?" *Presb* 20.1 (1994): 36-40.

Congdon, R. N. "Exodus 21:22-25 and the Abortion Debate." *BSac* 146 (1989): 132-147.

Cottrell, J. W. "Abortion and the Mosaic Law." *Christianity Today* 17 (March 16, 1973): 6-9.

Cowley, A., ed. *Aramaic Papyri of the Fifth Century B.C.* Osnabrück: Zeller, 1967.

Cranfield, C. E. B. *Romans*. 2 vols. ICC. Edingurgh: T & T Clark, 1975-1979.

Danby, H. *The Mishnah*. Oxford: Oxford University Press, 1933.

Dandamaev, M. *Slavery in Babylonia*. DeKalb: N. Illinois University Press, 1984.

Daube, David. *Studies in Biblical Law*. London: Cambridge University Press, 1947.

Davis, J. J. *Abortion and the Christian*. Phillipsburg, N. J.: Presbyterian and Reformed, 1985.

de Vaux, Roland. *Ancient Israel*. 2 vols. New York: McGraw-Hill, 1965.

De Vries, S. J. *Prophet Against Prophet*. Grand Rapids: Eerdmans, 1978.

Diamond, A. S. "An Eye for an Eye." *Iraq* 19 (1957): 151-155.

Dillard, Raymond. *2 Chronicles*. WBC 15. Waco: Word, 1987.

Doron, P. "A New Look at an Old Lex." *Journal of the Near Eastern Society of Columbia University* 1.2 (1969): 21-27.

Dorsey, D. "The Law of Moses and the Christian: A Compromise." *JETS* 34 (1991): 321-334.

Douglas, Mary. *Purity and Danger*. London: Routledge & Kegan Paul, 1966. New York: Praeger, 1966.

Dozeman, Thomas B. "The Book of Numbers." In *New Interpreter's Bible*. Vol. 2. Nashville: Abingdon, 1998.

Driver, G. R. and J. C. Miles. *The Babylonian Laws*. Oxford: Clarendon, 1952.

Driver, S. R. *The Book of Exodus*. Cambridge: Cambridge University Press, 1911.

Eichler, B. L. "Bestiality." Pages 96-97 in *IDBSup*.

Ellington, J. "Miscarriage or Premature Birth." *BT* 37 (1986): 334-337.

Evans, Craig A. *Word and Glory: On the Exegetical and Theological Background of John's Prologue.* JSNTSup 89. Sheffield: Sheffield Academic Press, 1993.

Falk, Ze'eb W. *Hebrew Law in Biblical Times.* 2nd ed. Provo, Utah: Brigham Young University Press, 2001.

Farrar, F. W. *The Second Book of Kings.* London: Hodder & Stroughton, 1903.

Fernando, G. C. A. "John 1:17 as Window to the Realities of Law and Love in the Fourth Gospel." *AJT* 13.1 (1999): 51-70.

Finkelstein, J. J. *The Ox that Gored.* Philadelphia: American Philosophical Society, 1981.

Firmage, Edwin B., B. G. Weiss, and John Welch, eds. *Religion and Law: Biblical-Judaic and Islamic Perspectives.* Winona Lake, Indiana: Eisenbrauns, 1990.

Fishbane, M. *Biblical Interpretation in Ancient Israel.* London: Oxford University Press, 1985.

Fowler, P. B. *Abortion: Toward and Evangelical Consensus.* Portland, Oregon: Multnomah, 1987.

Frame, John. "Abortion from a Biblical Perspective." Pages 51-56 in *Thou Shalt Not Kill.* Ed. R. L. Ganz. New Rochelle, New York: Arlington House, 1978.

———. "Toward a Theology of the State." *WTJ* 51.2 (1989): 199-226.

Fuller, R. "Text Critical Problems in Malachi 2:10-16." *JBL* 110 (1991): 47-57.

Gagnon, R. A. J. *The Bible and Homosexual Practice: Texts and Hermeneutics.* Nashville: Abingdon, 2001.

Garland, D. E. "A Biblical View of Divorce." *RevExp* 84 (1987): 419-432.

Garrett, D. *Rethinking Genesis.* Grand Rapids: Baker, 1991.

Geisler, N. *Christian Ethics: Options and Issues.* Grand Rapids: Baker, 1989.

Gentry, Kenneth L. *God's Law in the Modern World: The Continuing Relevance of the Old Testament Law.* Phillipsburg, N.J.: Presbyterian & Reformed, 1993.

Glueck, Nelson. *Hesed in the Bible.* Trans. A. Gottschalk. Cincinnati: Hebrew Union College Press, 1967.

Godet, Frederic. *Commentary on John's Gospel.* Grand Rapids: Kregel, 1978.

Good, R. "Just War in Ancient Israel." *JBL* 104.3 (1985): 385-400.

Goodfriend, Elaine A. "Could *Keleb* in Deuteronomy 23:19 Actually Refer to a Canine?" Pages 381-397 in *Pomegranates & Golden Bells.* Ed. D. Wright, et al. Winona Lake: Eisenbrauns, 1995.

———. "Prostution (OT)." Pages 5:505-510 in *ABD.*

Gordon, Cyrus H. *The World of the Old Testament.* Garden City: Doubleday, 1958.

Gordon, T. David. "Critique of Theonomy." *WTJ* 56 (1994): 39.

Gottwald, Norman K. "'Holy War' in Deuteronomy: Analysis and Critique." *RevExp* 61 (1964): 296-310.

Greenberg, Moshe. "Biblical Attitudes towards Power: Ideal and Reality in Law and Prophets." Pages 101-112, 120-125 in *Religion and Law: Biblical-Judaic and Islamic Perspectives.* Ed. Edwin B. Firmage, et al. Winona Lake: Eisenbrauns, 1990.

———. *Biblical Prose Prayer.* Berekely: University of California Press, 1983.

———. "More Reflections on Biblical Criminal Law." Pages 1-17 in *Studies in Bible: 1986.* ScrHier 31. Ed. S. Japhet. Jerusalem: Magnes, 1986.

———. "Some Postulates of Biblical Criminal Law." Pages 3-28 in *Yehezkel Kaufmann Jubilee Volume.* Ed. M. Haran. Jerusalem: Detus Goldberg, 1960.

Grelot, P. "La péché de 'Onan (Gn., XXXVIII,9)." *VT* 49 (1999): 143-155.

Grosz, K. "Dowry and Brideprice at Nuzi." Pages 161-182 in *Studies in the Civilization and Culture of Nuzi and the Hurrians*. Ed. M. A. Morrison and D. I. Owen. Winona Lake: Eisenbrauns, 1981.

Hamilton, Victor. *The Book of Genesis*. 2 vols. NICOT. Grand Rapids: Eerdmans, 1990-1995.

Harland, P. J. "Menswear and Womenswear: A Study of Deuteronomy 22:5." *ExpTim* 110.3 (Dec 1998): 73-75.

Harris, R. Laird. "*ḥesed*." Pages 1:305-307 in *TWOT*.

————. "Leviticus." Pages 499-654 in *The Expositor's Bible Commentary*. Vol 2. Ed. Frank Gaebelein. Grand Rapids: Zondervan, 1990.

Harrison, R. K. *Leviticus*. TOTC. Downers Grove: InterVarsity, 1980.

Hartley, John E. *Leviticus*. WBC 4. Dallas: Word, 1992.

Hays, J. Daniel. "Applying Old Testament Law Today." *BSac* 158 (2001):21-35.

Hays, Richard B. *The Moral Vision of the New Testament*. San Francisco: HarperSanFrancisco, 1996.

Herdner, A. "Nouveaux Textes Alphabetique de Ras Shamra." *Ugaritica* 7 (1978): 31-38.

Hobbs, T. R. *2 Kings*. WBC 13. Waco: Word, 1985.

Hoffmeier, James K. "Abortion and the Old Testament Law." Pages 57-61 in *Abortion: A Christian Understanding and Response*. Ed. J. K. Hoffmeier. Grand Rapids: Baker, 1987.

Hoffner, Harry A. "Incest, Sodomy, and Bestiality in the Ancient Near East." *AOAT* 22 (1973): 81-90.

Hoskyns, Edwin. *The Fourth Gospel*. 2nd ed. London: Faber & Faber, 1947.

House, H. Wayne. "Miscarriage as Premature Birth: Additional Thoughts on Exodus 21:22-25." *WTJ* 41 (1978): 108-123.

————, ed. *Divorce and Remarriage*. Downers Grove: InterVarsity, 1990.

———— and Thomas Ice. *Dominion Theology: Blessing or Curse?* Portland, Oregon: Multnomah Press, 1988.

Houston, Walter. *Purity and Monotheism: Clean and Unclean Animals in Biblical Law*. JSOTSup 140. Sheffield: Sheffield Academic Press, 1993.

Houtman, Cornelis. "Ezra and the Law: Observations on the Supposed Relation between Ezra and the Pentateuch." *OTS* 21 (1981): 91-115.

Hugenberger, G. P. *Marriage as Covenant: A Study in Biblical Law and Ethics Governing Marriage Developed from the Perspective of Malachi*. VTSup 52. Leiden: Brill, 1994.

Hyatt, J. Philip. *Exodus*. NCB. Greenwood, S.C.: Attic Press, 1991.

Instone-Brewer, D. *Divorce and Remarriage in the Bible*. Grand Rapids: Eerdmans, 2002.

Isser, S. "Two Traditions: The Law of Exod 21:22-23 Revisited." *CBQ* 52 (1990): 30-44.

Jackson, Bernard S. *Essays in Jewish and Comparative Legal History*. SJLA 10. Leiden: Brill, 1975.

————. "The Literary Presentation of Multiculturalism in Early Biblical Law." *International Journal for the Semiotics of Law* 8.23 (1995): 181-206.

————. "The Problem of Exodus 21:22-25 (*Ius Talionis*)." *VT* 23 (1973): 273-304.

————. *Theft in Early Jewish Law*. Oxford: Oxford University Press, 1972.

Jastrow, M. *A Dictionary of the Targumim, the Talmud Babli and Yerusalmi, and the Mishnaic Literature*. Brooklyn: P. Shalom, 1967.

Jepsen, A. "*'emet*." Pages 1:309-316 in *TDOT*.

Johnson, Luke T. "The Use of Leviticus 19 in the Letter of James." *JBL* 101 (1982): 391-401.

Jones, G. H. *1 & 2 Kings.* 2 Vol. NCB. Grand Rapids: Eerdmans, 1984.

Josephus, Flavius. *Josephus.* 13 vols. LCL. Cambridge, Mass.: Harvard University Press, 1926-1937, 1965 (Index).

Kaiser, Walter C. "The Blessings on David: A Charter for Humanity." Pages 311-315 in *The Law and the Prophets.* Ed. J. Skilton. Philadelphia: Presbyterian and Reformed, 1974.

———. "God's Promise Plan and His Gracious Law." *JETS* 33.3 (1990): 289-302.

———. *Hard Sayings of the Old Testament.* Downers Grove: InterVarsity, 1988.

———. *Toward Old Testament Ethics.* Grand Rapids: Zondervan, 1983.

———. *Toward Rediscovering the Old Testament.* Grand Rapids: Zondervan, 1987.

———. *The Uses of the Old Testament in the New Testament.* Chicago: Moody, 1985.

Kang, Sa-Moon. *Divine War in the Old Testament and the Ancient Near East.* BZAW 177. Berlin: Walter de Gruyter, 1989.

Kaufman, S. A. *Akkadian Influences on Aramaic.* Assyriological Studies 19. Chicago: University of Chicago Press, 1974.

Kaufmann, Yehezkel. *The Religion of Israel.* Trans. M. Greenberg. New York: Schocken, 1972.

Kaye, B. and G. Wenham. *Law, Morality and the Bible.* Downers Grove, Illinois: InterVarsity, 1978.

Keener, Craig S. *The Gospel of John.* Vol. 1. Peabody, Mass.: Hendrickson, 2003.

Keil, C. F. *The Books of Kings.* Commentary on the Old Testament by C. F. Keil and F. Delitzsch. 1877. Repr., Grand Rapids: Eerdmans, 1978.

———. *Pentateuch.* 1864. Commentary on the Old Testament by C. F. Keil and F. Delitzsch. Repr., Grand Rapids: Eerdmans, 1978.

Kellogg, S. *The Book of Leviticus.* 1899. Repr., Minneapolis: Klock & Klock, 1978.

Kline, M. G. "Comments on a New-Old Error [Review of Bahnsen, *Theonomy*]." *WTJ* 41 (1978-1979): 172-189.

———. "*Lex Talionis* and the Human Fetus." *JETS* 20 (1977): 193-201.

———. *The Structure of Biblical Authority.* Grand Rapids: Eerdmans, 1972.

Knauf, E. A. "Zur Herhunft und Sozialgeschichte Israels." *Bib* 69 (1988): 153-169.

Knoppers, Gary N. "Jehoshaphat's Judiciary and the 'Scroll of Yahweh's Torah." *JBL* 113.1 (1994): 59-80.

Koch, K. *The Prophets: Volume One: The Assyrian Period.* Philadelphia: Fortress, 1983.

König, F. E. *Historisch-comparative Syntax der hebräischen Sprache.* Leipzig: Hinrichs, 1897.

Levine, Baruch A. *Leviticus.* JPS Torah Commentary. Philadelphia: Jewish Publication Society, 1989.

Lindars, B. *The Gospel of John.* NCB. Greenwood, S.C.: Attic Press, 1972.

Liver, J. "The Wars of Mesha, King of Moab." *PEQ* 99 (1967): 14-31.

Lockshin, Martin I., trans. and ed. *Rashbam's Commentary on Leviticus and Numbers: An Annotated Translation.* BJS 220. Providence, RI: Brown University Press, 2001.

Loewenstamm, S. E. "Exodus XXI 22-25." *VT* 27 (1977): 352-60.

———. *Comparative Studies in Biblical and Ancient Oriental Literatures.* AOAT 204. Kevelaer: Butzon & Bercker, 1980.

———. "*Nešek* and *M/tarbît,*" *JBL* 88 (1969): 78-80.

Lohfink, N. "*ḥērem.*" Pages 5:180-199 in *TDOT.*

Longnecker, Richard. *Paul: Apostle of Liberty.* Grand Rapids: Baker, 1976.

Lorton, David. "The Treatment of Criminals in Ancient Egypt through the New Kingdom." *JESHO* 20.1 (1977): 3-64

Luther, Martin. *Luther's Works*. Vol. 22: Sermons on the Gospel of St. John. Chapters 1-4. Ed. J. J. Pelikan, et al. St. Louis: Concordia Publishing House, 1957. CD Rom Version: *Luther's Works on CD-Rom*. Augsburg, 1999.

Macht, D. I. "A Scientific Appreciation of Leviticus 12:1-15." *JBL* 52 (1933): 253-260.

Magonet, Jonathan. "'But if it is a Girl She is Unclean for Twice Seven Days. . .' The Riddle of Leviticus 12:5." Pages 144-152 in *Reading Leviticus*. Ed. J. F. A. Sawyer. Sheffield: Sheffield Academic Press, 1996.

Margalit, B. "Why King Mesha of Moab Sacrificed his oldest Son." *BAR* 12, no. 6 (Nov./Dec. 1986): 62-63.

McComiskey, T. E. "Hosea." Pages 1-237 in *The Minor Prophets*. Vol. 1. Ed. T. E. McComiskey. Grand Rapids: Baker, 1992.

McConville, J. G. *Ezra, Nehemiah, and Esther*. Philadelphia: Westminster, 1985.

————. *Law and Theology in Deuteronomy*. JSOTSup 33. Sheffield, JSOT Press, 1984.

————. "Narrative and Meaning in the Book of Kings." *Bib* 70 (1989): 31-49.

McMillen, S. I. *None of these Diseases*. Westwood: Revell, 1963.

McNeile, A. H. *The Book of Exodus*. Westminster Commentaries. London: Methuen, 1908; 3rd ed. 1931.

Melcher, Sarah J. "The Holiness Code and Human Sexuality." Pages 87-102 in *Biblical Ethics and Homosexuality*. Ed. R. L. Brawley. Louisville: Westminster/John Knox, 1996.

Merrill, E. *A Kingdom of Priests*. Grand Rapids: Baker, 1987.

Mikliszanski, J. K. "The Law of Retaliation and the Pentateuch." *JBL* 66 (1946): 295-303.

Milgrom, Jacob. *Cult and Conscience: The Asham and the Priestly Doctrine of Repentance*. SJLA 18. Leiden: Brill, 1976.

————. "Ethics and Ritual: The Biblical Foundations of the Dietary Laws." Pages 159-191 in *Religion and Law: Biblical-Judaic and Islamic Perspectives*. Ed. E. Firmage, et al. Winona Lake: Eisenbrauns, 1989.

————. *Leviticus*. 3 vol. AB 3, 3a, 3b. New York: Doubleday, 1991-2001.

————. *Leviticus: A Book of Ritual and Ethics*. CC. Minneapolis: Fortress, 2004.

————. *Numbers*. JPS Torah Commentary. Philadelphia: Jewish Publication Society, 1989.

————. "The Paradox of the Red Cow (Num xix)." *VT* 31 (1981): 62-72.

————. "Rationale for Cultic Law: The Case of Impurity." *Semeia* 45 (1989): 103-109.

————. *Studies in Cultic Theology and Terminology*. SJLA 36. Leiden: Brill, 1983.

Moloney, F. J. *The Gospel of John*. SP 4. Collegeville, Minnesota: Michael Glazier, 1998.

Montgomery, J. A. *Kings*. ICC. Edinburgh: T. & T. Clark, 1951.

Montgomery, J. W. *The Slaughter of the Innocents*. Westchester, Illinois: Cornerstone, 1981.

Morris, Leon. *The Gospel According to John*. NICNT. Grand Rapids: Eerdmans, 1971.

Morrison, M. A. "The Jacob and Laban Narrative in Light of Near Eastern Sources." *BA* (Sum. 1983): 155-164.

Motyer, J. A. *The Prophecy of Isaiah*. Downers Grove: InterVarsity, 1993.

Mowvley, Henry. "John 114-18 in the Light of Exodus 337-3435." *ExpTim* 95 (1984): 135-137.

Neufeld, E. *Ancient Hebrew Marriage Laws*. London: Longmans, Green, and Co., 1944.

Newman, Barclay M. and E. A. Nida. *A Translator's Handbook on the Gospel of John*. Helps for Translators. London: United Bible Societies, 1980.

Niditch, Susan. *War in the Hebrew Bible*. New York: Oxford University Press, 1993.

Noordtzij, A. *Leviticus*. Grand Rapids: Zondervan, 1982.

Noort, E. "Das Kapitualationsangebot in Kriegsgestz DTN 20,10ff. und in den Kriegserzählungen." Pages 197-222 in *Studies in Deuteronomy*. Ed. F. G. Martínez, et al. Leiden: Brill, 1994.

North, Gary. *Tools of Dominion: The Case Laws of Exodus*. Tyler, Texas: Institute for Christian Economics, 1990.

Noth, M. *The Deuteronomistic History*. JSOTSup 15. Sheffield: JSOT Press, 1991.

Oss, Douglas A. "The Influence of Hermeneutical Frameworks in the Theonomy Debate." *WTJ* 51 (1989): 227-258.

Otto, E. "Aspects of Legal Reforms and Reformations in Ancient Cuneiform and Israelite Law." Pages 160-196 in *Theory and Method in Biblical and Cuneiform Law*. Ed. B. M. Levinson. JSOTSup 181. Sheffield: Sheffield Academic Press, 1994.

————. "False Weights in the Scales of Biblical Justice? Different View of Women from Patriarchal Hierarchy to Religious Equality in the Book of Deuteronomy." Pages 128-146 in *Gender and Law in the Hebrew Bible and the Ancient Near East*. JSOTSup 262. Ed. Victor Matthews, et al. Sheffield: Sheffield Academic Press, 1998.

Patrick, Dale. "I and Thou in the Covenant Code." *SBLSP* (Missoula, Montana: Scholars Press, 1978): 71-86.

————. *Old Testament Law*. Atlanta: John Knox, 1985.

Paul, Shalom. *Studies in the Book of the Covenant in the Light of Cuneiform and Biblical Law*. VTSup 18. Leiden: Brill, 1970.

Payne, J. Barton. *Theology of the Older Testament*. Grand Rapids: Zondervan, 1962.

Phillips, Anthony. *Ancient Israel's Criminal Law*. Oxford: Blackwell, 1970.

Poythress, V. *The Shadow of Christ in the Law of Moses*. Brentwood, Tenn.: Wolgemuth & Hyatt, 1991.

Pressler, Carolyn. "Sexual Violence in Deuteronomic Law." Pages 102-112 in *A Feminist Companion to Exodus-Deuteronomy*. Ed. A. Brenner. FCB 6. Sheffield: Sheffield Academic Press, 1994.

————. *The View of Women found in the Deuteronomic Family Laws*. BZAW 216. Berlin: W. de Gruyter, 1993.

Ratner, R. and B. Zuckerman. "'A Kid in Milk'?: New Photographs of KTU 1.23, line 14." *HUCA* 57 (1986): 16-60.

Rofé, Alexander. "The Laws of Warfare in the Book of Deuteronomy." *JSOT* 32 (1985): 23-45

Romerowski, S. "Que signifie le mot *hesed*?" *VT* 40 (1990): 89-103.

Roth, Martha. *Law Collections from Mesopotamia and Asia Minor*. SBLWAW 6. Atlanta: Scholars Press, 1995.

Rushdooney, Rousas J. *The Institutes of Biblical Law*. Nutley, N.J.: Craig Press, 1973.

Ryrie, C. C. "The End of the Law." *BSac* 124 (1967): 239-247.

Sakenfeld, K. "Love (OT)." Pages 4:375-381 in *ABD*.

————. *The Meaning of Ḥesed in the Hebrew Bible*. HSM 17. Missoula, Montana: Scholars Press, 1978.

Saucy, R. L. *The Church in God's Program*. Chicago: Moody, 1972.

Schoneveld, Jacobus. "Torah in the Flesh: A New Reading of the Prologue of the Gospel of John as a Contribution to a Christology without Anti-Judaism." *Immanuel* 24/25 (1990): 77-86.

Schwienhorst-Schönberger, L. *Das Bundesbuch (Ex 20,22-23,33)*. BZAW 188. Berlin: Walter de Gruyter, 1990.

Scofield, C. I. *Rightly Dividing the Word of Truth*. 1886.

Sider, R. J. *Completely Pro-Life.* Downers Grove, Illinois: InterVarsity, 1987.

Smith, J. M. Powis. *The Origin and History of Hebrew Law.* Chicago: University of Chicago, 1931.

Smith, R. Payne. *A Compendious Syriac Dictionary.* Oxford: Clarendon, 1903.

Sonsino, Rifat. "Characteristics of Biblical Law." *Judaism* 33 (1984): 202-209.

Speiser, E. A. "The Stem *PLL* in Hebrew." *JBL* 82 (1963): 536-541.

Spieckermann, H. "God's Steadfast Love: Toward a New Conception of Old Testament Theology." *Bib* 81 (2000): 305-327.

Sprinkle, Joe M. *'The Book of the Covenant': A Literary Approach.* JSOTSup 174. Sheffield: Sheffield Academic Press, 1994.

————. "Deuteronomic 'Just War' (Deut 20:10-20) and 2 Kings 3:27." *ZABR* 5 (2000): 285-301.

————. "Law." Pages 467-471 in *Evangelical Dictionary of Biblical Theology.* Ed. W. Elwell. Grand Rapids: Baker, 1996.

————. "Old Testament Perspectives on Divorce and Remarriage." *JETS* 40 (1997): 529-550.

————. "2 Kings 3: History or Historical Fiction." *BBR* 9 (1999): 247-270.

Stahl, Nadette. *Law and Liminality in the Bible.* JSOTSup 202. Sheffield: Sheffield Academic Press, 1995.

Stamm, Johan J. and Maurice E. Andrew. *The Ten Commandments in Recent Research.* SBT. Naperville, Illinois: Allenson, 1967.

Stein, Robert H. "Divorce." Pages 192-199 in *DJG.*

————. "Is it Lawful for a Man to Divorce his Wife?" *JETS* 22.2 (1979): 115-121.

Stern, P. "Of Kings and Moabites: History and Theology in 2 Kings 3 and the Mesha Inscription." *HUCA* 64 (1994): 1-14.

Stott, John. *Divorce.* Downers Grove: InterVarsity, 1973.

————. *Involvement: Social and Sexual Relationships in the Modern World.* Old Tappan, N.J.: Revell, 1985.

Sutherland, John R. "The Debate Concerning Usury in the Christian Church." *Crux* 22.2 (June 1986): 3-9.

Thielman, Frank. *Paul & the Law.* Downers Grove: InterVarsity, 1994.

Thurston, T. M. "Leviticus 18:22 and the Prohibition of Homosexual Acts." Pages 7-23 in *Homophobia and the Judaeo-Christian Tradition.* Ed. M. L. Stemmeler and J. M. Clark. Dallas: Monument, 1990.

Tigay, Jeffrey. *Deuteronomy.* JPS Torah Commentary. Philadelphia: Jewish Publication Society, 1996.

Turner, Nigel. *A Grammar of New Testament Greek.* Vol. IV. Style. Edinburgh: T & T Clark, 1976.

van der Toorn, Karl. "Prostution (Cultic)." Pages 5:510-513 in *ABD.*

————. *Sin and Sanction in Israel and Mesopotamia.* SSN 22. Assen: Van Gorcum, 1985.

Watts, James W., ed. *Persia and Torah: The Theory of Imperial Authorization of the Pentateuch.* Atlanta: Society of Biblical Literature, 2001.

————. *Reading Law: The Rhetorical Shaping of the Pentateuch.* Biblical Seminar 59. Sheffield: Sheffield Academic Press, 1999.

Weinfeld, M. "The Decalogue: Its Significance, Uniqueness, and Place in Israel's Tradition." Pages 3-48 in *Religion and Law: Biblical-Judaic and Islamic Perspectives.* Ed. E.. Firmage, et al. Winona Lake: Eisenbrauns, 1990.

Weingreen, J. "The Concepts of Retaliation and Compensation in Biblical Law." *Proceedings of the Royal Irish Academy* 76 (1976): 1-11.

Wellhausen, Julius. *Prolegomena to the History of Israel with a Reprint of the Article 'Israel' from the Encyclopedia Britannica.* Gloucester, Mass.: Peter Smith, 1983.

Wells, Bruce. "Sex, Lies, and Virginal Rape: The Slandered Bride and False Accusation in Deuteronomy." *JBL* 124 (2005): 41-72.

Wenham, Gordon J. "*Bĕtûlâh, '*A Girl of Marriageable Age,'" *VT* 22 (1972): 326-348.

———. *The Book of Leviticus.* NICOT. Grand Rapids: Eerdmans, 1979.

———. "Christ's Healing Ministry and His Attitude to the Law." Pages 115-126 in *Christ the Lord: Studies in Christology presented to Donald Guthrie.* Ed. H. H. Rowdon. Leicester: Inter-Varsity, 1982.

———. *Genesis.* 2 vol. WBC 1-2. Dallas: Word, 1987-1990.

———. "Leviticus 27:2-8 and the Price of Slaves." *ZAW* 90 (1978): 264-265.

———. "The Restoration of Marriage Reconsidered." *JJS* 30 (1979): 36-40.

———. "The Theology of Unclean Food." *EvQ* 53 (Jan./Mar. 1981): 6-15.

Westbrook, Raymond. "*Lex Talionis* and Exodus 21:22-24." *RB* 93 (1986): 52-69.

———. "The Prohibition on Restoration of Marriage in Deuteronomy 24:1-4." Pages 387-405 in *Studies in Bible 1986.* ScrHier 31. Ed. Sara Japhet. Jerusalem: Magnes, 1986.

———. *Property and the Family in Biblical Law.* JSOTSup 113. Sheffield: JSOT Press, 1991.

———. *Studies in Biblical and Cuneiform Law.* CahRB 26. Paris: Gabalda, 1988.

Whitekettle, Richard. "Levitical Thought and the Female Reproductive Cycle: Wombs, Wellsprings, and the Primeval World." *VT* 46 (1996): 376-391.

Whitelam, Keith. *The Just King: Monarchial Judicial Authority in Ancient Israel.* JSOTSup 12. Sheffield: JSOT Press, 1979.

Williams, R. J. *Hebrew Syntax.* 2nd ed. Toronto: University of Toronto Press, 1976.

Williamson, H. G. M. *Ezra, Nehemiah.* WBC 16. Waco, Texas: Word, 1985.

———. *1 and 2 Chronicles.* NCB. Grand Rapids: Eerdmans, 1982.

Wiseman, D. J. *1 & 2 Kings.* TOTC. Downers Grove: InterVarsity, 1993.

Wright, Christopher J. H. *Deuteronomy.* NIBCOT. Peabody, Mass.: Hendrickson, 1996.

———. *God's People in God's Land: Family, Land, and Property in the Old Testament.* Grand Rapids: Eerdmans, 1990.

Wright, David P. *The Disposal of Impurity.* SBLDS 101. Atlanta: Scholars Press, 1987.

———. "Observations on the Ethical Foundations of the Biblical Dietary Laws: A Response to Jacob Milgrom." Pages 193-198 in *Religion and Law: Biblical-Judaic and Islamic Perspectives.* Ed. E. Firmage, et al. Winona Lake: Eisenbrauns, 1990.

Yamauchi, Edwin. *Persia and the Bible.* Grand Rapids: Baker, 1990.

Yaron, R. *The Laws of Eshnunna.* Jerusalem: Magnes, 1969.

———. "The Restoration of Marriage." *JJS* 17 (1966): 1-11.

Youngblood, Ronald. "Counting the Ten Commandments." *BRev* 10, no. 6 (December 1994): 30-35.

Zertal, Adam. "Mount Ebal." Pages 2:255-258 in *ABD.*

Zobel, H. –J. "*ḥesed.*" Pages 5:44-64 in *TDOT.*

Author Index

Subject Index

Aaron 22, 62-63
Abel 62
Abomination 104, 114, 116-117, 156, 163-164, 179
Abortion 69-70, 82, 84, 87-90
Abraham 7, 23, 41, 57, 61, 63, 67, 138, 150, 155-156, 160, 168
Absalom 199
Abstraction of principles 21, 23, 25
Achan 46, 93, 186, 197
Adam and Eve 62
Adultery 1-3, 5, 20, 53-54, 119, 130-132, 135, 139, 141, 145-146, 148-151, 153-154, 157-159
Altar laws 4, 51, 53, 58, 60-61, 63, 66-67
Amalek 177
Ammisaduqa, Edict of 44
Ammonites 139
'anâ 64, 160
Anabaptists 19
Animals 23, 54-55, 94-96, 98, 101, 103-105, 111-117, 165
Antinomianism 6, 11-12
Apodictic Law 2
'āsôn 69-72, 79-83, 85-86, 88
Atonement 22-23
Balaam 159, 178
Barrenness 155, 161
Baths, ritual 104, 107-112
Bathsheba 110
Ben-Hadad 34, 176-177, 185
Bestiality 53, 119, 165
Betrothal *see Marriage, Inchoate*
biplilim 70-71, 80-83
Blemishes (physical) 105, 115, 117, 125, 127, 169
Blood 4, 17, 21-24, 102, 107-108, 110, 114-115, 120, 125-128, 156, 168
Blood, eating 60, 114
Bloodguilt 55, 89, 98
Bondsmen 73, 76, 86-87
Book of Concord (A.D. 1580) 11

Book of the covenant 51-53, 57-59, 61, 64-66, 80-81, 84, 190
"Book of the law" 189-194
Brideprice 18, 42, 63-65, 136-137, 146-149, 156-157, 159-160, 170
Burials 103-104, 126, 144
Burning (as punishment) 103, 168
Burnt offering *see Offering, burnt*
Calvin, Calvinists 12, 19, 93, 163 *see also Reformed Theology*
Canaan, Canaanites 13-14, 17, 23, 61, 119-121, 139-140, 161, 164, 167, 173, 176-182, 194, 200
Capital punishment 3, 12, 15-17, 19-20, 24, 46-47, 71, 73-75, 79, 88, 94, 98-99, 102, 135, 157-158, 160-161, 165-166, 168
Carthage 172-173
Casuistic (case) law 3
Ceremonial (cultic, ritual) law 2-5, 8, 11, 13, 15, 21, 46, 51-52, 58-59, 61, 65-66, 111, 164-165
charis ("grace") 32-34, 38-39
Chemosh 171, 174-175, 183, 187
Chiasm 56-57, 59, 66
Child sacrifice *see Human sacrifice*
Childbirth 102, 107-108, 116, 155-156
Christian Reconstructionism *see Theonomy*
Church and state 3, 12, 14, 15-17, 19, 21, 25
Cities of refuge 3, 5, 17, 21-22
Circumcision 1, 7-8, 11-12, 17, 23, 65, 108-109, 121, 156, 197
Civil (judicial) law 3, 4, 5
Clean/unclean *see Purity laws*
Codex Sinaiticus 31
Common (as opposed to holy) 105, 116, 121
Composition, monetary 71, 73, 75, 78-79, 88
Confiscation 92
Corporal punishment 18-19

Scripture and Ancient Texts Index